INTERNATIONAL PRAISE for SURVIVE TO THRIVE

"If you don't believe in the spiritual side of life, you will after reading Mary Anne Dorward's new book, *Survive To Thrive*. Her personal stories are real, heartfelt, and convincing. Check this book out if you want to Thrive!"

~John Kremer, Author of 1001 Ways To Market Your Books and Founder of the Billion Dollar Initiative, North America

"With *Survive to Thrive* you get two wonderful gifts in one: a rollicking true life adventure story, and practical wisdom about how to live your best life. Mary Anne Dorward is a woman who's packed more amazing experiences into one life than 10 ordinary people do, traveling all over the world creating a life full of love and wonder. If you are looking for engrossing entertainment and profound wisdom, this is the book for you."

~Eric O'del, Minister and Theater Producer, North America

"Mary Anne's discussion of the dark night of the soul in her book *Survive to Thrive* speaks to the depth of her work and the wisdom of her heart. We all go through periods where the old story ends and we are thrown into the darkness of the unknown. In that holy darkness the seeds of our soul sprout. And like every seed we must first break open, turn inside out, come undone, and trust the innate wisdom of life to carry us through the process of transfiguration as we get planted in the Ground of our own Being. Mary Anne shares her intimate experience with that process. It is the only path from surviving to thriving. May we all have the courage to walk it."

~Vera de Chalambert, MTS, Author, Harvard-Educated Scholar Of Religion, North America

"Heartbreakingly honest, *Survive To Thrive* is truly Mary Anne Dorward's path to self discovery and redemption. This book is a testament to gaining courage and wisdom in the face of incredible adversity. Dorward's true self is humbly revealed, her struggles humanized, and her victories hard-won. This book is a treatise on the endurance of the human spirit."

~Mary Garripoli, Playwright, Women in Flames, North America

"*Survive to Thrive* is the perfect inspirational book. Reading it is life changing."

~Waiswa Festo, Pastor, Founder of Hope Harvest, Uganda

"Survive To Thrive is an extraordinary book and a must read. Mary Anne's journey of courage, determination and survival will be both enlightening and inspiring to anyone interested in learning how to live a purpose filled life. If there is one inspiring book you ever read in your life, make it Mary Anne's Survive To Thrive!"

~Amos Mutale, Writer, Coach, Motivational Speaker, Zimbabwe

"*Survive To Thrive* is an engaging, inspirational and motivating book for both men and women. In this powerful book, Dorward gives you the 11 Keys that will help you unlock the secrets to a truly Thriving life. *Survive To Thrive* demonstrates that any difficult circumstance we face can not only be overcome, but also transformed to help create a flourishing and Thriving life. Dorward's amazing stories from her life experience prove anything is possible with courage and faith. Highly recommended."

~Patrick Snow, Publishing Coach and International Best-Selling Author of Creating Your Own Destiny, North America

"As a Pastor and U.S. Marine, I can personally attest to not only the love, grace and peace of God, but also the strength, will and indomitable courage of the human spirit. I have known Mary Anne Dorward for nearly fifty years now, and her life is a shining example of all of the above. No matter what life threw at her, Mary Anne has always maintained her deep and abiding faith in God, which ultimately helped her learn how to truly thrive in her life. I know that this book, *Survive To Thrive*, and Mary Anne's faith and endurance will inspire you as it has me. Mary Anne shows us all how to live Christ's words, "Be still and know I am God." *Survive to Thrive* teaches us that God always sustains us, even in the darkest of times."

~Charles Louvau, Pastor, U.S. Marine, North America

"*Survive to Thrive* is an inspiring and engaging adventure story! Mary Anne shows us that *all* the experiences we have in life can become our most important teachers, and how with both time and compassionate reflection, each of us has the capacity to put our lives fully into perspective."

~Billie Taylor, Council Leader, Innkeeper, Mexico and North America

"Mary Anne Dorward has been through more trial and tribulation then most people will ever go through in one lifetime. I was truly captivated by Mary Anne's story, and in awe of the work she has done on herself. In *Survive to Thrive*, Mary Anne passes on the wisdom, knowledge and experience she has gained. Mary Anne also shares so many gold nugget skills and tips that will help anyone learn how to thrive. If you want to create a better life for yourself, read this book!"

~Paula Boucher, Health and Wellness Coach, Australia

"Mary Anne Dorward is an amazing example of a remarkably resilient human being. In her new book, *Survive To Thrive*, Dorward tells great stories from her amazing life, and then shares ideas that the reader can apply to their life if they choose. *Survive To Thrive* teaches us the tremendous potential we all have within us as human beings - if we know how to tap it. Dorward teaches us how to find our inner resilience so that we can create our own version of a thriving life. I highly recommend this book to anyone wanting to improve their life."

~Paul Goode, Widow, Cancer Survivor, North America, Ireland

"Ever since I met Mary Anne, I had no doubt in my mind that she was a special person and a remarkable fighter, with no ordinary or easy destiny. After having had the opportunity to read Mary Anne's captivating new book, *Survive To Thrive*, I am deeply touched by her story, so full of courage and resilience. I hope that many souls on the path will have the good fortune to consider Mary Anne's suggestions, and to be inspired by her tenacity as she shares the story of how she created the thriving life she both desired and lives today. My best wishes and blessings continue to be with her."

~ Urs Winzenried, Entrepreneur, Coach, Spain, North America

"In *Survive to Thrive*, Mary Anne Dorward has shed her ego to provide the reader a glimpse into some of her darkest moments and fears that many of us share, but normally keep hidden. She provides many lessons on how to survive the drama and trauma that life can bring, without judging what is right or wrong for any other individual. In sharing her life stories on how she managed through incredible physical and mental pain, she never claims to have the absolute or right answer. What she does provide for her reader is the encouragement to find their own path to happiness, peace and love through the numerous true life examples, relevant quotations, and valuable resources."

~Janice Barnard, Community Volunteer, North America

"In Mary Anne Dorward's newest book, *Survive to Thrive*, I was in awe that Mary Anne was able to share her own personal struggles in life with such honesty and integrity. I have known Mary Anne since our Junior High School days, and there were many parts of the book that left me deeply saddened by what she has had to endure. But, this book, *Survive to*

Thrive is truly uplifting. In sharing what she has gone through, we are able to know that she can relate to any of our own personal struggles. Although this is a fascinating "read," it really is also a workbook that we should all have by our bedside. There are so many wonderful ideas and exercises for the reader to practice in their own life. We can all learn so much from this book in our own journey through life, and as we become the thriving individuals we were meant to be."

~Cici Christiansen Lee, Grandmother, Community Volunteer, North America

"I first met Mary Anne Dorward in Elementary School, and coincidentally our fathers were also best friends in High School. Our lives and families have crisscrossed over the past 70 years. Mary Anne's life story is movie material. *Survive to Thrive* is a wonderful read - a roller coaster ride – that inspires the reader to closely examine their own life. This book also teaches us how to make positive changes to thrive. Thank you my friend for your courage and inspiration."

~Ellin Anderson Purdom, Friend, North America

"*Survive To Thrive* is a book filled with fascinating stories and great dialogue from one brave woman's life. Mary Anne Dorward has worked very hard to both survive and evolve in this life. I have enormous admiration for both her and her life journey."

~Catherine Eaton Skinner, Multidisciplinary Artist, North America

"*Survive to Thrive* is an engaging, inspirational and motivating book. This book is the story of the journey of a true hero. Dorward teaches us how we too can shape and live our best life. Thank you Mary Anne for your courage and inspiration."

~Tennyson Dube, Student, Zimbabwe

For more information about Mary Anne Dorward and her other books, please go to: www.WordsToThiveBy.com

SURVIVE TO THRIVE

11 KEYS TO UNLOCK YOUR THRIVING LIFE

MARY ANNE DORWARD

Powerful Voices Press

PVP

SURVIVE TO THRIVE: 11 Keys To Unlock Your Thriving Life
by Mary Anne Dorward.

Copyright © 2018.

US Trademark: Words To Thrive By ®
All rights reserved. No part of this book may be reproduced by any mechanical, photographic, or electronic process, or in the form of a phonographic recording; nor may it be stored in a retrieval system, transmitted, or otherwise be copied for public or private use—other than for "fair use" as brief quotations embodied in articles and reviews—without prior written permission of the publisher. The author of this book does not dispense medical advice or prescribe the use of any technique as a form of treatment for physical, emotional, or medical problems without the advice of a physician, either directly or indirectly. The intent of the author is only to offer information of a general nature to help the reader in their quest for emotional and spiritual well-being. In the event you use any of the information in this book for yourself, the author and the publisher assume no responsibility for your actions.

Powerful Voices Press

www.powerfulvoicespress.com

To book Mary Anne Dorward for a speaking engagement or coaching session, please visit: www.WordsToThriveBy.com.

FIRST EDITION

Cataloging-in-Publication Data is on file at the Library of Congress

ISBN 13: 978-0-9963691-4-5 Paperback

ISBN 10: 978-0-9963691-5-2 E-book

Gloria in Excelsis Deo!

TABLE OF CONTENTS

FOREWORD 13
THE JOURNEY OF SURVIVE TO THRIVE 15
INTRODUCTION 16
SURVIVE 18
THE ROUNDABOUT 19
THRIVE 21

BOOK 1
THE KEY OF CHOICES

INTRODUCTION 24
SURVIVE 25
THE ROUNDABOUT 35
THRIVE 40
CONCLUSION 54

BOOK 2
THE KEY OF GUIDANCE

INTRODUCTION 58
SURVIVE 64
THE ROUNDABOUT 75
THRIVE 77
CONCLUSION 79

BOOK 3
THE KEY OF HEALTH

INTRODUCTION 84
SURVIVE 85
THE ROUNDABOUT 94
THRIVE 131
CONCLUSION 138

BOOK 4
THE KEY OF LOVE
INTRODUCTION 142
SURVIVE 146
THE ROUNDABOUT 151
THRIVE 159
CONCLUSION 165

BOOK 5
THE KEY OF GRATITUDE
INTRODUCTION 172
SURVIVE 175
THE ROUNDABOUT 178
THRIVE 183
CONCLUSION 184

BOOK 6
THE KEY OF PEACE
INTRODUCTION 188
SURVIVE 189
THE ROUNDABOUT 194
THRIVE 205
CONCLUSION 209

BOOK 7
THE KEY OF ABUNDANCE
INTRODUCTION 216
SURVIVE 219
THE ROUNDABOUT 224
THRIVE 227
CONCLUSION 230

BOOK 8
THE KEY OF JOY
INTRODUCTION 234
SURVIVE 236
THE ROUNDABOUT 243
THRIVE 266
CONCLUSION 270

BOOK 9
THE KEY OF IMAGINATION
INTRODUCTION 278
SURVIVE 284
THE ROUNDABOUT 286
THRIVE 291
CONCLUSION 294

BOOK 10
THE KEY OF FREEDOM
INTRODUCTION 300
SURVIVE 303
THE ROUNDABOUT 308
THRIVE 310
CONCLUSION 321

BOOK 11
THE KEY OF POWER
INTRODUCTION 326
SURVIVE 329
THE ROUNDABOUT 334
THRIVE 344
CONCLUSION 348

ABOUT THE AUTHOR 350
ACKNOWLEDGEMENTS 351
FOR FURTHER EXPLORATION aka MY VIRTUAL BOOKSHELF 352
GLOSSARY OF TERMS 361

FOREWORD

When I wrote *If Life Is a Game, These Are The Rules*, (#1 New York Times bestselling book excerpted by Jack Canfield in his first *Chicken Soup for The Soul* book in 1994) I never imagined that I would meet a person who actually applied every single one of my *"Ten Rules For Being Human"* to their own life. Then I met Mary Anne Dorward. Mary Anne is the true example of Rules 8 and 9: "What you make of your life is up to you" and "All your answers lie inside of you."

I first met Mary Anne at a women's conference in Seattle in 2006 where we were both speaking as subject matter experts. We discovered that we shared a deep commitment to helping people become more empowered and fulfilled. Mary Anne and I have kept in touch over the years. I read and reviewed Mary Anne's first book, *Words To Thrive By: Powerful Stories Of Courage and Hope:* "It is rare that someone can take the events of their life, learn the lessons and then articulate those lessons so that others can benefit from their journey. Mary Anne has opened the door to her personal life lessons for all to benefit and illuminate your experience in the process called 'Life.' Her goal is for you to obtain meaning and relevance from everything that happens to you."

In her new book, *Survive To Thrive: 11 Keys To Unlock Your Thriving Life*, Mary Anne courageously reveals more of her personal life challenges and lessons, along with her pursuit of wisdom and truth. Her inspirational ideas are applicable to your own life as you move from survival to thriving. This is the story of Mary Anne's triumph over enormous odds, and is a testament to the endurance of the human spirit as we gain wisdom along the way. Mary Anne once again proves from her own life experience how we can obtain inspiration, truth, and relevance from everything that happens to us.

As with my *Ten Rules for Being Human*, when you lose your way, you can call upon Mary Anne's 11 Keys to help you both create and sustain your thriving life. I have great respect for Mary Anne as she encourages us all to have faith in the strength of our own spirits. Mary Anne reminds all of us how aspiring to be wise is really the greatest journey one can take in life. Since wisdom has been the ultimate goal of her life; she teaches how one's own innate wisdom within knows no limits other than those that you impose upon yourself. Mary Anne demonstrates in her own life and work, both personally and professionally, that she is an example of the words of the esteemed David R. Hawkins, M.D., PhD., "The realization of Absolute Reality and Truth is the greatest gift that one can be to the world and all of humanity."

Most importantly, Mary Anne's life journey and this book confirms what I have always said: our learning in life never ends, there are no mistakes only lessons, and each of our lessons is repeated until it is fully learned. Courage resides in all of us – and Mary Anne's life and this book prove that you can use that courage when you need it to do what's right for you. We all possess a strong natural power and adventurous spirit, which we can draw on to embrace what lies ahead. This new book will be a great companion to take with you in your lifelong journey.

~**Chérie Carter-Scott, Ph.D., MCC, Bangkok, 2017**

Chérie Carter-Scott, Ph.D., MCC is known as "The Mother of Coaching." She is the founder of MMS Coach Training, which is currently located in six locations around the world. Dr. Chérie is the producer of a new feature documentary, *LEAP* on coaching. She has been a frequent guest on Oprah and has appeared on numerous international media tours that include: *The Today Show*, *CNN*, and dozens of TV, radio, and print interviews. Not only is she a media personality who has worked on five continents, in more than 30 countries, she currently trains coaches in Europe, Asia, and North America. Dr. Chérie currently lives between Bangkok, Amsterdam, and California.

THE JOURNEY OF SURVIVE TO THRIVE

"Fairy tales are more than true: not because they tell us that dragons exist, but because they tell us that dragons can be beaten."

~G. K. Chesterton

INTRODUCTION

Every person's path to a Thriving life is unique. Contrary to what we may have been told in fairy tales from childhood, no handsome prince will come to rescue us, no genie will emerge from a bottle and give us three wishes, and there is no magic phrase that will open the door to a perfect life. Nevertheless, within each of us, there is a source power that often remains untapped and that we can access at any time if we choose to. Over the past nearly sixty years, I have discovered some valuable lessons about life. The most important, I believe, is that we can transform our challenges into assets that can be used to propel us forward.

In my quest to learn how to Thrive, I discovered 11 Keys that anyone can use to experience a more fulfilling and meaningful life. If you are asking yourself, "Where do I start?" or "How do I move my life to the next level?" this book is for you. Are you ready to shift your life from wherever you are now to a new and better place? That's wonderful! Reading this book is a great first step on your journey towards Self-realization. You may have already read your share of human potential books and have completed a number of self-help programs. You now want to step it up a notch and shift your life from good to great. Congratulations! You are on your way and this book will help you get there.

When I was in "Survival mode," I can remember saying to myself many times, "Uh Oh! This does not look good!" Often I felt as if I were some character in a horror movie. I saw my life completely falling apart before my eyes. I lost everything I cared about, and at one point, I felt like giving up on life entirely. But I did not give up. After a lot of trial and error, going around in circles and searching for a new direction, I discovered there were 11 Keys that I had used over and over to move past the obstacles I had faced. These keys were instrumental in getting me out of my Survival mode and on to the path towards the truly fulfilling and Thriving life which I live now.

As I learned to make better choices that moved me forward (even in small steps) the quality of my life improved. These moments of triumph gave me the strength and courage to continue in my quest to Thrive. In addition to making more informed choices in my life, I found that I could choose more positive thoughts, and this carried me even further. As I used my 11 Keys, my Thriving life became my new reality. This new life was full of new and unexpected opportunities, people, and adventures. I now live half a world away from where I was born with a man I love. I never would have imagined that when I started on my journey.

Many people choose to stay in what I call the "pity pit," where they feel that they will never escape from what has happened in the past, what is happening right now, or what may happen in the future. People who are accustomed to being the unfortunate victim in life seem to gravitate towards self-pity. Do these phrases sound familiar?

"Why does this always happen to me?"

"Poor me!"

"No one understands me!"

"I can't!"

"I'm not strong enough, brave enough, pretty enough, smart enough."

"I'll never be able to!"

These are the common refrains of people caught in the middle of the "pity pit." If we believe that we can't overcome an obstacle or improve our situation, we will work hard to justify that belief. As with any mistaken belief, we will effectively make sure that we remain stuck in that situation. Conversely, if we believe that anything is possible and that we can handle whatever difficulty comes into our life, we are much more likely to be open to achieve success.

We have all seen how some people allow various difficult life experiences to completely destroy them. We can make a different choice and accept the possibility that although life may be difficult at this moment, our situation can change and things can even improve dramatically. In spite of how things may look now, we can choose to move beyond just Surviving and transform our lives into an expression of Thriving.

How this book is structured

There are 11 Keys I used to unlock my Thriving life. Each key has three distinct phases:

1. Survive

2. The Roundabout

3. Thrive

SURVIVE

When we are surviving, we can feel stuck, thankful to have escaped the latest disaster. We might say things like:

"Well, that was awful."

"I hate my life, myself, my family, my friends."

"I don't deserve to be happy or successful or in a great relationship or doing what I love."

"I deserve to suffer, to be taken advantage of, to be humiliated, to lose."

"How could my life get any worse?"

When we get tired of just surviving and *decide to do something about it*, we move into what I call "The Roundabout."

THE ROUNDABOUT

The Roundabout is a period of transition during which we may open our minds to find we have more choices than we at first believed. Once we are in The Roundabout, we might discover we actually do have the courage to explore new and exciting places. As an example, these kinds of questions might signal our entry into The Roundabout:

"Why does this always happen to me?"

"I thought I understood this. But now, it seems as though I have just made one giant circle and I am back where I started. How did that happen?"

"Didn't I just pass that same exit a minute, a year, a decade ago?"

Or it might sound something like this:

"How did I get involved with that same type of person, again?"

"How did I make that same mistake, again?"

"How did I let that person get to me, again?"

"This always happens to me!"

We might circle The Roundabout quite a few times before we find the exit that takes us to where we really need to go. Perhaps we have tried every exit on The Roundabout except for one. I have found that this unmarked exit is that persistent thought, idea, direction or person that I have been dismissing as illogical or nonsensical. I have even said to myself, "It can't be that easy." But after having been stuck in that endless circle of disappointment and frustration, we might be ready to take our chance. Out of desperation, we might even find ourselves saying, "I have tried absolutely everything I can think of. Nothing has worked. Perhaps *now* I am ready to try something *really different*. Perhaps now I will follow that thought or idea, choose that person or take that improbable exit, since I've tried everything else."

It helps to ask ourselves the right questions. At first our questions might sound like this:

"How did I miss that?"

"Why didn't I follow my intuition?"

Then, we might ask, more constructively:

"If I had the chance to do this again, what would I do differently?"

"What would my ideal outcome look like?"

When we are ready to ask these kinds of questions and then *take action* on our honest answers to them, that's when things can really change for the better. You could say, at this point we are moving into our "Thrive Drive."

THRIVE

When we begin to truly Thrive, new jobs, people and other unexpected opportunities start showing up. When our life begins to improve, we may even be tempted to settle for "good enough" instead of pushing towards an even better life experience. Once we recognize that good enough isn't all there is, we can strive to live the life that we have always dreamed of but never really thought we could attain. At that point, things in our life seem to get even better.

You might find yourself saying things like:

"Wow!"

"This is amazing!"

"I had no idea I could have so much fun or be this happy or feel this fulfilled in my life!"

"I love my life!"

"Thank you Universe!"

When I realized that I had gone from just Surviving to Thriving I could not believe how good I felt. I now have much more energy. I feel that I am enjoying every day to the fullest and I sleep more peacefully than I ever have before. I also met the man of my dreams, got married and moved to Oceania, where I now live. I go paddle boarding and kiteboarding, take peaceful walks, create art and music, talk with people and write. This is my thriving life. What will yours look like?

Your Thriving Life

It is well within your power to achieve everything you have ever wanted in your life - and more! Whatever problems you may be having with your relationships, your career, your health or your life at this moment, you can change it all for the better. It is my hope that the gift of learning that I have found through my life experiences will spark some new ideas to help you discover and create for yourself the thriving life of your own dreams.

I can't, and won't, tell you what to do. As Cheryl Strayed says in her book *Brave Enough,* "I'm not trying to be the boss of you. I'm attempting to be a better boss of me." So, feel free to read this book in any order you wish. Follow your intuition and skip around. If any of the 11 Key sections of this book don't interest you, skip 'em. Seriously. You're the boss of you.

Staying open to learning something new is without a doubt, the most important thing to bring along with you for the ride we are about to take together in this book. Actually, that's not a bad idea to keep in mind for also living a thriving life in general.

Are you ready to unlock your own thriving life? This book will give you the keys you need to open the doors to a happier, healthier and brighter future.

From Me To You

A Course In Miracles suggests, "Use this moment to be free."

What might freedom look like for you in your life right now?

BOOK 1

THE KEY OF CHOICES

"It's not our abilities that define us. It's our choices."

~Alfred Dumbledore, Harry Potter and The Chamber Of Secrets

INTRODUCTION

Not long ago I sat by the bedside of a dying woman named Helen who was just shy of her 90th birthday. As I was meditating sitting next to her, it occurred to me that each of us are the sum total of the choices we have made. I opened my eyes and looked at my friend. Helen struggled to leave her body, gasping for her last breaths. Helen exemplified the qualities of devotion to her family, kindness and generosity towards others. Now, at the end of her life, Helen was surrounded by flowers all around her room from family and friends, people like myself, whom she had welcomed into her family as if they were her own.

Helen had indeed lived a very full and rich life. I thought, "This is what this person's choices look like after 90 years." Later that afternoon, I looked in the mirror at my face. I thought, *This is what my choices look like after 54 years.* I looked into my eyes and asked myself out loud, "What do you see in the mirror at this point in your life?" This is what came to mind at that moment:

Here is a woman who has tried, to the best of her ability, to always be kind, compassionate, loving and empathetic. This woman does not have a lot of possessions, but she has had an abundance of wonderful life experiences. This is a woman who has valued wisdom over money. I see a woman who has run into some tough obstacles in her life. As she encountered each hurdle, she might have stumbled or even fallen down multiple times, but she always sought the opportunity or knowledge she knew was there within each roadblock she encountered.

This woman knew that the opportunity for personal growth was always waiting behind each of life's challenges. This precious jewel of wisdom often required some digging in order to find it. But what she found was always exactly what wisdom she needed at that moment. Once the solution presented itself, this woman applied the wisdom, took the opportunity and carried on with her life.

From Me To You

Each of us is the sum of the choices we have made up to this point in time. **What do you see when you look in the mirror? How have your decisions - up to now - shaped you? What would you do differently in this moment now to create a new and more Thriving future for yourself?**

SURVIVE

The Key Of Choices is the Master Key in our journey from Survive to Thrive. Our choices determine the outcome of everything we do and have in our lives. One of my best teachers in the Key Of Choices was a man I met by chance. I believe I met this man at just the right moment because I trusted my instincts and decided to follow them.

The trip to Alcatraz

When my children were young, we went on a tour of Alcatraz, the former maximum-security prison in the middle of San Francisco Bay. We were at the top floor of the prison touring the individual cells when the PA system crackled: "For those of you on the Alcatraz tour today, we have a very special opportunity. Leon 'Whitey' Thompson, one of only four men who were released from Alcatraz prison directly to the San Francisco streets, is here with us today signing his books. If you would like to meet Mr. Thompson he will be on the second floor for the next hour. Feel free to stop by and say hello."

The kids and I looked at each other and said, "Cool! Let's go!" As we stood in line I suggested that each of us think of a question we would really like to ask Mr. Thompson. This was an unusual and rare opportunity to meet someone who had actually been imprisoned at Alcatraz.

When we finally got to the head of the line, Mr. Thompson greeted us warmly and said politely to me, "What fine-looking children you have, Ma'am." Mr. Thompson did not fit the image I had in my mind of an ex-convict. He was well dressed in a suit. In front of him were stacks of the two books he was selling and signing.

"Thank you very much, Mr. Thompson. I would like to buy both of your books. Would you please inscribe them to my children?"

"I would be happy to do that, Ma'am. But please, call me Whitey. And what are your children's names?" At that, he pulled out one of each of his books and opened the front cover.

"Whitey, their names are Sarah and Joshua. While you are doing that, do you mind answering a few questions?" I asked, with some hesitation.

Whitey Thompson looked up, put down his pen and gave us his full, undivided attention. "Of course. I would be happy to answer any questions you have, if I can. What would you like to know?" he said with a warm, genuine smile. He looked back and forth between the three of us. Silence.

"Who's first?" Whitey asked.

Sarah shook her head vigorously, lips tightly closed, signaling a strong "*No.*"

I looked at Joshua. "Okay, Joshua. Your turn. What would you like to ask Mr. Thompson?"

Joshua did not miss a beat. "Mr. Thompson. Uh, Whitey. Sir. Can you please tell me what possessed you to rob those thirty-nine banks in the first place?"

Whitey smiled at Joshua, and then at me. "My, he is quite direct isn't he?"

"Yes. He certainly is," I said, blushing.

"How old are you, son?" Whitey asked.

"I'm eight years old, sir. I mean, Whitey. So why did you do it? Thirty-nine banks is a lot of banks. I'd really like to know why you did that."

The bottom of the barrel

"Well, Joshua, first of all I want you to know that your question is a good one. And without going into a whole lot of detail, I can tell you that I was in the war and I came out of it a very angry man. But I am living proof, son, that you can get to the bottom of a deep, dark barrel and pull yourself out." Whitey gave Joshua a warm smile.

Then he turned to me. "Ma'am?"

I took a deep breath, and then let out a careful sigh. I wasn't sure how honest I could be with a complete stranger. I had been depressed for quite some time, largely because of my recent divorce. I decided to risk it. "Whitey, as we were walking around, I was listening to the audio program that tells the history of Alcatraz and has interviews with several former prisoners."

"Yes Ma'am, I know it well," Whitey said.

"Well, I remember your interview in particular. You said that when you arrived here at Alcatraz your heart was cold as a stone."

"Yes Ma'am, that was true." Whitey said, without any trace of bitterness.

"I have to admit I am also very familiar with that 'cold as a stone' place. What I want to know is, do you remember the moment when things began to change for you? You know, from cold as a stone to something else?" Privately, I was hoping he could help me do something about the cold stone I felt had replaced my own heart. I hoped that he had some words of hope to help me out of the self-imposed solitary confinement I had been trapped in for so long.

The moment when everything changed

Whitey looked at me with the kindest expression and then said, "I absolutely do remember that moment, Ma'am. It was just about the most important moment of my life. It was the moment I realized that I was the only person who had gotten me in here, and I was the only person who was going to get me out."

Whitey leaned forward, looked right into my eyes and then said, "And after that moment, Ma'am, everything changed for me. My decision to be really honest with myself, and to change my focus shifted my entire future. Instead of being angry and bitter and resentful about my past, I put all my thoughts on what I, personally, was going to do to get me out of here.

"I began thinking about how I was going to build a different, more productive future for myself. And here I am today. I'm happily married and I am doing work that I love. It all started right here in this prison years ago.

"Who would have thought an inmate from Alcatraz would now be a best-selling author? I talk in schools, helping kids stay out of trouble so they never do the kinds of things I did, or have to go through what I had to go through. I figure that's the best kind of work I could do now, you know, to help others out of my own personal experience. I want kids to stay out of prison." Whitey concluded, and then he sat back in his chair.

I was too stunned to speak. I had not expected his answer.

After we left Alcatraz that day, I kept thinking about what Whitey had said about the moment he realized that he was the only person who had gotten himself into Alcatraz, and that he was the only person who was going to get himself out. At the time we met Whitey, I was feeling so helpless that I might as well have been behind bars myself. I imagined that Alcatraz couldn't have been any worse than the cruel and punishing prison I had put myself in. I kept asking myself, *How am I going to get myself out of this?* I also kept saying to myself, *If Whitey could change his stone cold heart, and then build a new life for himself starting as a prisoner on Alcatraz Island, I should certainly be able to overcome my own problems.*

Whitey Thompson was a powerful example of how our choices make the difference between remaining hopelessly trapped in a prison of our own making or taking control of our situation and moving on to a new life of possibility and achievement. As I told Whitey, I too had been consumed with rage, anger and knew well that feeling of being "cold as a stone" inside. My meeting with Mr. Thompson was the inspiration I needed to turn things around, reimagine who I was and what my life could become.

His story reminded me that since I was the one responsible for my own prison of anger, rage and frustration, I was the only one who would be able to get myself out. I was the one who had to make different choices in order to create a new life for myself and move forward. I was the one who had to seek out a new environment where I could get the help and support I needed. I was the one who had to work through my issues in order to move on to living a healthier, happier and more fulfilling life.

Whitey taught me how important my daily choices were. I felt graced and inspired by his hard-earned wisdom, determination, and the decision he made to turn his life around. His inspiring story demonstrates our capacity as humans to rethink the life choices we make and then, take responsibility for building the kind of future we really want to create.

Whatever you are experiencing right now in your own life, you must accept that it is the result of the choices you have made. If you are stuck in survival mode, as I was when I met Mr. Thompson, your life can transform in an instant if you accept that you alone have the power to change your life for the better. If you feel as though you are at the "bottom of the barrel" in your own life right now, know that you are the only one who is going to get yourself out. Everything depends on the choices you make from this moment forward. Choose wisely.

The lunch

Some of the choices I made when I was young had a big impact on the rest of my life, both great and not so great.

When I was twenty years old and was preparing to move to New York City to pursue my dream of becoming a Broadway actress, my father asked me to join him for lunch. At this lunch, my father asked me to make him a promise. Before we shook in it, my Dad told me the following story from his own life.

His father had been a very successful man who owned the only deep-water dock for offloading oil from the largest tankers coming into the San Francisco Bay from around the world. My father was expected to go into "the family business." His father took him to lunch, as my Dad was doing with me that day.

My father explained, "At that lunch, my father told me that he wanted me to promise him that I would pursue the business of my choice for the next five years. If I was sufficiently passionate about my own choice during those five years, I was free to pursue that as my livelihood. If not, he would create a spot in the family business for me as a back-up plan.

"I took my father at his word. I really had no interest in the family business and I certainly didn't want to be in the oil business. I had a passion for advertising, so that's what I did. Eventually, as you know, I became very successful in the world of advertising, started my own business, made a lot of money and this brings us to today and to you. I would like to propose that we make the same agreement I did with my father. This means that I don't expect you to be a part of my business, even though you are already quite good at doing commercials and voice over work."

I was flattered. "Thanks Dad. I appreciate that."

My father continued, "When you get on that plane to New York next week, I want you to focus 150% on your goal of becoming an actress on Broadway. Keep your focus on being a success at that for the next five years. At the end of that time we will have lunch again. If you are ready to let that dream go, I will pay for you to go to graduate school and study something else you are interested in. Deal?"

I hadn't expected this from my father. But I put my hand out over the white linen tablecloth, being careful not to knock over my wine glass and said, "You've got a deal Dad. Let's shake on it!" He put his hand out and we shook on it.

He smiled and said, "You know what I always say: **get up and get after it!**"

I smiled back at him. "I will, Dad. You know I will!"

At that moment, knowing we had created a backup plan really eased my mind. On my way home, I thought to myself, *I could work at this for five years at 150%. I can let loose with all of my drive and determination. Those five years will be over in a flash. Who knows where I'll be by then?*

Leaving on a jet plane

After I had checked two large suitcases at the airline counter, I hugged my father and mother goodbye. Then I walked onto the plane to New York City with my backpack and my sewing machine, which I tucked under the seat in front of me. I was so scared I almost threw up on the plane! *New York? Yikes! What was I thinking?* I kept repeating this to myself until I fell asleep.

That first month of my life in New York, I slept on the couch of a family friend, Meg, whom I had known since I was born. Meg had been my father's secretary and I adored her. When I was a little girl, Meg used to let me sit next to her and pretend to type like a grown-up just outside my Dad's office. I had not seen Meg in many years and it was extremely generous of her to let me sleep on her couch for my first month in New York while I searched for an apartment. She helped me get acquainted with New York and taught me how to read a subway map. She also vouched for me for my first apartment.

But from the day I started renting and I was fully on my own for the very first time in a huge new city, I was too scared to go out of my apartment on 23rd Street and 9th Avenue except to get groceries. After a month of that, I figured I really had to get out. I challenged myself to get on the subway, and take just one single ride. As I marched myself toward the subway station nearby, I kept telling myself, over and over, *You can do this Mary Anne. You can do it!* When I got to the station, I bought my first subway token and boarded my very first subway train in New York City. *I'm now officially A New Yorker!* I chuckled to myself as the subway car rattled north.

After I mastered the subway, I decided it was time to get started with my acting career. I did not have an acting agent to represent me, so I spent a part of every day writing cover letters, enclosing my photo and resume and then marching these packages off to the post office. I read the trade papers daily, which is where all New York auditions were advertised. I would circle the auditions that were right for me, then get on the subway, and find the theatre where the auditions were being held that morning or afternoon. Then, I would sign my name on their "open call" auditions list usually located out front of the theatre. On any given day, of all the actors who were auditioning for a play or musical show, I might be number 500, 800 or even 900 on the list.

Every morning Monday through Saturday, once I knew what the acting part was I wanted and had signed up to audition for, I came home, put on the outfit for the audition I expected would come up first in the queue. Depending on the number of auditions that day, I would gather and then put any other appropriate outfits for each role into my duffle bag. After the first audition, I would find the nearest hotel and pretend to be a guest so I could use their bathroom to change clothes and adjust my makeup if needed. Then I would go to the nearest park bench or coffee shop to study the written material called "sides" for the next audition. I would also mentally practice the best monologues I had prepared in case anyone asked for them. If it was a musical I would mentally rehearse my audition songs in my head. By the time I had waited in line for most of the day and completed all my auditions it was time to go home.

I did this routine for a full month before I got my first job, an Off-Off Broadway show at the well-known La Mama Theatre. This first show was the play TNT, which stood for *Tricephalus Neurosylogistic Training*. The play was a spoof on the personal transformation movement very popular at that time called EST. The first review I read of the show began with, "TNT is not genuine dynamite, but it is a real bomb." My first thought was, *Nowhere to go but up from here!*

After that less than successful first play, I decided that I would look for the best actor training school I could find. I enrolled for acting classes at the Lee Strasberg Theatre Institute in New York City.

One day, I was sitting in class watching the directing unit. A woman came up to me and asked, "Are you an actor?"

"I sure am!" I replied, cheerfully.

"Well I need someone just like you to do a scene in this class for Lee. Would you help me out?" she asked hopefully.

"I would be happy to!" I replied, full of hope and excitement. After she walked away, I thought to myself, *Oh my God! I will be performing for the famed and well known founder of the Actors Studio, Lee Strasberg!*

We did many rehearsals in between classes for the upcoming scene. After we had performed the scene in front of Lee Strasberg, he was silent for a moment and then sat forward in his chair and asked, "Who are you and where did you come from?"

"I'm Mary Anne Dorward and I came from California, Sir." I replied, not sure what he wanted to know.

"No. *Who* are you and *where* did you *come* from?" He yelled.

"Uhhhh. Sir, I'm Mary Anne Dorward and I came from California?" I said as I sunk lower in my chair. From his tone, I thought he hated the scene, and was about to throw me out of the room.

"I want you in my class, and I want you there tomorrow." he said.

"Excuse me?" I asked sheepishly.

"I just said, I want you in my class and I want you there tomorrow." With a wave of his hand, then he said, *"Next!"*

Thus began my training as the last protégé of Lee Strasberg, Founder of the Actors Studio. In addition to my classes at the Lee Strasberg Theatre Institute, I was invited to his and his wife Anna Strasberg's home every Sunday for the next 4 years until he died. My favorite piece of advice from Lee, in both life and work was, "You don't have to *be something*. You just have to *be*." I continue working on that one to this day.

From Me To You

For me - success, happiness and abundance are determined by these three choices:

1: What I choose to do.

2: Where I choose to do it.

3: Whom I choose to do it with.

What determines success and happiness for you? What are the choices you are making right now that will get you there?

THE ROUNDABOUT

Our belief system is formed from the thoughts we think over and over. This is true regardless of the accuracy or truthfulness of what we think. We make our choices based on what our mind believes and is convinced is true. For example, have you ever said to yourself something like: "I'm such an idiot." "I'm so stupid." Our belief system defines what we believe, how we feel about ourselves, and also what is possible for us to achieve. When we repeat negative thoughts like those above, we are actually shaping our future. Did you know that the words that you think or speak daily have the potential to transform your life?

Dr. Robert O. Becker tells us in his groundbreaking book, *The Body Electric: Electromagnetism and the Foundations of Life*, that words are actually a form of stimuli that generate thoughts, and that each thought produces a "unique electromagnetic biofield." This means that every word we choose to say or think has its own unique energy signature and that our words have a direct effect on our body. The latest brain science shows that most average people have over 50,000 thoughts a day, and most of them are negative. Depending on the words we use, this energy can have a profoundly positive or negative effect on us.

Dr. Richard Davidson, a neuroscientist, has spent the last ten years devoted to neural cartography, the science of mapping out the brain's unconscious "word-activated" emotional pathways. Dr. Davidson's fascinating neural cartography research reveals that when we speak negative words, our brain's right prefrontal cortex becomes neurologically activated; when we speak positive words, our left prefrontal cortex becomes activated. The researchers have further discovered that negative word signatures create a right prefrontal dominance and this generally results in anxiety and depression (un-ease). On the other hand, speaking positive word signatures creates a left prefrontal dominance, which, more often than not, manifests as happiness and confidence (ease).

This means that neuroscience has actually proven that the words we use, our daily inner dialogue, generates correlative emotional patterns, and these emotional patters influence our daily lives in a huge way. Dr. Davidson says, "Our words produce a matching chemistry." So, the next time you find yourself saying, "I'm a failure," remember that you are transforming your chemistry with those negative words and ideas. This shift in chemistry sends your body into feelings of anxiety, depression and worthlessness. Isn't it amazing to think that each of us, at any moment of our lives, have control over our body chemistry? By simply changing the words we choose, we have the power to transform our lives. In addition to the words we choose, it's also helpful to take a good look at the people who are in our lives as well.

Crabs in a bucket

One day, I heard a story about a woman who was taking a walk along the beach, and noticed several crab fishermen casting their nets, waiting a few moments, and then **pulling in a few crabs at a time. One fisherman had a bucketful of five or six crabs.** As she stood there watching, she noticed that one of the crabs from his bucket was climbing on top of the rest. This ambitious crab slowly gained height, and then extended his front legs upward toward the lip of the bucket to pull himself up. This little guy was trying to make a break for it! At this point, the woman asked the crab fisherman if he was aware that this cheeky little crab was about to hoist himself up and over the edge of the bucket.

THE KEY OF CHOICES

He smiled and calmly said, "Watch what happens."

As this ambitious crab started pulling himself up to get over the edge of the bucket to freedom, all of the other crabs reached up, grabbed his hind legs and pulled him down back to the bottom of the bucket.

At the moment of hearing that crab story, I suddenly realized that a similar thing had occurred in my life. When I began to make different choices, to experiment with more positive new ways of thinking, and my life began to shift toward in a more positive direction, that's when I noticed more judgment, criticism and push back from the familiar "crabs" in my life. The people who had called themselves my friends seemed to prefer I stayed the same as I had been.

We've all heard that old saying, "Misery loves company." When I truly committed myself to pursuing a Thriving life, these people, like the crabs I had seen in the bucket, continually tried to pull me back into conversations focused on the familiar "pity pit" territory of disappointment, failings and insecurities. Has this ever happened to you? Did you notice when you made a decision to finally change something in your life for the better, that other people in your life seemed to like to drag you back to the old familiar way of being or doing you used to share?

It has been said, "you are the average of the five people you spend the most time with." I began to notice that there were certain people in my life who consistently really drained me, and I also felt really tired after being around them for any length of time. I noticed others who tended to be very judgmental or critical. These people would tend to put me down in a joking way with phrases like, "Well aren't you just so special." or "Who do you think you are?" and "Well easy for you to say." Still others didn't seem to share my excitement or ambition for change at all. It appeared that these people really just wanted me to stay the same so we could all remain in "the pity pit" together. They preferred to complain how bad things were all the time, instead of taking steps to change their life.

Even though the process was hard, I committed to cutting out all of "the crabs" from my life. While I felt love and compassion for them, I was always getting caught in their negative or judgmental downdraft. More and more, I could see that being around them was not good for my health or overall well-being. I needed to find a new group of friends. Anyone who was more committed to staying the same than they were to exploring positive change in their lives had to go.

As I look back now, I can see that it was a three-step process. First, I challenged myself to imagine what truly supportive, loving, and kind friends could be like. Second, I decided that moving forward I would choose only people who were truly supportive, inspiring and encouraging. Finally, I committed to waiting for them to show up in my life. Eventually, I discovered new people to support me in all areas of my life - personal, professional and spiritual. These people in my life now are all very positive and encouraging. Choosing to spend time with the people who truly love and support you is **one of the very best, and most healthy, choices you can ever make for yourself.**

Cutting out all "the crabs" in my life also taught me some valuable principles, which I have chosen to follow ever since:

1. Choose to take advice only from a person who has triumphed over what you want to overcome, not one who doesn't have the slightest idea how to get out of the mess they are in.

2. Choose to take financial advice from a person who is financially abundant, not from someone who doesn't have any money.

3. Choose to take relationship advice from someone who has successful relationships, not from someone who consistently fails in their relationships.

4. Choose to take business advice only from someone who is successful, not from someone who isn't.

5. Choose to take life coaching from someone who is healthy in body, mind and spirit, not from someone who lives from their wounds, or who is stuck in the "pity pit."

People who are not successful in giving advice in finances, relationships business or life cannot give you the answers you seek, as they don't have the answers to give. They haven't solved their own problems and challenges. If you have people in your life who are draining you or holding you back, one of the most important things you can do is to make the choice to remove them from your life as soon as possible.

While this may sound a bit scary, remember that every second you spend around negative or toxic people is one second of your precious life that you will never get back. It is said, "Nature abhors a vacuum." Parting ways with negative or toxic people will make space for new people to come into your life who actually do inspire and support you.

Letting go of the past

Another important choice is to let go of the past. Even though the past is over and done, and we know for a fact that we cannot change anything, isn't it amazing how much time we all spend inside our heads beating ourselves up over it? Why not consider trying a different approach? Instead of beating ourselves up for making what we consider now to be a poor decision or choice, we can choose to say instead, "Well it seemed like a good idea at the time." This approach contains great wisdom and compassion. Saying to ourselves, *Well it seemed like a good idea at the time,* allows us to see, and hopefully accept, that whatever we did or said in our past, we were doing the best we could with what we knew at that moment in time.

This approach also helps us learn how to reframe the past and then, "use this moment to be free" as *A Course in Miracles* suggests. We obviously cannot change what we said or did in the past. But rather than beatng ourselves up now in the present, we can choose to learn from the past and as a result of that learning create a new and different future. We can now choose a new perspective on whatever it was that happened. In this moment, since we have grown in experience and knowledge, we know better and so we shall do better, simple as that. With this new insight, anything in our past thus becomes of tremendous value, rather than the relentless self-flagellation, recrimination and blame we normally tend to heap upon ourselves.

From Me To You

What negative thoughts of your past are you still beating yourself up with today? Can you see now that what you said, thought or did was the best you could do with what you understood at that time? In truth, whatever we choose to do or say, at any given moment of our lives, always "seems like a good idea at the time." Forgive yourself for any harm you may have caused in the past, and now create a more positive future. Now, is our only point of power. How we choose to use that power is always up to us.

THRIVE

As I moved into a more Thriving life, I began making very different choices in my words, decisions, and the actions. I also challenged myself to try new things. For example, little by little, I became more comfortable traveling alone as a single woman. As a result, I was then able to follow through on my childhood dream of traveling and exploring distant lands. I made plans in my mind to travel to the places I had always been curious about such as Spain, Greece, Portugal, Africa, Egypt, the Middle East, and the islands of the Aegean.

I also stopped waiting for that "perfect moment" to arrive. Instead, I chose to say, "Yes!" to spontaneous and unexpected opportunities as they presented themselves. For example, a business colleague found out last minute that she was unable to use her summer time share in Spain due to her work commitments. At a meeting of a business networking group we were both members of, she offered her home in Spain to anyone who was interested, able and willing to travel in a week. I jumped at the chance. I had never been to Spain and it was on my "travel bucket list." This trip became a spontaneous spring break holiday and was a really fun trip that my kids and I all really enjoyed.

In other trips, I was more open to a sudden, unexpected inspiration for a radical change of plan, as when I travelled to Egypt in 2007. On that trip, I had been on a cruise that had taken me from Istanbul, through the obscure Greek Islands of the Mediterranean and ending in Athens, Greece. I had been scheduled the day after I arrived in Athens to go to the Temple of Delphi. Ever since I was a child, in addition to the Parthenon, I had always wanted to see the ancient temples where the words "Know Thyself" were inscribed in the arch of the stone entry gate.

However, in my hotel room in Greece, as I was meditating on this idea of "Know Thyself," I had a sudden inspiration to instead travel to Egypt to find the face of the woman I had drawn in a school art class when I was ten years old. During the art class, I had gone into a kind of trance state. I began to draw, quite spontaneously, an Egyptian woman's face. The drawing just poured out of me, far above my art skills level; it was as if I was drawing from memory. I came out of the trance, looked down at the drawing I had just done there on the desk and I had absolutely zero idea who she was.

So there I was, sitting on my bed in my hotel room in Athens, Greece, almost fifty years later and quite unexpectedly, this memory of the Egyptian woman's face I had drawn when I was ten years old came to my mind. It hit me like a ton of bricks: *I have to find her.* So, I got on the phone and made the necessary arrangements to fly to Egypt the following day.

As I boarded the plane and sat down in my seat, I thought, *Who does something like this?* Just as quickly, I caught the negative tone of judgment, smiled and said to myself proudly, *I do.* As I looked out the window of the plane as it was landing, I had this sudden sense of familiarity, as if I was returning "Home" in some very strange way.

When I met Neera, the tour guide I had hired for my two days trip, she asked, "So what would you like to do with your two day trip here in Egypt, Miss?"

I cheerfully replied, "We are going on an adventure to find the face of a woman I drew when I was ten years old."

I wish I could have captured this woman's expression on film that moment. It was somewhere between, "Oh how nice." and "You are definitely a crazy woman."

Neera picked me up at the hotel the next morning. When she asked what I would like to do first I replied, "Well, I would like to begin my search at the Pyramids of Giza."

When we got there, Neera dutifully went to buy me a ticket. She returned a few minutes later and said, "I am sorry, Miss. The entry tickets to the Great Pyramid are all sold out for today."

Suddenly I felt a huge force of energy overtake me. I looked Neera in the eye and said evenly and firmly, "I don't care what you have to do. I don't care what it costs. *Get me into that temple.*"

Quite intimidated, Neera nodded her head, turned on her heels immediately and left. She returned again a few minutes later with my ticket to the Great Pyramid. "Will 1:00 suit you Miss?" she said, as she handed me my ticket.

The Great Pyramid of Giza

At the appointed hour, I was at the door to the Great Pyramid of Giza and allowed to pass. It was very quiet and soon I realized I was the only one there. *What are the odds of that?* I thought to myself as I began to climb the nearly vertical rope ladder causeway toward what was called, the main burial chamber.

When I entered the room, I saw a large black empty marble sarcophagus. This was one of the main tourist attractions in Egypt, it was the middle of a normal tourist day, and yet I was the only one there. *Had Neera pulled some strings perhaps to get me a private viewing?* I wondered to myself.

A sudden *Knowing* then came to me: *No one was ever buried here.* I do not know to this day what came over me at that precise moment, but as if I just knew what to do, I climbed over the edge of the ancient sarcophagus and laid my body down flat on the bottom. There could have been any number of deadly spiders inside the sarcophagus, but I didn't care in the least. Next, I laid my head down and closed my eyes. Immediately, I dropped into a deep meditation.

The sound of the word "Om..." spontaneously burst forth from my mouth, resonated all through my body, reverberated off the walls of the sarcophagus and then seemed to spill out and reverberate off the walls of the room. That first tone of "Om..." began to amplify and reverberate even more around the entire chamber. That sound kept going and going and going, and it seemed as if it was without end.

I quite spontaneously added a second tone, about one third higher in pitch. This second overlapped the first tone I had made, in perfect harmony. It too seemed to keep going and going and going without end. I added a fifth and a seventh, a ninth and an eleventh and a thirteenth tone in pitch on top of the other tones.

All of the tones just kept going and going and going on top of each other in what became a beautiful cosmic harmony. A fleeting thought of *Was this room actually some sort of an ancient sound chamber?* drifted by while I was swimming in this musical symphonic melody of tone on top of tone, the room humming with sound.

The words, *I have never truly heard my own real voice before this very moment* drifted through me, as the overlapping tones entered my body, which also began to hum with vibration. I completely drifted into total bliss as this divine symphony of tone continued to reverberate off of the walls and all throughout my body.

Suddenly my reverie was interrupted by what sounded like a distant male voice. At that moment, I didn't know if I was dreaming or not as I was so lost in this heavenly cosmic symphony of sound. I vaguely heard the male voice again so I opened my eyes and saw a man standing over the sarcophagus who was looking down at me.

As I looked up from the bottom of the sarcophagus, he seemed a bit blurry. As I slowly came back into consciousness, the man's face came more sharply into focus. I realized, in a flash of memory, that this man was one of the guards who I had passed standing at the entry door on my way into the pyramid. He looked very angry.

With a sudden jolt, I realized that this man was screaming at me, "Get out you! Get out you! No meditating in this temple! Illegal! Illegal to mediate here! Out! Out! Out!" He began clawing at me from above. Lucky for me, laying flat on the bottom of the sarcophagus, I was just out of reach of his fingernails.

All at once, I pulled myself into a ball and exploded with the word, "No!"

The guard looked like he had seen a demon and awkwardly backed away from me. This gave me time to hoist myself up and out of the sarcophagus. As soon as my feet hit the ground, I backed away from the guard as quickly as I could until my back hit the wall on the other side of the room.

After a few quick moments, the guard seemed to get his bearings. Once again, his eyes flared and his mouth burst open wide with rage, "I will arrest you right now!" he shouted as he rushed forward, grabbing at and then taking hold of my shirt.

I raised both my hands instinctively, breaking his grasp and shouted back, "So sorry! I am stupid woman! So sorry! So sorry!" At that I took off as fast as I could to my left and through the door out of the room. With the guard close behind me, I quickly scrambled down the steep rope ladder the way I had come in, and then ran as fast as I could down the hallway. At last, I could see the light of the opening of the doorway. I ran faster.

"Arrest her!" I heard him shouting from behind me, in close pursuit. Before the other men could flick their cigarettes or pick up their machine guns, I bolted through the doorway to the Great Pyramid and out into the blasting Egyptian heat.

"Arrest her!" I heard the guard shout again.

I did not look back. I ran as fast as I could, away from them all over the hot sand and stone. As I ran, my eyes were frantically scanning the road ahead, looking everywhere for my driver and Neera. With great relief, I finally spotted the unmistakable long black town car and Neera in the distance. Neera and the driver were both waving to me with their arms stretched high over head.

As I got closer to them, I noticed that Neera had a very strange expression on her face, and she began waving even more frantically. I had not looked behind me, but there were four male Egyptian guards with machine guns right on my heels. Neera opened the car door and I dove in with her right behind me.

Neera slammed the door shut as I screamed to the driver, "Drive! Drive! Drive!"

Just as the guards caught up, my driver quickly pulled our car out on to the road, creating a large cloud of dust. All we heard was one last slamming sound of what must have been the butts of their machine guns hitting the rear of the car. We roared away out of their reach, leaving them behind shouting angrily with their fists in the air.

"What were you doing in there? Those men looked very angry. They almost caught you! What were you up to in the Great Pyramid Miss?" said Neera.

"Nothing!" I replied, giving Neera a feeble smile as I tried to catch my breath and get my heart to stop racing.

"Well Miss, from the looks on their faces and the way they were chasing you it did not look like nothing to me!" Neera replied.

When I calmed down after a few minutes, I told Neera and the driver the story of what I had done. The driver rolled his eyes and Neera turned very red.

"Lucky for you that you got away, Miss. What you did is just not done here, Miss. It is illegal Miss. You could have gotten us all in a lot of trouble. You realize, yes, that you could have been put away in jail for a very long time for what you did?"

Until that moment, I had not realized how close I had come to being thrown into an Egyptian jail. Neera reached into the cooler in the back seat and then handed me a bottle of cool water. I realized at that moment I was desperately thirsty. After a few gulps of water, I asked cheerfully, trying to change the subject, "So, where are we headed to next on our tour today?" It was only then that I noticed my hands were shaking.

"We are headed to the Ancient Capital of Egypt called Memphis." Neera replied. "I will keep a close eye on you so you don't get into any more trouble."

"That sounds interesting." I said, as I settled into the back seat of the car. After all that excitement, I tried to let my mind drift. In the cool air conditioning and safety of the car, I watched through the window as we passed hundreds of huge date palm trees laden with dates. These ancient date palms lined the streets as far as my eyes could see.

Memphis

When we arrived in Memphis, Neera stayed close by me. "No more trouble from you here in this place." she said wagging a finger in my direction.

At our first stop, there were several huge ancient statues from many centuries ago. There was one male statue two stories high that quickly caught my attention. He was a very imposing figure standing in a very stately pose. I wondered who he might have been. He had a huge pointy head piece and was carrying a large spear which was even taller than he was. I looked around the rest of the room and could not find a single female statue equivalent to this large male statue anywhere.

"What happened to all of the women statues of Egypt? Where are the statues of them? Why aren't there any female statues like this tall guy here?" I asked Neera as I pointed to the large stone man with the spear and huge hat.

At this, Neera gave me a slight smile and then beckoned me to look at a particular spot on the male statue. "See that?" She said as she pointed to the upper inner thigh of his leg, the leg that was stepping forward.

"What?" I couldn't see anything where she was pointing.

"That! Those hieroglyphs right there." Neera said, pointing to a group of drawings that were etched into the upper thigh of the male statue. "Do you know what that means?" she asked.

"Nope. I don't have a clue what any of that means." I answered in all honesty.

"Well you asked what happened to the women of Egypt. That hieroglyph there is the cartouche of his wife. Symbolically, that hieroglyph in that specific location of the upper inner thigh of the forward stepping leg means that man could not take one-step forward without his wife. You understand now? You understand now what happened to the women of Egypt?"

I nodded, suddenly feeling very sad. It seemed that the male patriarchy in Egypt had taken over the women here too just as they had all over the world. But it would appear that the women still knew where to leave evidence of their authority and power, even if it was done quietly and they didn't have a huge egotistical statue of themselves to show for it.

At that moment, I had the feeling I would never find what I had come here looking for, that face of the woman I had drawn when I was ten years old. I was certain that she too had long ago been erased just like all the other important women in history had been. Feeling a bit depressed at that thought, I began wandering around, looking at pieces of broken statues scattered all over the grounds. Neera struck up a conversation with the driver of our car over in the shade. I guess by this point she thought that I wasn't going to get into too much more trouble.

The Sphinx

I rounded the corner on a far section of the grounds and for some reason I felt drawn to look up. I had to blink in the bright sunlight. There was a huge sphinx there in the courtyard. *Was this possible? There, without a doubt, was the face of the woman I had drawn when I was ten. But this could not be possible. All the sphinxes of Egypt were statues of men weren't they?* I felt suddenly faint. I put my hands to each side of my head, as I suddenly had a splitting headache.

I thought, *I must truly be crazy. Why had I wasted all this time and money on a pipe dream? Looking for the face of someone I drew with I was ten. What was I thinking? What kind of person does something like this? I'm such an idiot!*

My knees began to buckle from under me. I must have looked rather odd, as Neera came running toward me as fast as her legs could carry her. She gripped my right arm, and put her other hand at the small of my back. "Are you all right Miss? Are you all right? Please! Please come sit down over here in the shade. This heat!" When we sat down in the shade, Neera asked again, "What is troubling you Miss? Please tell me."

I shook my head. Then a moment later I said, "Well I know you have thought since the moment we met that I was crazy. Especially when I told you that I was looking for the face of the woman I drew when I was ten."

"Yes, Miss." Neera said with a little chuckle.

I pointed to the large sphinx in the middle of the yard where I had just been standing. "Well that face, over there, on the sphinx was the face. But of course it couldn't be the face now could it, because all the

Sphinx's are all men right so ..." At this, I noticed all the color drained right out of Neera's face. "What is it?" I asked.

Neera took a few moments to answer, and then said pointing to the sphinx in the middle of the grounds, "Not that one."

"What one?" I asked.

"That one. The one you were just pointing to. The one who you said was the face of the woman you had drawn when you were ten. That sphinx over there is a woman."

"What?" I said, suddenly close to tears. "That sphinx over there is a woman?" I cried.

Queen Hatshepsut

"Yes. She was one of the most powerful and great rulers Egypt has ever known. Queen Hatshepsut." Neera said proudly. I tried to pronounce the name as Neera had just said it. Neera shook her head. "In English, her name is pronounced close to the words, "Queen Hot Chicken Soup." We both laughed.

"Please tell me more about her." I asked.

"Queen Hatshepsut was one of the great rulers of Egypt as I said. She was also one of the greatest art patrons Egypt ever had. Queen Hatshepsut is responsible for some of the greatest art and buildings Egypt ever had created. Much of it still stands today." Neera then pointed once again to the sphinx in the middle of the yard. "Queen Hatshepsut was also the only woman in Egyptian history to have her face carved as a sphinx. So yes. That sphinx is a woman. Are you sure it is the face you drew so long ago?" Neera said, frowning.

"I am more sure of that than I am of anything in my life." I answered, with tears streaming down my cheeks, as I stared at that giant and magnificent sphinx who I now knew was Queen Hatshepsut, the face I drew when I was ten.

"Well then Miss." Neera said squeezing my arm. "You found what you came for. Yes?"

"Yes." I replied. "I can go home now."

When I returned to America, I called a psychic friend of mine named Rina, and asked, "Can you please help me understand what happened in Egypt? Why was I so incredibly drawn to go there? Why did it seem so utterly familiar to me? It was all so bizarre."

Rina laughed and said, "You mean, other than the fact that you hadn't been back for nearly 3,500 years and wanted to see your old home again, not to mention revisiting an old sound chamber and a sphinx or two?" I nearly fell off my chair.

This story of my finding Queen Hatshepsut is just one example how the spontaneous decisions and choices that I began to make in my new life led me on fascinating adventures, which I could never have predicted or planned.

How our choices change the world

Mahatma Gandhi had many wise things to say about our choices, and how we can change the world as a result. Gandhi said,

1. Choose to change yourself first. "You must be the change you want to see in the world."

If we change ourselves, we will change our world. If we change how we think then we will change how we feel. New feelings will change what actions we take. If we change our thoughts and our actions, the world around us will change. Our greatness lies not so much in being able to remake the world, but in in being able to remake ourselves.

2. Choose to be in control of yourself and your feelings at all times: "Nobody can hurt me without my permission."

What we feel and how we react to anything is always up to us. No one outside of us can actually control how we feel. We choose our own thoughts, reactions and emotions to anything and everything. It's always our choice.

3. Choose to forgive and let it go: "The weak can never forgive. Forgiveness is the attribute of the strong."

Choose to forgive. By making the choice to forgive we release ourselves from the past. This allows us to live a more joyful, and fulfilling present. Choose to forgive others not because they deserve it, but because you deserve peace.

4. Choose to take care of this moment: "I do not want to foresee the future. I am concerned with taking care of the present. God has given me no control over the moment following."

Staying in the present moment as much as possible gets better with practice. When we are fully in the present moment, we don't worry about the next moment, which we can't control anyway. Spending our time imagining negative future consequences, or reflecting on past failures, wastes the very valuable now of the present. Our only point of power is *Now*.

6. Choose to see everyone as human: "I claim to be a simple individual liable to err like any other fellow mortal. I own, however, that I have humility enough to confess my errors, and to retrace my steps."

Everyone is just a human being no matter who they are. We all do the best we can, with what we know at the time. When we consider past errors, it is helpful to remember that if we could have done better we would have. Now is the time to forgive our humanness and move on.

7. Choose to persist: "First they ignore you, then they laugh at you, then they fight you, then you win."

When we find what we really believe in, we discover inner motivation with the potential to drive us to accomplish great things. One of the reasons people don't get what they want in life is simply because they give up too soon. Success or victory seldom comes as quickly as we would like it to. Dare to dream and make new choices; this will take you farther than you ever imagined possible.

8. Choose to see the good in people and help them: "I look only to the good qualities of men. Not being faultless myself, I won't presume to probe into the faults of others."

My mother always told me, "Everyone has good in them. But with some people you may have to dig a little deeper to find it." Each of us has the power to decide what things we choose to focus on. Focusing on the good in people is an empowering choice as well because they will often rise to the level of your positive expectation.

9. Choose to be congruent and authentic: "Happiness is when what you think, what you say, and what you do are in harmony."

Happiness begins from within. When our thoughts, words and actions are aligned, authentic and sincere, other people are more likely to listen to and trust us.

From Me To You

Everything begins with our choices. I always ask myself, "Is this choice I am about to make bringing me closer or farther away from what I truly want in my life right now?" This question focuses all of my decisions and always leads me to the more loving and empowering choice for myself.

CONCLUSION

The constant social media bombardment from all over the world at all hours of the night and day has the net effect of ultimately dulling our senses. In the current charged political climate, we are bombarded with propaganda from every political point of view. However, if any person or country sets a long-term intention, it remains empowering no matter what.

The "long term view" can become our new daily practice, as when we choose respect for all beings, peace in the world is possible. A.T. Ariyaratane, a Buddhist Elder and considered the Gandhi of Sri Lanka., presented a beautiful example of just such a long-term intention. His Sarvodaya movement combines Buddhist principles of right livelihood, right action, right understanding, and compassion and has organized citizens in one-third of the nation's villages to dig wells, build schools, to meditate, and collaborate as a form of spiritual practice.

A 500 Year Peace Plan

For over twenty-five years there was a terrible civil war in Sri Lanka. The Norwegians eventually brokered peace. Once the peace treaty was in effect, an Elder of the Sarvodaya movement, a man named Ariyaratane, called his followers together. Over 650,000 people came to the gathering to hear how he envisioned the future of Sri Lanka. At this gathering he proposed a 500-year peace plan, saying, "The Buddha teaches we must understand causes and conditions. It's taken us 500 years to create the suffering that we are in now."

Ariyaratane went on to describe the effects of 400 years of colonialism, of 500 years of struggle between Hindus, Muslims and Buddhists, and of several centuries of economic disparity. He went on, "It will take us 500 years to change these conditions." Ariyaratane then offered solutions, proposing a plan to heal the country.

The plan began with initial years of cease-fire, and the first years of rebuilding roads and schools. Then his plan went on for ten, twenty-five, fifty years with specific programs to learn each other's languages and cultures, to right economic injustice, and to bring the islanders back together as a whole. Every one hundred years he proposed that there would be a Council Of Elders to take stock of how the plan was going. This is a beautiful example of a sacred intention, the long-term vision of an Elder.

Other nations around the world could use some truly wise Elders right now. These Elders would be those people, male and female, who step forward with a long-term vision for the world. Today, when many people believe that the world is teetering on the edge of WWIII and the traditional nuclear détente appears to be failing to hold the peace, we need a long-term vision now more than ever in the history of the world.

To empower this long-term vision, we need to start now and be willing to plant seeds however long it takes in order to benefit both our society and ourselves. Gandhi reminds us: "I claim to be no more than an average person with less than average ability. I have not the shadow of a doubt that any man or woman can achieve what I have if he or she would simply make the same effort and cultivate the same hope and faith."

Each person can choose to offer their unique vision and energy to support the world no matter where they live. We can also choose to empower the people around us. If we don't, change won't happen. Do not doubt for a moment that that positive change in the world can be born from your choices and your life right now.

From Me To You

There is a woman in the Middle East, completely unattached to any political agenda, who decided one day to begin planting date palms. This woman has planted a date palm daily for many decades.

She will not live to eat a single date from any of those date palms that she has planted. However, she envisions the people of the future with a bountiful harvest as a result of her daily practice. This woman made a choice to set a long-term intention of the heart.

It is a powerful act to stay true to our values, and also to live by them. Thomas Merton taught, "Do not worry about immediate results. More and more you must concentrate on the value, the rightness, the truth of the work itself."

This one woman who plants date palms in the Middle East set her compass of the heart on food for future generations. Taking the "long term view" can become a daily practice for all of us. This daily choice to act with integrity demonstrates a profound belief in our deepest shared human values.

BOOK 2

THE KEY OF GUIDANCE

"I wish I could show you, when you are lonely or in darkness,
the astonishing light of your own being."
~Hafiz of Shiraz

INTRODUCTION

I have always had this feeling that "someone" or "something" was watching over me, guiding me with very loving gifts of ideas, images and inspirations. These images in my imagination began when I was little, and continue to show up now in my life, often when I'm listening to or playing music, kiteboarding, doing art or simply sitting quietly looking out over the ocean. Some people call this loving presence their Guardian Angel. I'm not sure what it is. All I can say is that my intuitive guidance, this gift of continual creative assistance, comes from a place I know loves me.

Meet Aunt JaneAnn

It was my Aunt JaneAnn who first called my attention to this way of living life guided by intuition. Aunt JaneAnn taught me from the age I was barely able to walk, that I could always close my eyes, go inside my heart and pour my questions out to God. She assured me that God would always answer if I called, but that His answer would not necessarily come in words. Aunt JaneAnn instructed me that I was to always keep my eyes open for what she called, "Signs." These Signs could come through the words of other people, in a song, or could even be found on a billboard. Most often these days, my most frequent and consistent Sign of Love from God, The Source, shows up as a heart shaped rock.

From a very young age, I often visited my Aunt JaneAnn at her home in Los Angeles. We had this special ritual we did together every time I came to visit. We hopped into her yellow mustang convertible, put the top down and then drove to the Zen Bakery. There we bought blueberry muffins and every kind of cookie they sold. From the Zen Bakery, we drove down to the Self Realization Fellowship in Malibu.

The Self Realization Fellowship was founded by Yogananda. On the Self Realization Fellowship grounds there is a big lake which has a lovely path completely surrounding it, and where there are benches in various spots. Aunt JaneAnn and I always chose the bench closest to the spot where a portion of Ghandi's ashes was buried. We would sit together on the bench and talk, looking out over the lake and at the many colored water lilies, as we ate the muffins and cookies from the Zen Bakery.

Next, we would walk over to the Self Realization Fellowship Lake Shrine. There we would meditate together, sitting quietly with eyes closed for about half an hour. Next, we'd walk back to the car, and then drive over to the Bohdi Tree Bookstore. This was always my favorite part of our ritual journey together. At the Bohdi Tree Bookstore, Aunt JaneAnn always gave me the very same direction. "Wander around the bookstore and see what book jumps out at you. If one looks particularly interesting, bring it up to the counter and start making a stack. Trust your instinct about how many books are enough. Just let me know when you're done."

For about the next hour or so, I would wander around the new and used book sections, waiting to see what books "called" to me. There were times when a book seemed to glow to get my attention in a particular bookshelf. Other times, a book might actually fall off a table or shelf just as I was standing there and then land close to my feet. These books clearly wanted to come home with me and most definitely went into my stack at the counter. Eventually I might have a stack of anywhere from three to ten books. When I had collected a particularly large stack of books, I would look at Aunt JaneAnn with a question mark in my eyes.

My Aunt JaneAnn never asked me why I chose a particular book. She would simply say, "Did each of these books "call" to you?

I would nod and say, "Absolutely."

"Wrap 'em all up please." Aunt JaneAnn would tell the person at the cash register.

When we got home, I would take my book treasures into the guest room, disappear for the rest of the day and read. Invariably, there was a book I had not chosen myself, but that Aunt JaneAnn had slipped into my bag of books for me to discover as a surprise.

When I came out later in the afternoon, Aunt JaneAnn would ask with a knowing smile, "So did you learn anything interesting from your book treasures?" Then we would talk and talk and talk about the new ideas I had discovered.

One particular trip to the bookstore, I had chosen a book about people who had had what were called, NDE's or "Near Death Experiences," and OBE's which were "Out Of Body Experiences." That day, I asked Aunt JaneAnn about near death experiences, and she told me about hers.

Aunt JaneAnn's out of body experience

When Aunt JaneAnn was twenty-four years old, she fell off a horse and broke her neck. By the time the ambulance got her to the Emergency Room and on to an operating table, the doctors saw the heart monitor flat line. She was clinically considered dead. By the time they got their paddles to her chest, she remembered seeing herself floating above the operating table watching from above. Aunt JaneAnn watched the doctors try to shock her back to life a few times and then throw up their hands in frustration. Next she felt herself being dragged away into a very bright light.

"What was that Light like? I asked. As Aunt JaneAnn described the light to me, she got a very wistful expression on her face and then seemed to be far away, lost in thought. "So, what was it like?" I asked again, eager to know.

Aunt JaneAnn returned from her reverie, "Well you know me and how much I love my animals, Uncle Scott and my kids. But I swear, I could have left everything behind in an instant just to be in that incredible feeling of amazing Love and Light. The Love was completely unconditional and the Light was like nothing here on earth. Honestly, it's all pretty hard to describe. It was like nothing I had ever experienced before, or have experienced since."

"Tell me more!" I insisted, leaning forward in my seat.

Aunt JaneAnn went on, "Well, I begged to be allowed to stay in that beautiful Light and Love. But then I heard this really warm and loving Voice say, 'I'm sorry to tell you, Jane Ann but you're not done yet. You are going to have to go back to earth.' Again, I begged to be allowed to stay but this beautiful loving Voice repeated, 'Right now is not your time to come Home. Not yet.'

"What happened next was rather strange. I found myself leaving the warm and Loving Light and gradually returning back toward the hospital operating table. For some odd and unexplainable reason, I hovered over the operating table just long enough to read the serial number of the light fixture located directly over the operating table. I then found myself back in my body again.

"Suddenly I was in terrible, absolutely agonizing pain. It felt like I was trapped in a suit that was entirely too tight. Then I opened my eyes."

"What did the doctors say to that?" I asked.

"Well as you might imagine, they were quite surprised to see me open my eyes. They had given up on me and were all just about to leave the room. It was one of the nurses who shouted, 'Oh my God! She's alive! She's back!'

"So there I was on the operating table, with my head and body strapped to the table so I couldn't move. My neck had been broken by the fall off the horse, and they told me later that I had been only about only one centimeter from being completely paralyzed. But at that time in the operating room, everybody was just pretty happy to see me open my eyes!"

Aunt JaneAnn laughed out loud at the memory. "But you know me. I never can resist a joke. Before we left the room, I told the group that I had seen God."

"You didn't!" I exclaimed. "Did they believe you?"

"Nope. They thought it was the anesthetic talking and no, they didn't believe me. So I told them I could prove it to them. 'You all know you have had me strapped to this table all this time since I have been in this room? Well, I left my body while you were giving me those shock paddles over there. While I was out of my body, I hovered above my body and all of you standing here in this room. In fact, I can tell you the exact serial number of that light over this table.' They all looked at me like I was crazy." Aunt JaneAnn laughed.

"So what did you do next?" I asked.

"I proceeded to give them the exact letters and numbers I had seen on the light fixture above the operating table. I even made one of the nurses go get a pen and write it down on her hand."

"Did they believe you?" I asked.

"Nope. So next, I made one of the other nurses climb up on to the table next to me and read out loud the numbers from the light fixture over my operating table. Of course, the numbers on the light fixture and the numbers on the other nurses hand were a perfect match."

"Seriously? You made them climb up?" I said.

"Well of course, they still didn't believe me and thought it was some sort of trick I had played on them." Aunt JaneAnn said shaking her head. "But that trip into the Light changed both my life and also my light energy. I was never the same after that."

"In what way?" I asked.

"Well for one thing," Aunt JaneAnn smiled wistfully, "I knew without a doubt what true unconditional Love felt like. That experience changed the course of my life.

"I began to work with kids who were very ill and many of whom were dying of cancer and other illnesses. I formed my foundation, The Kite Foundation, which stands for Kids In Transitional Experience. I got my PhD and helped a lot of kids from this side of life over to the other side called Home.

"I also went out of my way to always reassure these kids from my own personal experience that The Other Side, or Heaven or Bliss or Home or whatever belief system they came from, was a great place, very safe and loving. I told them that they didn't have to stick around here on earth feeling guilty, or to take care of their parents, or even worry about anyone in their family anymore. I basically reassured them that they could leave their bodies whenever they felt ready and die in peace."

"Wow. That's' so cool. I bet those kids loved you and were so relieved not to have to worry about sticking around for their parents." This made me think about our family, and especially the recent death of my favorite brother.

Then, I asked my Aunt JaneAnn the question most important in my mind, "So, as you look back, what was the most important thing you learned from your out of body near death experience?"

Aunt JaneAnn thought for a moment. Then she took my hand tenderly and said with great love and understanding, "I never, ever, ever, feared death again."

As tears began to stream down my face, I said, "Thank you for that. Thank you."

From Me To You

When my Aunt JaneAnn was dying for real at a very ripe old age, we were sitting together reminiscing about our time together sitting at Yogananda's Lake Shrine and how she had taught me to always look for The Signs.

She asked me what was the best sign I had ever received. I replied that my best Sign from God came in all shapes and sizes of heart rocks.

When I asked her what she thought it meant that I found heart rocks everywhere, and had found them all over the world wherever I travelled, Aunt JaneAnn smiled and said, "It's quite clear to me. You see in The Universe what The Universe sees in you."

SURVIVE

Guidance can come from within us as a hunch or an intuition as to what we should do next. Sometimes, guidance comes from other people or in our dreams at night.

One night in New York, I had a powerful dream. My favorite brother Bob, and I, were sitting on twin beds and we were laughing so hard that tears were streaming down our faces.

Finally, catching his breath, Bob said, "Oh. My. God! Life! You can't live in it and you can't live out of it. So I guess ya might as well enjoy it, right?!"

"Right!" I said, and we burst out laughing again.

Then I woke up.

I had every intention of calling my brother the next morning to tell him about this funny dream, but I had several important auditions that day and didn't make the time to call. As I was going to sleep that night, I thought to myself, *I'll call Bob tomorrow. He will just love hearing about that dream.*

The sudden death that rocked my world

The next morning as I was having breakfast, the phone rang. It was my older brother John. The first thing he said was, "Ok Sis. Are you sitting down because you might want to before I say anything more."

I chirped, "What's up Bro?"

There was a long silence. "I'm sorry to be the one who has to tell you this but Bob is dead."

My head started to swim, my knees buckled and I slid to the floor in my kitchen. "What?" was all I could manage to get out of my mouth.

John repeated, "He died sometime early this morning."

"What?" I repeated again, refusing to grasp this news.

John repeated it. "He's dead, Mary Anne. Bob is dead. You will probably want to get on a plane and come home as soon as you can."

"What happened?" I asked. "How did he die?"

"Well that's a long story but right now it looks like he was with friends, got drunk and took a lot of drugs and they didn't walk him around before he went to bed. He died of a drug and alcohol overdose. I'm so sorry."

"Uh, yeah, me too. I'll get on a plane as soon as possible." I said numbly.

"Are you OK?" John asked.

"Are you?" I shot back.

"Not really. This is one hell of a horrible day."

"You got that right." I replied.

"Look I have other calls to make. You know. About Bob. I'll call you back later and we can talk more." John sighed.

"Thanks for calling John. I really appreciate it. I know this can't be easy for you either. Are you OK?" I asked.

"Not really." John said. "But I'll get through it." John sighed again.

"I know you will John. We all will. Somehow." I said and then we hung up.

As the tears began to fall, all I could think of was, *I should have called him. I should have called him and told him my dream. Maybe he wouldn't have died* All my life my brother Bob and I had always felt like two sides of the same coin. Whenever I was in trouble, sad or confused, he was the person I always called.

"What will I do now?" I sobbed. "What will I do now?" I sat there, on the floor, with tears streaming down my face and the phone in my hand for quite some time, repeating, over and over in my mind, *This can't be happening. Not Bob.*

Life after Bob

This next section, like all the sections in this book, is optional reading. It is about an encounter with my deceased brother Bob. If you are uncomfortable with the idea of speaking with departed spirits, or you have trouble with the idea of the afterlife and reincarnation, then you may wish to choose to move on to reading the next chapter.

On the other hand, even if you are uncomfortable, you may want to read it anyway. What I will describe here is an event that actually happened. I am including this story in this book because so much of who I am today, and how I look at life, came from this experience. You may be surprised by what you discover about your own beliefs after reading this. Take what you will from this chapter and if you wish, consider applying it to your own life.

My first visit to a psychic medium

I struggled for years after losing my younger brother, Bob. He was only 22 years old when he died and I was 24. Sadly, after Bob's funeral our father refused to allow his name to be spoken at the dinner table. No toasts were allowed. There was no talking about Bob. We were all expected to keep our grief private.

After a week of this torture, I called my Aunt JaneAnn. She simply said, "Get on a plane, Mary Anne. Today. I'll pay for it. I'll pick you up in a few hours at the airport. Got it?"

I smiled for the first time in a long time. "Got it." I said. I took the next possible flight to LA to be with my Aunt. Perhaps she could help me make some sense of this terrible loss. When I arrived in LA, we took our usual field trip to the Zen Bakery, the Self Realization Fellowship, and the Bohdi Tree Bookstore.

Next, Aunt JaneAnn insisted that I go see a psychic medium, a lady whom she knew and trusted. I hesitated, because I knew that my brother Bob would never show up through a psychic, and I told my Aunt so.

Aunt JaneAnn laughed and said, "Maybe. But sometimes souls on the other side will take whatever opportunity they can to communicate with us on this side. Personally, I think he'll show up."

I insisted, "Bob would consider the whole idea of yours total and complete bunk."

Aunt JaneAnn said gently, "You will never know unless you try it."

So I went. I was apprehensive about the meeting. What if this person was a total and complete fake? Conversely, what if this woman could read my darkest secrets? In any case, since this was my first experience with a psychic, I have to admit I was curious to know what it would be like.

I was certain of one thing: My brother Bob wouldn't show up.

As the psychic went into a trance, her body went limp for a moment and then she began channeling an entity by the name of Indira. Indira's voice was completely different from the female voice of the psychic. When Indira started speaking, I was taken aback and a bit frightened.

This new deeper, more male sounding voice of Indira started speaking in an Indian accent, "This is a bit difficult for me to explain to you. Your brother is standing beside you right now, somewhat awkwardly, as if he is not sure about being here or is feeling quite uncomfortable. He is holding out a red rose for you. He thinks you will understand this symbol. Do you?"

I was still unconvinced and uncomfortable. I replied, "Well, my brother Bob knows that I have always loved roses."

"Well this is part of it." The voice of Indira said. "Wait one moment. Your brother is recalibrating himself to connect better with this channel's energy. This is new to him, he says. Please wait one moment."

I sat absolutely still in the chair opposite her, not saying a word. Then, much to my astonishment, my brother Bob's voice came through the mouth of this psychic, and he started talking to me just like old times. It was very strange to hear Bob speaking through someone else's mouth, especially considering that he was dead.

Bob's message

"Ok. First thing here. You know me M.A. When I was alive, I didn't believe in these kinds of people, these psychics. I thought they were all total and complete bull. But Aunt JaneAnn created this opportunity on your side and so I took it. I love you so much. I'm so sorry you have been in such pain since I left. But I had to go. I had to." Bob said through the mouth of the medium.

The sound of Bob's "voice," even through another person, made me cry. "Oh My God! Is it really you Bob?" I said, tears streaming down my face. I missed my brother so much.

"Look, M.A., I know this is totally weird: me talking through someone else! It feels so weird to me too, trying to fit my voice into someone else's mouth. It's totally bizarre. But I really needed to talk to you."

"Me too you." I replied. When he was alive, my brother and I always said these words to each other on the phone when we talked, and he was the only person in the world who called me M.A. Oddly enough, at that moment, I felt kind of like I was speaking to him by telephone again.

"I need you to know two very important things about what's real in life and what's not. OK?" Bob said urgently. I nodded in response to what he was saying. "It's all about Love. Everything. All of it. Can you believe that? It sounds so simple, I know. But I guess it isn't or we would have figured it out by now, right?"

I laughed. "Yeah, you're right there."

Bob went on, "Remember this, OK? Never pass up a chance to show Love. It might be a kind word, a note, a phone call or a little gift. Let people know that you Love them. That's what the universe is all about. I know it's rough where you are with all the positive and negative stuff going on. But in truth it is all about Love."

"OK. I got it. Thanks. What's the second thing you wanted me to know?"

There was a pause, and then he continued. "The second thing is a real mind blower. It was for me anyway once I came Home. Oh, by the way, that's what it's called over here: Home.

"Anyway, you know how everything looks so incredibly solid where you are? Like when you walk around and bump into things - walls, tables? That sucks. It hurts like hell; you know what I mean? I really hated that about life on earth.

"From my new perspective here now I can tell you this. Everything around you isn't actually real. It's all energy. Everything. What you see with your eyes is not as solid as it seems. If I had realized the power of my mind to move all obstacles out of my way, I would have done things very differently in my life there...." There was another long pause.

"Did you have to face any judgment when you left for the choice you did make here, you know.... dying like you did...as in you know, killing yourself?" I asked. My brother had died from what had appeared to be an accidental overdose of alcohol and drugs.

Bob continued, "No, there actually is no judgment here at Home. There is only complete acceptance and total Love. In the world where you are, people are so totally critical and judgmental. They only think in terms of positive and negative. But here it's all just Love. It's so hard to put into words. But I know now that if I had understood this Love when I was alive - that everything is energy, anything is possible and I could literally move mountains with my mind alone - I believe that I would have made some very different choices.

"Anyway, I could not continue the way I was going. As you know, I felt totally trapped. So I decided to make the choice to leave that life and start over again. After I died, I came home and met with my Advisors – they are kind of like your soul's Board of Directors here - to rethink my life plan for the next time around. I'm totally cool, so please don't worry about me, OK? Nothing, absolutely nothing bad happens to you after you die. It's all good."

I sighed in relief. "OK. I was wondering about that, especially considering how you, you know, you chose to leave your life." I was so glad to know that my brother had not been punished or faced some sort of fiery Hell out of Dante's *Inferno* for killing himself.

"No actually M.A. there's no such thing as hell here. None at all." he said, as if he had read my mind. "Yeah, I can read your mind. It's one of the very cool things that you can do from this side. People's thoughts broadcast like sound coming from a radio there and we can hear them easily from here.

"Anyway, people create their own hell in their minds and with the choices they make on earth. Hell is a fictional place that religious people want you to believe exists so they can control you and take your money. Here at our true Home it's nothing but unconditional Love, Peace and Acceptance. Got it?"

A big smile bloomed on my face, and then I said, "Got it." I used to smile a lot when I was with Bob; he was always so irreverent. I hadn't smiled in a while. In fact, I hadn't smiled since he died. "God, I miss you Bob! It's not the same here without you. I don't know if I can make it here on my own without you."

Bob replied, "Yeah, I hear that. In fact, I brought that up with my Advisors when I got over here. They told me that this was our original plan before either of us were born. The purpose of the plan we created, and both of us agreed to, was to give you a chance to learn the lessons of grief and loss. I tried to send you a dream about that. Did you get it?"

I was stunned. "Oh my God! Wow! I thought it was just a dream. It never occurred to me that you sent it to me as a message. This is amazing! But I have to ask, why in the world would we plan your death like that? This hurts. Missing you hurts so much!" I said, tears beginning to stream down my face.

"I know it doesn't feel like it makes any sense right now. But you and I did plan it that way. You were very clear that you wanted to experience great loss and sorrow, so you could gain the strength that comes from struggling with profound grief. Taking away your favorite brother seemed the quickest way to help you move forward in the growth and learning of strength that you wanted. Does that make sense to you?"

I sighed. "Yeah, I suppose. But I still don't like it - not one bit. You get to experience unconditional Love over there and I still have to deal with all the crap over here. It just doesn't seem fair."

Bob suddenly became very firm, "Stop whining M.A. You're not a whiner, and you're not a quitter. You are strong and you have to go on. Promise me that you'll finish that big audacious plan you have for the rest of your life."

"I promise." I said. "But I don't like having to go through it without you. I need you!"

Bob then reassured me, in the way only he could, "You don't have to like it. You just have to work through it. One step at a time M.A. Just one step at a time."

"I'll try." I promised.

"Good." Bob said. "Back to what I was telling you before, since I have to go soon. I actually have another meeting with my Advisors about my next life. Doesn't that sound weird?" He laughed again.

"Yeah it does. Totally." I replied with a grin. "Go ahead and tell me what else you wanted me to know before our time is up." I said.

"OK. Now that you know these two important things - that love is the most important thing and that everything is energy - you have to live your life based on these principles."

"How in the world can I do that?" I said.

Bob tried his best to explain, "Focus on being Love, and using the power of your mind to move all obstacles out of your way. Remember that nothing is solid and everything is energy. The bottom-line it this: *Everything is Love. Use the power of your mind to move all obstacles out of your way.* That's what I want you to take away from our meeting." There was another long pause. Then Bob said, "I love you MA."

"I love you too Bob." I answered. There was another pause.

"It's time for me to go." he said.

"Please don't leave me Bob!" I cried.

"I'm sorry but I have to go now. And you have some big mountains to move, M.A."

"I'll do my best Bob. Will I ever be able to talk to you again?" I asked hopefully.

"If you put a rose by your bedside at night, I'll know that you want me to communicate with you. I will reach you through your dreams. Then we can talk again. OK?"

"OK." I said. "Can you stay with me just a bit longer?" But, he was gone.

The deep voice of Indira, the channel, returned. "That was an interesting visit was it not?"

"Yes it was." I replied, feeling comforted by having been with Bob, but also profoundly sad that he was gone.

Now, whenever I want to speak with my brother Bob, I buy a red rose or cut one from my garden and the put it on my bedside table. Before I fall asleep, I close my eyes and say these words in my mind, *I'm ready, Bob.*

If you are missing a special relative, like I miss my brother Bob every single day, try asking for a dream to connect with them. You could even try writing your deceased relative or friend's name on a piece of paper and then put that piece of paper under your pillow at night as a "signal" that you wish to speak with them. You may think this is a total fantasy or even a little crazy, but I urge you to consider trying it. As my Aunt JaneAnn always said to me, "You'll never know until you try."

From Me To You

Our inner wisdom is our most trustworthy ally. That inner wisdom is also the source of reliable, infallible guidance at all times. I have adopted a practice of Listen. Trust. Act.

THE ROUNDABOUT

I've been truly blessed by many wonderful teachers along my life path. The people I consider my true teachers have come in many types: from mentors, friends, therapists, healers, doctors, books, spiritual leaders and a wonderful supportive husband, to cruel and unkind family members, psychopathic employers, violent rapists and narcissistic ex husbands. While it may be hard for you to see these types of people as blessings in your own life, I can assure you that all of these people have been true blessings in my life.

Every difficulty, difficult person and difficult encounter along our path of life contains within it the possibility and the potential for many things: an awakening, a new valuable awareness, rebirth, joy, survival and yes, even Thriving. Each person in my life, especially the tough ones, has played a very important role in guiding me along the way to a clearer sense of both what I did and did not want to manifest in my life. I can honestly say that I would not have learned how to move beyond Surviving, nor learned how to Thrive without each one of these people having been a valuable part of my life journey.

When it comes to changing their life for the better, many people ask me, "Where should I start?" I always ask them, "As a soul, do you know what your soul lessons are? In other words, what you came here to learn?" For many people, this is a bit of a foreign concept. "What is a soul lesson?" they invariably ask. You will find a clue about what your soul lessons are from becoming more aware of what shows up in your life in three specific areas:

1. What are you most afraid of?

2. What really frustrates you?

3. What make you really angry?

Once you know what those things are, you can begin to notice how they show up in your life, over and over, until you learn how to deal with them.

Most of our biggest lessons in life show up first in negativity. Then, as we begin to deal with them, we move more and more toward learning what changes we need to make in our lives. As we make more healthy choices and learn to fully live our days always listening to our inner guidance, we begin to make more healthy choices and then we feel more tranquility and inner peace.

From Me To You

The great music genius B.B. King said, "The beautiful thing about learning is nobody can take it away from you."

What are the things you have learned so far in your life that you value the most? Remember, no one can ever take that learning away from you. You carry that beautiful wisdom with you for the rest of your life.

THRIVE

As I paddle on my paddleboard, kiteboard on the ocean, walk along the beach or on a mountain trail, I often let my mind wander. The human mind is our central processing unit but here's the astonishing thing: Did you know that the more that doctors, scientists, academics, and researchers discover about the human brain—the less they understand the human mind?

You might assume that the brain and mind are more or less the same thing. But actually, our brain is only the physical part of us. It has neurons, dendrites, synapses, and grey matter constantly firing messages in all directions throughout our body. But the mind is not physical; it's our inner consciousness. Moment by moment, our minds create how we think and behave, our deep emotions, and more or less everything else that defines how we feel, and act. Our minds also have a profound impact on all the decisions we make.

Each of our minds has a very distinct and unique map that is much like a blueprint. I was totally shocked when I learned that each of us acquired this unique blueprint and it was installed in our subconscious like a program in our mind's computer, before the age of 7. This means that before the age of 7, our brains were actually programmed by our parents, teachers, churches mosques or synagogues, and society in general. These programs were all to do with what is considered "acceptable" or "preferable" behavior according to the specific culture that we were born into.

According to psychologists, this programming has been filed away in our subconscious minds and actually now drives a full 95% of our daily decisions, thoughts and actions in present time. Here is the most amazing part of all: even as our subconscious blueprint drives the majority of our daily decisions and actions, *70% of those subconscious programs are negative*. This information totally blew my mind.

The beggar sitting on a box of gold

There is an old story about a beggar sitting on a box on the side of the road holding out a begging bowl. Unknown to him, the box he was sitting on was filled with gold, which would have relieved him completely of the need to ever beg again. But because he didn't know that, and believed that he was sitting on an ordinary box, day after day he complained of how hard, difficult and unfair life was. All the while, this beggar was sitting on top of infinite riches.

I never imagined that I, like the beggar sitting on that box of gold, had an incredible power within me to change my own life. It had always been there, right inside me all along. All my answers about how to change my life were hiding right there within me. I just had to understand what my attachments and aversions were, and then figure out where and whom they had come from. I learned that most of the time, we get the majority of our unconscious programming from our family and the culture we grew up in. I realized that all my programming in my subconscious wasn't even mine, and that is was all a form of propaganda, which had actually come from someone and somewhere else! Once I understood this very important truth, I realized that if a program or programming I had chosen to believe up to that point wasn't mine, I could choose to discard or change it. Once I changed some of my limiting beliefs about myself, which had been located in my subconscious blueprint from the past, my life in the present began to shift and change dramatically.

These days, I do my very best not to beat myself up for things that happened in my past, as in the past I truly did not known any better. It was a relief to realize that I had actually done the best I could with both the information and programming which I believed at that time. If I could have done better, I would have done better. Every single choice I have ever made seemed like the best idea at the time.

From Me To You

Whenever I get anxious about the future, I remind myself, "I don't need to know. My inner guidance guides me as I go." The job of our inner guidance is always to direct us toward our highest and greatest Good. We can choose to learn from our choices of the past and apply all that great learning toward better living in our present reality. We don't have to know how everything in our lives is going to unfold in our future. All we need to do is trust that out inner guidance always guides us wherever we go.

CONCLUSION

As we learn how to trust our inner guidance, how do we know who or what we can truly trust? The poet, Maya Angelou, suggested, "When people tell you who they really are, believe them the first time." I know this is easier said than done. Over the years, I have listened to the positive words people say, but not really paid enough attention to their actual negative actions. I once heard a great story that speaks to this. It's a great reminder to always pay attention and trust our own inner guidance.

The Lady and the Snake

A woman was walking along the road one day when a snake crossed her path. The Snake stopped, looked at her, and said, "Please lovely Lady, please pick me up."

The woman looked at the snake and said, "No way. I'm not picking you up. You're a snake. I know what snakes do. You will bite me."

The Snake replied seductively, "Oh beautiful Lady. I am just a lonely snake looking for a little warmth. You have that beautiful cloak around you. All I want is a little hug. Can you just give me a little hug? That's all I need. I am just a little, old, lonely, snake. Please, please pick me up?"

The woman looked dubiously at the snake, and replied, "You're kidding right? Do you really think I am that stupid? I'm not picking you up. You're a snake. You will bite me, I know it. Forget it."

"But I am not like every other snake. I am a good snake. I don't bite people, especially a lovely Lady such as you. I am just cold and you have that beautiful warm cloak. All I want is a little hug, just for a moment. Please. Please. Take pity on me."

The woman suddenly felt compassion for the snake and said, "So. That's all you want? A little hug? That's it? If I pick you up, you promise you won't bite me?"

The snake said, "Of course not lovely Lady. If you pick me up, I give you my word: I will not bite you."

"Really? I have your word? You won't bite me?" the woman repeated.

"Really. You have my word." the snake replied.

The woman thought to herself, *What the heck. It will only be for a moment. He gave me his word.* She picked up the snake and wrapped him in her cloak. At that moment, the snake struck her with his fangs, right on the neck. "Ouch! That hurt! What did you do that for?" the woman exclaimed, as she threw the snake to the ground. "You gave me your word you wouldn't bite me?!"

The Snake hissed and laughed, "Lovely Lady, what do you expect? I'm a snake. Snakes bite. That's what snakes do. It's our nature. You knew I was a snake when you picked me up." At that, the snake slithered off into the bush, leaving the woman to die.

Don't we all at times choose to deal with people who are like the snake in this story, knowing it is their nature to bite us? We still choose to give them another chance, even when we know from our actual previous experience that certain people are not going to be good, kind, or act with integrity towards us. Sometimes we have to learn the hard way that a snake is a snake, will always be a snake, and will always behave like a snake. If given the opportunity, a snake will always bite us. That's what snakes do. It is their nature.

When you stop and think about it for a moment, we cannot fault the snake for behaving just how it is: a snake. We are the ones who need to change our behavior and our choices in relationship toward the snake. We can choose instead to remember the old adage, "Once a snake, always a snake." We can respect the fact that a person who is a snake will always behave like a snake. We can choose to respect ourselves by not listening to that snake, not dealing with it by picking it up, and make the wiser choice to just keep walking.

From Me To You

Do you trust your gut instincts about other people when you meet them, or have they repeatedly burned you? Ever hear that expression, "Burn me once, shame on you. Burn me twice, shame on me." Do you choose to pick up snakes some times in your life, even after you have been metaphorically bitten or burned by them?

These days, I live my life by the adage, "Trust. But verify." Whenever I meet or begin to do business with someone new, I listen to what they say, but I also watch closely how they behave. Their actions, not their words, tell me everything I need to know about who they really are, and whether they are trustworthy or not. People's actions also tell me everything I need to know about how they will undoubtedly treat me in the future.

BOOK 3

THE KEY OF HEALTH

"Don't give up. Normally, it is the last key on
the ring which opens the door."
~Paulo Cohelo

INTRODUCTION

This book, The Key Of Health, is in no way intended to help you diagnose or treat any illnesses or health issues you may be facing in your life right now. In this key, I will share with you some of my own personal health challenges, the choices I made in response to them, and the obstacles I ultimately overcame in order to solve them. The stories and experiences I share in this book are primarily intended to demonstrate my strong belief that any health problem, no matter how severe, contains within it an important life-changing lesson that will further us along our path to self-fulfillment.

I want to make it absolutely clear that I am not suggesting that you need to approach any health challenge, exactly as I did. Trust your own inner guidance about the path that feels right for you, and then follow that. Unlike others who may preach or teach that there is only one way (their way) to achieve good health, increased personal awareness or enlightenment, I want to emphasize that what has worked for me might not be what will work for you. We each have our own walk and we must find our own answers to vital health questions along the way. Always follow the path that feels right for you.

From Me To You

No matter what is happening at any given moment, I have always relied on the power of prayer.

"Prayer is sitting in the silence until it silences us, choosing gratitude until we are grateful, praising God until we ourselves are a constant act of praise."

~Friar Richard Rohr

THE KEY OF HEALTH

SURVIVE

Years ago when I had some health concerns, I met a healer named Dan, a well-respected massage therapist at the Miraval Spa in Tucson, Arizona. I asked the Spa staff whom they would recommend as the best massage professional and they told me that talk show host Oprah Winfrey used to fly Dan out to Chicago to work with her and her friends. Hearing that, I made an appointment with Dan for the following day.

When I first sat on the massage table, Dan made what I thought was a very bold statement: "Healing is possible, no matter what your circumstances." He said this with such conviction and certainty that it was hard to argue.

However, I chose to question it: "How do you know that for a fact?"

"It is a spiritual law. You must first heal yourself on the inside. Only then can healing take place on the outside, where you can see it." Dan answered.

"But how do you know this?" I insisted.

Dan smiled. "I have seen it time after time. Once a person is truly ready, they can be reborn from the inside out. They can heal themselves."

Of course I wondered if I was ready for this. In response to my puzzlement, Dan said, "Yes, you are ready. The time is now."

Was he reading my mind I wondered?

I was really surprised by his next question. "If you could walk away from it all and start your life now with a clean slate, chuck everything and start again, what would you do?"

"You mean all of it? As in, *ALL of it?*" I replied, wishing that what he had suggested could be true.

"All of it!" he said emphatically. As Dan looked at me, I felt as if he was looking right into my soul.

The next words flowed from my mouth without hesitation or forethought. "Oh God I know exactly what I would do! I would talk to people and I would write. That's it." I gave a huge sigh of longing at the thought.

"And why are you not doing this now?" Dan asked, his piercing blue eyes looking straight into mine.

"Uhhhhhh…" was all I could manage.

"Now you see!" Dan exclaimed. "By postponing your own joy in life, you will remain stuck in this position. You could change everything right now if you wanted to. Until you are ready to give birth to this new self your life will stay the same, and you will remain in a state of dis-ease. So you need to ask yourself how long are you willing to put up with this? When are you going to awaken the you that has been waiting a lifetime to be born?"

With a few words he had pierced me to the very core and my tears began to flow. With my head down I cried, "I don't know. I don't know. I don't know!"

After a minute or two he said gently, "You know, Mary Anne, you can make this change in an instant." Dan snapped his fingers. "An instant! That is all it takes to make this shift. It happens first in your mind, then in your words and actions, and then in your life. And it can all begin in a flash with a simple decision, just like that!" Dan snapped his fingers again.

I was stunned. "That's it?" I asked. "That's all it takes to finally take charge of my destiny?"

"Yes." Dan replied. The word reverberated through my soul.

"Somehow I thought it would be much more complicated than that." I said.

"Nope" he replied with a smile.

"So by changing your thoughts you can change your world?" I asked.

"That's it. Exactly." Dan said. A profound sense of relief began to permeate my entire body and I could feel my tension ebbing away.

Dan went on, "You must understand how important it is to listen to yourself. There is nothing I or anyone else can give you, tell you, or do for you.

"You have been searching your whole life for someone or something outside of yourself to give you the answer and yet it has been inside you all along. It is there now. Your inner guide will tell you what you need to do at any given moment.

"Stop looking outside yourself for the answer. It is now, and always has been, within."

I was reminded of an old Hindu legend that I had heard years ago:

There was once a time when all human beings were gods, but they so abused their divinity that Brahma, the chief god, decided to take it away from them and to hide it where it could never be found. Where to hide their divinity was the question.

Brahma called a council of the gods to help him decide. "Let's bury it deep in the earth." said the gods.

Brahma answered, "No, that won't work because humans will dig into the earth and find it."

Then the gods said, "Let's sink it in the deepest ocean."

Brahma said, "No, not there, for they will learn to dive into the ocean and will find it."

Then the gods said, "Let's take it to the top of the highest mountain and hide it there."

But once again Brahma replied, "No, that will not do either, because they will eventually climb every mountain and once again take up their divinity."

Then the gods gave up and said, "We do not know where to hide it. It seems that there is no place on earth or in the sea that human beings will not eventually reach."

Brahma thought for a long time and then said, "Here is what we will do. We will hide their divinity deep in the center of their own being, for humans will never think to look for it there."

All the gods agreed that this was the perfect hiding place, and the deed was done. And since that time humans have been going up and down the earth, digging, diving, climbing, and exploring, searching for something already within themselves."

I came back from my reverie to see Dan smiling at me. "Yes. That's it. That's it exactly."

Once again I was startled by his ability to seemingly read my mind. I had heard that shamans had special powers but it was another thing entirely to have someone pierce my inner thoughts. Again, in response to my inner thoughts I had not spoken out loud, Dan said, "Oh don't worry about that. You project your thoughts far more than you are aware. And by the way, those same thoughts are forming your reality. So pay close attention to the language in your head because that determines the future of your life."

I was floored by this notion. Dan went on, "Remember that Biblical verse that says, 'In the beginning was the Word, the Word was with God, and the Word was God.' (John 1:1)"

I nodded.

Dan continued, "If we are all made in the image and likeness of God, then our words should have that same power. But most people don't have this kind of faith, and so they are careless with their thoughts. This keeps them traveling in the same circle, never able to break free and truly experience their own divinity. Kind of like you right now."

I had to laugh at this. "You got that right!" I felt myself relaxing even more as I let his words sink in. I stopped worrying about him reading my mind. Maybe I didn't need to take myself so seriously, either. I had a revelation at that moment. It dawned on me that everything I ever wanted in my life was only a thought away.

Dan responded to my thoughts again. *"Yes. Exactly.* So watch your thoughts carefully and choose only those thoughts that conform to the reality that you want to create.

"Accept this - that we are all held in the Sacred Womb and our birth is more than just our entry into this world as infants. You can have a rebirth of consciousness when you pass a new threshold of understanding about yourself and the nature of your reality. You are doing so right now at this moment.

"If people understood how important it is to be mindful of their thoughts they would be amazed at how profoundly they could transform themselves and the world around them. You have that power inside of you, Mary Anne.

"If you would just write about what you are experiencing on a daily basis, many people could benefit from your experiences, thoughts and meditations.

"Be an example of how we can all manifest the life of our dreams and you will do a great service for humanity. If not, you would be just another example of a life not fully realized. It's always your choice. And you will always have another chance to get it right. Always."

Our massage session was over and although Dan had barely touched me with his hands, his words had transformed my world. I bowed to him in gratitude and then left the room.

As I was walking back over the beautiful Miraval grounds to my room, I was reminded of one of my favorite quotes by Julian Of Norwich, who recounted a revelation she received from Jesus Christ, ending with his words: "All shall be well, and all shall be well, and all manner of thing shall be well."

My visit with the shaman named Dan assured me that all shall be well if I said so. All shall be well if I decided so and all shall be well if I acted so. But first, I had a few bouts with cancer and some other health challenges to overcome.

The bike accident

After I was raped after a business meeting, one of the ways I dealt with the experience was to take up cycling. I bought a road bike, got my friend Eric to teach me how to ride it, and then joined the Native Planet Cycling Club. These people were serious hard-core cyclists. Some had ridden the Tour de France. Eventually, I was up to riding 100 miles a week.

One day I was the lead cyclist in a pace line of 8 expert cyclists on my Seattle Native Planet team. In our bright read black and yellow cycling jerseys we were hard to miss as our pace line was heading down the very steep hill by Bastyr University just outside of Seattle. Our tires were within a few inches of each other as we picked up speed heading down the hill. A car passed all eight of us on our left. Then, at an intersection in front of us that had a green light, the driver suddenly turned to the right and stopped, blocking our way through the intersection.

I had less than three seconds to react. All I could do was scream *"HEY! HEY! HEY!"* as I squeezed on my brakes hard, trying not to hit the car directly in front of me. Before I crashed, something very curious happened. All of a sudden time slowed down to what felt like taffy. There was total silence as time seemed to stretch out. I also saw everything happening in slow motion.

I turned my head and saw my Mother who had been dead for 20 years standing at the side of the road at the intersection. Suddenly as if by thought alone, I found myself standing next to her, both of us observing me, the car and the bike accident just about to happen.

I heard my Mother say very calmly, "If you would like to leave the planet, now would be a good time."

There was a split second pause, and then I screamed out the words, "I'm not leaving my children!"

As soon as these words left my lips, some sort of crucial, life altering "Decision" appeared to be made. Suddenly I was back on my bike heading toward the car windshield again. I remember clearly what happened next because it was equally bizarre. I had never been in a bike accident and no one on my team had prepared me for something like this.

In slow motion, my right hand seemed to act of its own accord. "Something" took control of my right hand just before impact with the car window, pulled the front, right handle bar back towards me. This caused my bike to slant to the right, and continue it's forward motion trajectory toward the car. But, instead of going through the window, I began to slide sideways under the car. As the bike slid under the car, my body was suddenly completely catapulted up and off the bike. Rather than going right straight into the glass window, where I was headed before my Mother's appearance at the side of the road, my entire body changed trajectory mid air and started moving upward. I was being lifted up on to the top of the car as if by some magic.

As soon as my body landed on top of the car, "time" sped up. I bounced off the hood of the car, and then my body ricocheted off the roof of the car, landing on my head on the asphalt in the middle of the street. The car took off the moment I hit the ground. It was a hit and run. As I was lying in the street, my fellow expert cyclists, with Tour de France speed, cycled after the car as it sped away from the scene of the accident. Each of them took one part of the license plate and thankfully we were able to track the man down. I spent the next five years fighting in the legal system to successfully sue this man for "hit and run" to cover my medical expenses, and for the excruciating and unrelenting physical pain of the accident lasting a full three years.

Sideways blessings

If we consider this same "hit and run" accident from a different perspective, there was a life saving "sideways blessing" which also came out of it. After many months of excruciating pain and also PTSD from this scary bike accident, my doctors were mystified as to why my chest pain had not fully resolved. My doctor ordered a mammogram to try to figure out why. As a result of that mammogram, and several biopsies of chest tissue she took from around the surrounding area of my bike injury, breast cancer was discovered. This discovery made it possible for the breast cancer to be surgically removed at a very early stage.

I am deeply grateful now for that bike accident. The breast cancer surgeon later told me that those random biopsies most likely saved my life. She went on to further explain that the type of cancer I had would not have even been visible on a mammogram for another two to three years. By that time, the cancer would have most likely metastasized to elsewhere in my body. The surgeon guessed that I most likely would have been dead by around age 60, the same age my mother had been when she died from multiple metastasis of breast cancer throughout her entire body.

You never know why things happen in life. You could say that the bike accident, and my mother's appearance from the "Other Side" that day, gave me an opportunity to save my own life. I obviously needed to learn how truly powerful I was to effect my own healing. For example, little did I know at that time of the bike accident that tumors could talk and I would be given a message of hope and empowerment beyond my wildest dreams. Someone else might say that all of these events were totally random and unrelated flukes. Either way, whatever difficult health challenge you might be facing now, please remember this: What may look like the worst possible thing that could ever happen to you right now might turn out to be a sideways blessing which later saves your life in some way.

From Me To You

I have usually taken more than one trip around The Roundabout until I found the right answer, or the right teacher, to help me see the right exit. Looking back now, I can see that my typical pattern was that I waited far too long, or been far too stubborn to ask for any help at all. The consequence of that choice was that I suffered much longer than I really needed to.

Help is not just a four-letter word. Use it when you need to.

Even if we manage to get ourselves to the place where we feel at the very last shred of hope, there is always another possibility, choice or direction available to solve any problem or challenge. Don't give up. Ask for help.

THE ROUNDABOUT

There is always a transition period between any great change in one's life. This period of change can feel much like we have entered a roundabout on the road of our lives, where we keep going around and around until we find the right exit. Sometimes we keep going around, and around and around, waiting for our lives to change for the better. One thing is certain, when we finally find the correct exit and make the necessary changes we need to make to put ourselves on the right path for us, things in our life start to get better and then, we are able to Thrive.

My most important teachers always appear exactly at the time when I need them most. Whenever these people have appeared, they have always guided me to a new idea or approach to help me find a way out of my current difficulty. When I was diagnosed with breast and cervical cancer at the same time, my three teachers in the realm of health were a Reiki healer, a Qigong Master, and a Minister.

Mammograms, biopsies and pap smears

After the bike accident, I was in brutal and unrelenting pain. None of the drugs I was given made much of a dent in this pain. I had to sit and sleep in a zero gravity recliner chair just to get any relief. Shortly after the bike accident, I was scheduled for a mammogram. It was excruciating but I somehow managed to get through it. Dr. Dee, the radiologist from my mammogram the year before heard from the nurse that I was still in severe pain. Dr. Dee, a road cyclist herself, had remembered my case from the year before. She told me that it was not normal a full year after a cycling accident to still be in such extreme pain. She scheduled a random biopsy just to try to see what was going on. Dr. Dee took a random biopsy of tissue, telling me, "I'm 99.9% sure you do not have cancer, but I wanted to do this just in case to totally rule it out."

A few days later Dr. Dee called and told me that she was in shock. I did have breast cancer; she had snagged a piece of breast cancer tissue during the random biopsy. She had shown my breast X ray to her colleague Dr. Hanson, and he confirmed not one, but two tumors in my left breast.

The moment after I received the breast cancer diagnosis and hung up the phone with Dr. Dee, I got a call from my gynecologist, Dr. Joki, with the results from my recent pap smear. He told me that the results were not good. We already knew that the man who had raped me the year before had transmitted one of the deadly strains of the HPV virus to me. Dr. Joki had been monitoring this, and told me that my particular form of HPV had now mutated into cervical cancer.

It was a complete trifecta of bad news. After scheduling an appointment to mark the two breast cancer tumors at the hospital and another to remove the cervical cancer, I can remember thinking that I had suddenly stepped into the children's book I used to read over and over to my kids when they were little, "Alexander and The Terrible, Horrible, No Good Very Bad Day." We all used to laugh so hard every time we read that book. Now it appeared that I was having one of those days myself, and I really didn't feel much like laughing.

Talking tumors

I immediately picked up the phone again and called my dear friend Camille. Camille is a Reiki healer, and a wise friend of many years. When I told Camille that I had cancer, this time breast and cervical cancer at the same time, the first thing she said was, "Have you talked with your tumors yet?"

I wasn't sure if she was kidding or not. "Excuse me?" I said, truly puzzled.

"Have you talked with your tumors yet?" Camille repeated.

"Camille, I didn't know that tumors could talk. I mean, that's a real first for me." I replied, chuckling a bit.

"Oh yes, tumors can talk." Camille replied, ever so matter of fact. "As a healer of many years, I know that cancer tumors always come with a message. Usually, I do a Shamanic journey into my clients body and have a conversation with the tumor to learn what that message is."

"You're kidding right?" I said, totally skeptical.

"No I am not kidding one bit. When I do my journey into the body of my client, I always ask the tumor what message it wishes to deliver. Then I assure the tumor that I will give that message to my client on their behalf. Next, I thank the tumor for its message, and lovingly release the tumor to go on its way saying, 'In the name of Love and Light, I release you to the place from where you came, preferably, somewhere outside the body of my client.'"

"Do the tumors actually listen to you? By that I mean, do the tumors usually leave?" I asked, somewhat in awe.

"Oh sure. Tumors often leave after I have delivered their message, but not before my client makes some very significant changes in their lives."

"What kind of changes?" I asked, really interested now.

"Well," Camille began, "usually the tumor's message refers to some long held pain, grief, anger or something else that the person has been hanging on to for some time and now really needs to release or let go of.

"Normally, my client and I discuss what pain, grief or anger they think the tumor is referring to. Some clients know immediately what they are holding on to, and others don't. I help each client with the process of figuring out what his or her specific issue is based on each tumor's unique message. Then together we design a way for them to let go of whatever that is. This process heals it once and for all." Camille replied cheerfully.

This was fascinating so I asked, "Well Camille, could you please talk with my tumors for me and tell me what they say?"

Camille was firm. "Mary Anne, unlike most of my clients, you are quite connected spiritually. You are perfectly capable of going within yourself and asking that question directly of your tumors."

"Well what kind of question do you even ask of a tumor?" I asked, truly puzzled. "So sorry Camille, but I'm having trouble wrapping my head around this new fact that tumors can even talk."

Camille laughed and then said, "I know it sounds really weird, but it's very simple and straightforward actually. Just close your eyes, go within and ask each tumor specifically, 'Why are you here, and what do you want me to know?'"

"Will I hear some booming voice of The Dark Force Of Cancer?" I joked.

Camille laughed. "Well, in my experience, the message from the tumor usually comes in some sort of word, sentence, image, picture or a moving picture like a scene from a movie. In my healing work, I am shown these things in my imagination; they suddenly show up on my internal screen, inside my mind. I know it sounds a little weird, but that's what happens."

"A little weird?" I laughed. "You aren't kidding me, are you?"

"No I am not kidding you. I'm dead serious. But you can decide for yourself what you want to do." Camille said.

"I'm not too sure I want to go in there all by myself and talk to my tumors. It actually sounds a little scary. What if they say something really bad?"

Camille reassured me, "I know what you mean, but these tumors are just there to get your attention so you can begin to heal whatever is causing you pain. You might want to think of them as really just messengers."

"Won't you just go in for me?" I pleaded.

Camille was adamant; "Actually, I really believe that you will be able to get whatever message your tumors have brought with them on your own. In fact, I'm absolutely sure of it. So call me later and tell me what you hear. I have to go to work now." I hung up the phone and I just sat in my chair, looking out over the Ballard Locks watching several boats go by.

Then I thought to myself, *What the heck. Let's give it a go. If Camille thinks I can do it, I probably can.*

I closed my eyes and tried to picture a phone cord connection between my mind and the first tumor, which Dr. Dee had told me was located in my left breast near the center of my chest. I asked Tumor Number One, *Why are you here and what do you want me to know?*

Tumor Number One speaks

What I heard in my head next totally surprised me. It was like a direct phone line to Tumor Number One:

I am the part of you that is cold as a stone.

I thought to myself, *What? What did it say? Cold as a stone? What the hell does that mean?*

The voice of Tumor Number One repeated, *I am the part of you that is cold as a stone.*

This time as I heard the words in my mind, I also saw a picture of a grey stone in my imagination. *Yikes.* I thought. *Am I cold as a stone? What does this mean?*

Tumor Number One spoke the same exact words for a third time: *I am the part of you that is cold as a stone.*

Now, I had heard the same exact sentence three times, like the clanging of a cathedral bell. I thought to myself, *Well now I wonder what Tumor Number Two has to say?* I closed my eyes again.

Tumor Number Two speaks

Tumor Number Two was located in my left breast, near my armpit. I focused my mental attention there. What I saw next completely surprised me. It was a memory from my childhood that I had completely forgotten about, and clearly had repressed until that moment.

In my mind, it was like I had stepped into an old home movie of my family. I was five years old:

I saw myself alone, sitting on the living room couch of our home in Oakland, watching a program on TV. I could hear my parents were fighting in really loud voices in the kitchen. Periodically, a loud screaming voice would turn into the sound of a dish smashing and crashing.

Then, suddenly it was silent.

A moment later I looked up and saw my father coming around the hall corner into the living room. He was sweating, his face was beet red and he had a bit of white froth at the corner of his mouth, as he always was when he was really mad. He was carrying a large butcher knife and I could see that there was some red liquid on the knife blade.

I suddenly knew that the red liquid was blood, and I quickly got up off of the couch. My father marched straight up to me, holding the bloody butcher knife out in front of him. Next, he placed the butcher knife right under my chin, and turned his head to the side. I saw a trickle of blood coming down his face from his ear to his chin.

"Look what your mother has done! Look what she's done!" he kept repeating, while at the same time punctuating each statement with a shake of the bloody butcher knife under my chin.

My first thought was, *Is Mommy dead?* My next thought was, *Is Daddy going to kill me?*

I didn't scream. I didn't run. The last thing I remember was the feeling of suddenly being very cold as I stared down my nose at the blood on this huge butcher knife under my chin, and my feet feeling like they were both cast in two large blocks of concrete.

Then the movie ended.

When I opened my eyes, I felt like I had just come out of a movie theatre, after having seen a very scary movie. I felt cold and my hands were shaking.

I had no idea what to make of all that I just saw, but I knew who would.

I picked up the phone and called Dr. Sun, my Quigong teacher. When Dr. Sun, also a prominent doctor at Bastyr University answered the phone and I told him about the cancer diagnosis, he told me to come up and meet him at his office immediately. I decided to save the bloody knife story for later.

The Minister

Before I left the house to meet Dr. Sun, I made one last quick call to my friend Eric, a Minister at the Amazing Grace Spiritual Center. When I told him I had just been diagnosed with cancer his first words were, "How do you feel about that news?"

"Pretty scared and depressed actually." I answered feeling really glum.

"Where is it written that cancer has to be depressing?" Eric asked.

"What are you talking about, Eric? I called to get some sympathy here." I pouted.

"I'll ask you again, Mary Anne, can you show me where it is written, *exactly*, that *cancer has to be depressing*?" Eric asked.

I replied a little testily, "Well I am sure I don't know. But it sure feels depressing to me."

Undeterred, Eric chirped in the way only Eric can, "Yeah I hear that. But *where is it written that cancer has to be depressing?*"

I could tell he was going all New Age Ernest Holmes spiritual on me with this line of questioning, but I still wanted sympathy. "I have no idea." I replied honestly.

"Good! Me either!" Eric chirped. "I challenge you to be the Joy Ambassador for Cancer."

I hadn't expected this response in a million years. I wasn't feeling too joyful at that moment either. "You have got to be kidding me." I said sourly. I was obviously not going to get any sympathy from him.

"Nope! Not kidding! But I do have to go right now to see a client. So think about that will you, my dear? Love you! Bye!" At that, Eric hung up.

Well this is certainly shaping up to be a very interesting day so far. I thought to myself. I didn't have time to go into the third cervical tumor to find out what message it had for me. I grabbed my purse and car keys and headed out the door to go see Dr. Sun at Bastyr University.

The Quigong Master

I knew Dr. Sun, my Quigong teacher loved fresh fruit and I had just picked some gorgeous peaches over the weekend. When I arrived at his office, I handed him a large bag filled with fresh peaches as I said, "Thank you so much for seeing me today, and especially on such short notice."

We sat down at his desk and the first words out of Dr. Sun's mouth were, "So have you talked with your tumors yet?"

I couldn't help it. I started laughing. "You know Dr. Sun you are the *second* person in the last two hours who has asked me if I have talked to my tumors."

"Well have you?" he replied quite seriously.

"As a matter of fact, I have." I replied, equally serious now.

"What did they say?" he asked as he leaned forward in his desk chair.

I told him what I had seen so far, that one tumor said I was cold as a stone and the other showed me a horror movie.

Dr. Sun was unfazed. "Cold as a stone…very interesting." he mused.

"So, Dr. Sun do you think I'm actually a very cold person, you know, like cold as in a stone, cold, grey stone? Am I a cold person and just don't know it?" I wondered out loud.

At that, Dr. Sun put his hand up as if to say *stop* as he did in our Quigong classes. "Actually the messages from tumors are not always literal. They can also be metaphorical in nature. This message from the first tumor sounds more like one of frozen grief to me."

"Frozen grief? What's that?" I asked curious.

Dr. Sun began, "Let me explain a little about ancient traditional Chinese medicine to you for a moment before we go on. In Chinese medicine, we mentally divide the body in half of a patient who has a tumor. If a tumor has shown up on the right side of the patient's body, it is most likely a belief system that they themselves have created which is in error and that we need to help them correct.

"If the tumor appears on the left side of the patient's body, this usually tells us that the tumor carries a message for the patient most commonly that they have taken on a belief system or idea about themselves from outside themselves.

"In other words, a tumor on the left side of the body indicates that the mistaken belief system that the patient has taken on as their own could actually have come from someone else, such as a teacher, a parent, society or the like.

"The most important thing to understand about tumors, whichever side they appear on, is that the belief system the patient has accepted as truth about themselves is actually an error. Once we identify that error, then we help the patient correct that mistaken belief system about themselves. Make sense?"

I smiled and said, "Well, Dr. Sun, I have tumors right now on the *right, the center and the left* sides of my body. Do I get the bonus prize?"

We both had to laugh at that, but very quickly, Dr. Sun returned to his questions, "So, which tumor would you like to work with first?"

I really wasn't sure how to answer that question, so I said, "Let's start with the one in the middle over my heart. That's the one that says I'm as cold as a stone." I said.

"OK. Is there anything you have not grieved in your life?" Dr. Sun asked.

"Well, you mean like did somebody die and I didn't deal with it?" Dr. Sun nodded. I started to ramble again, as I often do when I need to figure something out. "Let's see. Well I was pretty pissed off when my brother died. I was 24 and he was 22 at that time. But I think I dealt with that pretty well."

Dr. Sun nodded. "Go on."

I thought for a moment and then said, "Hmm. Well, I did have a miscarriage at four months, and then was pregnant again very soon after that. Then that child died at full term. His name was McKenzie and he died at birth."

"That experience must have been very hard for you. Tell me more about that." Dr. Sun said gently.

"Well, after McKenzie died, I was pregnant again six weeks later. Since I thought it was all my fault the first baby and then McKenzie had died, at that point I made a pact with God. I told God that since it was clearly my love that had killed both the first and second baby, I would try a new strategy of holding back .001% of my love from the next child. I thought that perhaps this might protect the next child from death. If that child lived, I would know I was right.

"So I did that and Sarah was born alive and well 10 months later. She lived so I thought this totally confirmed that both the first baby and then McKenzie's death were all my fault. Since Sarah continued to live and didn't die, I chose the same strategy of holding .001% of my love back from the next child. That next child was Joshua whom you know of course. Joshua didn't die either, so I figured I had done a really smart thing, you know, holding my love back from both of them. So in an effort to continue to protect both of them, you know, from my obviously toxic and deadly love, I've just kept that same strategy up ever since. It seems to have…."

"Stop! Stop, Mary Anne!" Dr. Sun spoke louder than normal, just to get me to stop talking. "STOP!" Dr. Sun finally yelled. "Are you listening to yourself?"

I stopped talking, mid sentence and said, "Huh? What? Listening to what?"

"What you just said!" Dr. Sun said again.

"What about what I just said?" I said confused.

"That part about your son McKenzie's death being all your fault?" Dr. Sun repeated.

"Yeah, what about it?" I said, not understanding the question. The fact that my son's death was my entirely fault was pretty obvious to me.

"Was his death, in fact, all your fault? Did you actually do something and then he died?" Dr. Sun asked.

"Oh no. The doctors said it was a thing called, chylothorax that actually killed him. Chylothorax basically means water in the lungs. The doctors told me that they don't really understand it, and they don't even know what causes it actually. The doctors also said that any intervention they had tried for it so far was either fatal to the mother or fatal to the child." I explained.

"So McKenzie's death was not, in fact, a direct result of something you did?" Dr. Sun said.

"Well no, but..." I started to say.

"No *buts*. So you *did not, in fact, kill him*." Dr. Sun said.

"But Dr. Sun. Don't you see? There is something seriously *wrong with me*. In fact, I think that *my love is actually tainted*. I couldn't save my brother or my mother or my first baby or my son… Don't you see? It's a fact: If I *love* someone, I am a *curse on them* and they *die*."

"Wait!" Dr. Sun said as he put his hand up, palm facing toward me. "Stop! Are you listening to yourself Mary Anne? Are you?"

"What do you mean, Dr. Sun?" I asked, not understanding the question.

"You just said a moment ago, that when you *love* someone you *kill* them. Is that in fact *true*?" Dr. Sun asked.

"Well, I thought it was true at the time." I went on, beginning to ramble again, "And I guess, when I stop and think about it, I still believe it on some level. I mean, Dr. Sun, I have *proof* right? My two living children have both lived *after* I decided to hold back that .001% of love from them, right? So my toxic love must have been the problem."

Dr. Sun paused, and then continued, "Well, first of all, I think that it is impossible for a mother to hold back their love from their children, any part of the 100% of it. It must have taken enormous strength for you to even try to do a thing like that, holding back love from your beautiful children."

"Well I don't know about that Dr. Sun. Actually I honestly think I am pretty weak overall. But I can say that I was always telling myself, even when they were both babies, *Now don't get too close now, because your love will hurt them and then something really bad will happen, and then they will die too just like their brother.*"

Dr. Sun again put up his hand, palm facing toward me. "Stop." Then he went on more gently, "Well, Mary Anne can we agree that now that both of your living children are old enough to keep themselves safe, that you can now give that .001% of your love back to them? Would it be possible for you to let yourself love them 100% now? Can you do that?"

I started to cry. "But what if they *die*?" I wailed.

"It is not them who are dying now Mary Anne. My professional opinion is that the .001% of your love that you have been trying so terribly hard to hold back from your children for so many years has now hardened into the tumor over your heart that *is now killing you instead.*"

I was flabbergasted when I heard this. "Seriously? So, you're saying that the message of this tumor is what then?" I asked.

"Give it back." Dr. Sun said quietly.

"Give what back?" I asked, still unclear.

"The *love*. Give your love back to both of your children. Tell them that when they were born, you created this *idea*, this *belief system* really, to hold back .001% of your love in order to *keep them safe*. But now you know that they are all grown up and perfectly capable of keeping themselves safe. You understand now that you as their mother no longer need to protect them and so now you are *giving back to them the .001% of love that you have withheld all these years.*"

Dr. Sun paused for just a moment and then said simply, "And then, and this is very important, tell them, *'I love you with ALL of my heart.'*" With that, Dr. Sun sat back in his chair.

"Oh my God, Dr. Sun, my kids will think I have totally and completely gone off the rails if I do that." I said shaking my head.

"Well this is a life and death matter for you right now. You have created a *false belief system* for yourself that has now hardened into a cancer tumor directly over your heart in order to get your full attention. *That tumor, right now, is killing you.* Does it really matter at this point what your children think?" Dr. Sun said.

"Well, when you put it that way, I guess not." I replied.

Dr. Sun sat forward in his chair again. "Good. Now, I want you to go to each them, take them by the hands, look them straight in the eye and say, 'I love you with ALL of my heart. ALL of it. Not .999%. ALL of it.' Then, let's see what happens. OK? Can you do that?" Sun reached out and put his hands gently over mine, both of which were gripping the side of the table.

Tears were streaming down my face. After a deep breath I said, "Well, I'll certainly try."

"OK. Let's move on then. Now tell me, what did the *other* tumor say?"

When I finished explaining the movie from Tumor Number Two, I said, "I realize now that there was something else that second tumor said after it showed me the movie."

"What was it?" Dr. Sun asked.

"Tumor Number Two said, 'I am the part of you that despises your femininity.' I have absolutely no idea how to apply your Chinese Medicine tumor methodology to that one."

Tears of deep connection and compassion were welling up in Dr. Sun's eyes as he looked at me and said, "A parent is the child's entire world at the age of 5. The parent is also the one person who is supposed to *protect* their child from any and all harm. Do you realize that a traumatizing experience like you had with your father at that very young age - having a parent who looked and sounded like they were threatening to kill the other parent, and then threatens you, the child, with a bloody butcher knife — is psychologically and emotionally traumatizing enough to *give* you cancer later as an adult?" Dr. Sun then dropped his head and slowly shook it from side to side. "It's no wonder you have breast cancer."

Then Dr. Sun looked up, and his eyes were deep and penetrating as he asked: "So what do you think your Father's *message* was when he shook the bloody butcher knife under your chin?"

"I have no idea." I replied honestly.

But Dr. Sun pressed on, "Think Mary Anne. *Think!* When someone puts a *bloody knife* under your chin, shakes it, and screams, *'Look what your mother has done!'* what is he *telling* you?"

I thought for a minute, and then said, "'You better do exactly what I say or else?' That kind of thing?"

"Exactly." Dr. Sun said, nodding his head. Dr. Sun and I sat together in silence for quite a while.

Finally I said, "Well this explains a lot to me."

"In what way?" Dr. Sun asked.

"Well it's a funny thing you should say all this today, Dr. Sun. Well it's not funny actually. Really interesting is more like it. Right before I came up to your office, I was out there." I pointed to the parking lot outside his office window. "I took a few minutes and called my Dad on the phone to tell him I had both breast cancer and cervical cancer. He exploded on the other end of the line. He actually started screaming at me."

"Really? What did he say?" Dr. Sun asked.

"Well he went on and on about how I didn't need my breasts. He also said what the hell did I need either breasts or a cervix for because I wasn't ever gonna have children again. He said I should 'just have everything cut clean off.'" I paused and then continued. "I think he meant I should just take off both my breasts and have a hysterectomy.

"Then when I said, 'Well Dad I kind of like my feminine parts,' he cut me off and said really harshly, 'Just cut 'em out. You don't need 'em. Just cut 'em out.' He seemed like he was actually mad at me for having cancer. It was all just so weird."

"Do you see how all this is tied together Mary Anne?" Dr. Sun said, leaning even more forward in his chair.

"No. Not exactly." I replied honestly.

"Well your father, when you were five years old, comes in with a bloody butcher knife, delivering the message you felt was, 'My way or else.' And then later, when you have a feminine type of cancer, he tells you to have everything cut clean off. It's really quite classic, actually. Quite."

"Classic? In what way?" I asked, quite confused.

Dr. Sun smiled. "*Who is it that actually despises femininity?*"

I wrinkled my brow. "I don't know. I thought it was me. Are you saying that it is him?"

"Yes. Him. And blaming all his rage on your mother, what kind of message does that send to a five year old girl child?"

I guessed: "Women are bad?"

"Yes. And since you are a woman, how did this make you feel about yourself?"

I thought for a moment. "Bad."

Dr. Sun nodded his head. "Exactly. And now what message has he given you today, in the present, right out there in the parking lot?"

"Let me see if I can wrap my head around this Dr. Sun. Could my Dad be saying that women's feminine parts like mine are dispensable once they have performed their service as baby makers? Or maybe could he be saying that women like me should all be neutered or become more like men because there is no more need for any of those feminine parts?" I said slowly trying to put the pieces together.

Dr. Sun asked, "What did the second tumor say again?"

"The second tumor said, *I am the part of you that despises your femininity.*" I answered.

"Now think Mary Anne. When did you first receive the message that femininity should be despised?" Dr. Sun asked.

"From my Dad at age 5?" I was beginning to see where Dr. Sun was going.

"Well you probably got that message loud and clear way before that age. This father of yours sounds like he really despises women. Would you say that is true?" Dr. Sun asked.

"Well, he certainly beat my mother into submission. In the middle of the night one time I heard my mother crying. I came in to find out what was wrong, and she was holding her hand over her face. She said she had run into a door, and I should just go back to bed. I knew she was lying. I was always waking up in the middle of the night hearing my father scream at her."

I took another deep breath and continued, talking faster and faster. "But other than her, he failed at every relationship he had with women, well, other than his current girlfriend Nan. But even Nan actually told me one night when we were alone, 'Your dad can be a real asshole at times, but I'm a 78 year old woman and I'm too afraid to be alone. So I stay with him.' So, I guess that relationship isn't really working too well either. But….." my voice drifted off.

"But what?" Dr. Sun asked gently.

Suddenly I was sobbing. I tried to talk through my choking sobs. "But he was my Dad…and I loved him…and I wanted to please him….and I was the only girl…and my Mom…" my voice drifted off again. Dr. Sun handed me a tissue.

"What is it?" Dr. Sun asked.

"The last thing my mom said to me before she died was, 'One of the great regrets of my life is that I did not protect you from that man.' Dr. Sun, it was just all so confusing…." I hid my face with both of my hands, trying to get a hold of myself.

"But the underlying message was?" Dr. Sun probed.

I pulled my hands away from my face as I continued, "Well I think it was 'I despise women, so you better agree with me and *despise your mother* as much as I do… and also yourself, because you are a woman too…And you better do things my way or else something *really, really bad is going to happen to you.* I hold all the power and you don't. And you *never will.*"

Dr. Sun nodded, and then paused to let what I had just said sink in. "Mary Anne, the most important thing right now is that you *identify the belief system that he gave you, which was in error, so you can let it go.* What is it?"

"Well I don't really know what the exact belief system was, but I think as a result of whatever that was I've been really angry all of my adult life. I can see now that I've taken The Old Boys on any opportunity I could. I've always had this rage and drive that I somehow had to *beat them all.*" I shook my head. "Looks like now that I was just trying to do was beat my father, over and over."

"And how did that work out for you?" Dr. Sun asked.

"Well, not too well." I replied in all honesty. "All that The Old Boys ever did, once they used my brain, my body or my strategy to get whatever they wanted - money, power, prestige - was to close ranks, crush me, make death threats on my life and send other male rapists to punish me for standing up to them.

"Now that I think about it, my first marriage was like marrying my father all over again. You know, during the first time I had sex with my husband, I actually saw an apparition of my father's face? You would have thought that I would run like hell away from that. But even that vision wasn't warning enough. I didn't listen. I walked right into that marriage, left my career, which I loved, and served him instead. Oh my God. How *stupid* could I be?"

Dr. Sun reached over, took my hand and held it. "Is that really such a surprise to you now, after what happened to you when you were five? Wouldn't you subconsciously try to replicate the same relationship you had with the primal male in your life?" he said gently.

"Well, I guess so. From that point on, I did everything according to my father's rules." I took another deep breath and then exhaled. "In my marriage, I felt that my only worth was in how I served, took care of the children, cooked the food, did the dishes, and most importantly, taking care of my husbands every need, both personally and professionally. I always worried that if I didn't do everything up to his standards of perfection, he would leave me." I paused for a moment to take a breath. A pattern was beginning to come clear to me as I spoke.

I continued, "My father had multiple affairs with other women. My husband used to call me on the phone from every movie location, some jobs went on for months at a time, and he would tell me that he was attracted to yet a new younger woman. I never knew quite how to respond to that. But since I had given up my own career, and he was supporting us all, I became really afraid of losing both him and the security of his income. So, even if holding our family together meant living a lie, and sacrificing both my pride and self-esteem, I was willing to pay that price. Obviously, now looking back, I can see that I chose to wear the "golden handcuffs," and do my best to both protect our children and our community from the truth.

"I never told anyone what was going on, not even my closest friends. I chose to handle it all privately, by you know, just holding my head up the best I could, being a loyal and good wife, devoting my full focus and attention to our two children. Honestly, I didn't know what else to do. I didn't see any other options available to me at that time.

"Eventually, my husband and I tried marriage counseling, but then he had another affair, this time with a woman twenty five years younger than him, when he was 44 and she was 19. It's a long story but after fifteen years of marriage, I finally divorced him and then he married her. She was nine years older than our daughter, just as my father's new wife was eight years older than me. So you are right, Dr. Sun. The same history just repeated itself in two generations." I gasped at this sudden awareness.

Dr. Sun still had my hand in his and he gave a little squeeze of support as he said, "That's a lot for anyone to have to deal with. It also completely ties in with the message that your second tumor is trying to get through to you now so that you can heal it once and for all: 'I am the part of you that despises your femininity.' What else do you think that could possibly mean?"

"Well, Dr. Sun, if that's the message that needs to be healed, I can see how all my life I have totally despised myself, and everything female about me. I've told myself that I am worthless, and I've even believed that I totally deserved the kind of unkind treatment I got from men, that it was somehow all my fault. In fact, I always felt that I was born the wrong sex, because men seem to have all the power and freedom to do what they wanted in life. I've lived my entire life this way, you know, believing that I was a failure and that being born a woman I was even lower than a speck of dirt." I heaved a heavy sigh as a single tear rolled slowly down my check.

"Is that true?" Dr. Sun asked.

"That I'm a failure? That being born a woman I'm even lower than a speck of dirt? That I should despise myself because I'm a woman? Well, I can definitely see now that all those things are pretty cruel things to say. But honestly, I guess I've believed them all for so long it just seems normal now." I sighed again.

Dr. Sun went on, "Well, I believe that your second breast tumor is here now to call your attention to all of these mistaken beliefs you have about yourself as a woman so that you can finally heal them. Don't worry. We will work on those beliefs too. For now though, let's focus first on the tumor over your heart. I think that tumor is also here to help you learn how to love yourself. So, please drive right now to wherever your children are and tell them what we talked about. Then call me and let me know how that goes. Whatever happens, together we will go on with our healing work from there. OK?" Dr. Sun got up and took my hand.

"Good Work Mary Anne. I'm proud of you. This is very challenging stuff you are dealing with."

Meeting with my children

I went to both my children that afternoon and did exactly as Dr. Sun suggested. After nearly twenty years, I was finally able to say, *"I love you with all of my heart."* I gave each of them back the 0.001% of my love that I had been holding back in an effort to keep them safe.

After speaking with my son, I got into my car and began to drive away. About halfway down the block, I felt this giant *Poof!* in the middle of my chest where the tumor over my heart was located. It was a very odd feeling, but it wasn't painful. The *Poof!* felt like a sudden, and quite unexpected energetic blast from within. I had no idea what this *Poof!* was.

The MRI

The next day, I had an appointment at the hospital with the radiologist to have both tumors marked for the upcoming surgery. As I was lying face down on the MRI machine waiting to be rolled into the tube, I wondered what they would find. I asked the nurse, "So, excuse me, but what happens, say, if you don't find a tumor in there?"

This nurse was a bit surly, "Well Honey, if there's no tumor, we can't measure it now can we? But I've been assured by Dr. Hanson that there are two tumors that we are measuring today so don't you worry Honey. Just relax and let us do our jobs OK? Are you ready to go into the MRI machine? If so, then put your headphones on so you can listen to some nice music and we will begin."

When I got into the MRI machine, the loud noises began to ping off the sides of the tube in addition to the music playing in my earphones. Quite unexpectedly, I heard a loud *Voice* say in my mind just like the tumors had talked to me the day before, *Now do you believe in the power of your mind to move all obstacles out of your way?*

Excuse me? I replied silently in my mind. *Who are you?*

The Voice repeated again, *I will ask you again. Now do you believe in the power of your mind to move all obstacles out of your way?*

Before I could answer, the nurse was pulling me out of the machine again.

"What's wrong?" I asked the nurse.

"Honey we're just having a bit of trouble with this one tumor of yours, particularly the one over your heart area. I just want to readjust your body a little bit so we can get a better shot of it."

"Well what if it is not, in fact, actually there?" I asked.

The nurse snorted at the very thought. "Well, Honey, if we can't find it, then we can't measure it now can we?"

I countered with, "But..."

She quickly replied, "But nuthin' Honey. Even I looked at the previous X-ray. I can assure you that there is most definitely a tumor there. We just need to mark it today for size and location for the surgeon. That's all. Here we go. Be absolutely still now." Before I could say anything more, I was being rolled back into the machine.

Again I heard the same Voice as before: *Now do you believe in the power of your mind to move all obstacles out of your way?*

This time, in my mind I replied immediately, *Yes! Whoever you are, yes!* I certainly didn't want to offend whoever it was.

Are you sure about that? boomed the voice over the banging sounds of the MRI machine.

Yes I'm sure! YES! I screamed back in my mind.

At this point the machine rolled back again and the nurse said, "Honey we can't find it. You can go now."

I was stunned. "What do you mean you can't find it?"

"It appears to be gone." said the nurse.

"The tumor? It's gone?" I whispered.

"Yes its gone." she replied.

"What happens now?" I asked, still in total disbelief.

"Well Honey, now you can go on home!" she said.

The radiologist puts handguns to his head

At this point Dr. Hanson, the radiologist, came into the room. He stood there in the doorway, with his hands at the side of his head one finger pointing to his ear on each side, like imaginary handguns aimed at his own brain. I am not sure if he was even conscious of what he was doing, but next both of his thumbs started moving, like he was pulling the triggers of the two imaginary handguns, each gun aimed at the sides of his head.

He started yelling: "What did you do? What did you do? I know that tumor was there! I saw it with my own eyes on the original X-Ray! What did you do?"

I smiled, remembering the Voice I had heard so clearly inside the MRI machine. "How much time have you got?"

Dr. Hanson actually sneered as he said, "Not much. What did you do? I want to hear it." Dr. Hanson demanded.

"Well this might be a little hard for you to believe, but I dissolved it." I replied.

"You what?" he said, again pulling the triggers of his two imaginary handguns on both sides of his head.

Even though I wasn't sure he really wanted to know, I continued, "Well, actually for these past two weeks, I worked on that specific tumor with Dr. Sun, a Chinese medicine doctor and I dissolved it. It's kind of a long story."

Dr. Hanson's face was flushing with rage. "Well whatever the hell you did, we are still going to operate on the other tumor. I know that one is still there. I saw it with my own eyes today."

Undeterred, I said, "Well then, I'll get to work on that one right away." I started to get up from the bench of the MRI machine where I had been sitting.

"Oh please!" Dr. Hanson said with a complete sneer, "You don't mean to tell me that you think that in *another two weeks* that you can *dissolve that other tumor* on your breast that's *even bigger*? Oh *really*?"

I replied, completely matter of fact, "Well if I can dissolve one tumor, I ought to be able to dissolve the other one right?"

As he turned and then marched down the hall, Dr. Hanson yelled out to no one in particular, "This is absolutely ridiculous! Dissolving cancer tumors! That just does not happen, do you hear me? Does not happen!"

Wanna bet? I thought to myself a bit smugly as I watched him storm down the hall of the hospital until he was out of sight. When I got into the elevator, I suddenly remembered the words that my brother Bob had said to me through the trance medium nearly thirty years before: "Believe in the power of your mind to move all obstacles out of your way." I now I had proof that Bob was right about that power which had at first seemed rather outrageous to me; I had actually dissolved a cancer tumor.

The morning of breast cancer surgery

Two weeks later, I entered the hospital for the removal of the remaining breast cancer tumor. On the morning of breast cancer surgery, the radiologist injects the breast containing the tumor with a blue radioactive dye. It takes about two hours for the blue radioactive dye to be fully absorbed by the body so that the surgeon can later identify what is known as "the sentinel node" during surgery.

During normal routine breast cancer surgery, first the surgeon removes the cancerous tumor. Then, following the path of the radioactive dye, the surgeon progressively removes node after node from the patient's body that shows any sign of breast cancer cells. If the dye goes to the first node, what doctors call "the main sentinel node," and there is no cancer detected there, the surgeon removes just that one node as a safety measure, and then stops. If the main sentinel node has cancer cells detected, the surgeon removes that node and then progressively more nodes until the surgeon get a fully clear one.

However, the morning of my breast cancer surgery, before I would even allow the radiologist Dr. Hanson to inject me with the customary radioactive dye, I told him, "I want you to measure the tumor."

Dr. Hanson was incredulous. "Why? Oh God. Here we go again with you." he said as he rolled his eyes to the ceiling. I could tell that not many people gave orders to Dr. Hanson.

However, I was firm: "Why? Because I want to see how much progress I have made working on dissolving my second tumor over these past two weeks."

"You really don't think you actually eliminated that second tumor of yours too do you?" He said snidely.

"Well I have no idea." I replied evenly. "That's why I would like you to measure it."

"Why should I?" Dr. Hanson demanded, sounding like a pouty child.

I looked him squarely in the eye and said, "Because if you *don't*, I will call the entire surgery *off*. You will *not* inject me with the radioactive dye. I will *leave* this hospital right now, and *there will be no surgery. So measure it. Now.*"

For a moment, Dr. Hanson appeared to go a bit cross-eyed. Then he said begrudgingly, "All right. If you insist." Dr. Hanson moved the ultrasound wand he held in his hand over my left breast. Quite to my surprise, the next thing I heard come out of his mouth was "*Shit!*"

"What do you mean by '*Shit!*' Dr. Hanson?" I asked, not sure if he meant "good shit" or "bad shit."

"I mean *Shit* as in *Damn!*" Dr. Hanson exclaimed, with wide eyes as he stared at the ultrasound monitor to our right. "*Shit!*" he said again, a little louder this time. At this point, the two nurses who had been on the other side of the room the whole time rushed over to see if Dr. Hanson needed help.

In front of all three of them I asked, "So is the tumor still there?"

"Of course it's still there." Dr. Hanson sneered, still staring at the ultrasound machine as he shook his head from side to side. He looked a bit dazed, confused and bewildered all at once.

"Well then *why* did you just say, *'Shit!'* and *'Damn!'* Dr. Hanson?" I snapped back.

Dr. Hanson unglued his eyes from the ultrasound machine and turned his face toward me. "I said that because I just measured your other tumor, and compared it to the size it was two weeks ago when I last saw you. That second tumor is now a full 25% smaller. *How in the hell did you do that?"* Dr. Hanson was still shaking his head slowly from side to side, his words hanging suspended in the air between us.

At that moment, I was crestfallen. The tumor was still there after all my efforts working with Dr. Sun, doing absolutely everything he had assigned me to do over the previous two weeks' time. I had been so dedicated and determined, following his every instruction to the letter. I had also felt so deeply hopeful that I would be successful in my goal. Now, suddenly I had to accept the actual fact that I had failed to fully dissolve Tumor Number Two. It was a crushing blow.

But I sure wasn't going to let Dr. Hanson know anything about my profound disappointment. I held my head up and with as much pride as I could possibly muster said, "OK Dr. Hanson. My tumor is 25% smaller. That's good. I made some progress. That's good. OK, you may now proceed with the radioactive dye injection and the surgery. Go ahead. Inject me now. I'm ready." Even though I felt like bursting into tears at that moment, I didn't break.

After the injection, I held myself together until I got to the waiting room. Once I was there I called Dr. Sun on the phone. The moment Dr. Sun answered "Hello," that's when I began to cry. A river of tears began flowing down my face, dropped off my chin and into my lap. "Well, I failed." I announced.

"What do you mean you failed?" Dr. Sun asked. "What did the doctor say?"

"He said Tumor Number Two was 25% smaller."

"That's wonderful!" Dr. Sun exclaimed.

"But, Dr. Sun, *I still failed to dissolve it 100%*. It's as simple as that. *I failed!* I can't tell this story to anyone now, even after all our hard work! They will think the fact that I dissolved that first tumor was an accident."

"What do you mean by an accident, Mary Anne?" Dr. Sun said calmly.

"Dr. Sun think about it!" I exploded in frustration. "If I had dissolved *two* tumors, right in a row, well then *that* would have been *proof positive*. Dissolving one, and not the other *looks like an accident*. I'm so sorry. I clearly didn't work hard enough. I failed you, Dr. Sun. I failed myself. I failed period." Hot, salty, humiliating tears streamed down my face, as I sat there in the waiting room.

"Mary Anne," Dr. Sun said gently, "This news is far from a failure. There are a few things I didn't tell you."

"Like what?" I asked.

"Like the fact that I normally work with a client 8-12 months to dissolve a single cancer tumor. You dissolved one in two weeks. Then you got another second tumor down by 25% in an additional two weeks' time. Think about that for a moment. That is actually quite an amazing accomplishment!"

"But I didn't get the whole thing soon enough to avoid the surgery now did I?" I sulked.

"Well in this respect," Dr. Sun began, "I have two things to say to you. The first is if you did not get this surgery on that breast cancer tumor, *your children would never forgive you*. If you were to die from this cancer, *always* in the back of their minds, they would have believed that you chose not to do everything you could to save yourself.

"And I'll tell you another thing on that matter. I couldn't absolutely guarantee that I could help you get the second tumor fully dissolved, even in 9-12 months' time. Your children would never forgive either of us if we didn't succeed. And since we already know that at this moment your cancer tumor cells are already located outside of the cell wall and on the move, the choice now of continuing to work together to dissolve the second tumor would be putting your life at risk. It's best now to let Western Medicine do what it does best. You know what that is, right?"

"What?" I asked, trying to take in all he was saying.

"To cut is to cure, Mary Anne. That is what Western Medicine does best. *To cut is to cure!*"

"Really Dr. Sun?" Tears of gratitude were now flowing down both my cheeks instead.

"Really, Mary Anne. You did amazingly well and I am really, really proud of you and all of the very hard work you did. You did absolutely everything I asked of you. From my perspective you achieved extremely positive results. Now you hold your head up, march in there, and let Western Medicine get the rest of that tumor out!" Dr. Sun then said, more gently, "And, please Mary Anne, call me when it's all done, OK?"

"OK, I will. Thanks for all your help, Dr. Sun. I really appreciate it. More than words could ever say." I felt so incredibly grateful to Dr. Sun at that moment.

"You are most welcome Mary Anne. It has been my privilege to work with you. As always." Dr. Sun hung up.

The next moment, the lady hospital volunteer arrived with a wheelchair to wheel me over for the surgery. On the way over to the surgery side of the hospital, I got into a lively conversation with her. After a few minutes, she laughed and said, "Hey, aren't I the one who is supposed to be cheering you up here? You are the one going into surgery after all! Honestly, I have to say thank you to you Sweetheart. Before I met you today, I was having kind of a rough day myself. But now, after talking with you I feel so much better! I have really enjoyed this conversation with you so much. Aren't you just one big bundle of joy!" At that moment, I remembered what Eric the minister had challenged me to do when I told him I had been diagnosed with cancer. I smiled to myself, and thought, *Well, despite everything, perhaps I've become the Joy Ambassador For Cancer after all.* This also gave me another idea.

Always look on the bright side of life

In the operating room, right before I was placed under anesthesia, I insisted that the entire surgical team sing a chorus of *Always Look On The Bright Side Of Life*, from the Monty Python movie, *The Life Of Brian*. Everyone in the surgery room couldn't believe I was even serious. But I was insistent, "Hey c'mon everybody, aren't I entitled to at least one last request before going under the knife?"

Not much they could all do then but sing. So before I was put under, everyone in the room - doctors, nurses, everyone - sang a chorus of *Always Look On The Bright Side Of Life*, complete with the whistle part. After we all finished laughing, I said to the anesthesiologist, "You don't happen to have any morphine in that cocktail of yours do you? I remember that one from my son's C-Section. That drug was really great!"

He replied with a grin, "Honey, there's morphine heading to a vein near you." That's the last thing I remember of my surgery.

After the morphine and other anesthesia came down the IV, I was out, and everyone else began the surgery in high and lighthearted spirit. The cancer was removed successfully. I went through 33 radiation treatments and the standard chemo treatment pill of daily tamoxifen for five years. I also got my wish to fly first class to Paris, climb the Eiffel Tower, and eat a chocolate croissant at the very top.

The stair fall

Two years after the bike accident and cancer, I had to sell my home to pay all the massive doctor and hospital bills. I rented a small apartment on the ground floor of a building in Ballard. I had spent the first day there unloading all my furniture and boxes into my new apartment using the side of the building that had a ramp. I took myself out to dinner that first night, and by the time I was done eating, it was drizzling outside. The rain became heavier on the drive home. So due to the rain, I decided to enter my new apartment for the first time from the other side of the building which was closer to my assigned parking place.

I had no idea how slippery the stairs would be in the rain. As I stepped down the first stair, I slipped at the top due to its awkward (and what later proved to be illegal) steep pitch and fell straight down to the bottom of the ten wooden stairs on to the concrete below. I knocked myself completely unconscious, and to this day, I do not know how long I lay there in the rain.

When I woke up, I was completely soaked and it slowly dawned on me that I was in a lot of pain. Somehow, I dragged myself over to my new front door, got the door open and then dragged myself into the kitchen. My head, back and left ankle were throbbing so I pulled myself up the refrigerator to the freezer, grabbed a bag of frozen peas I had bought on my earlier grocery run, and then dragged myself over to the couch. Somehow, I managed to get myself up on to the couch, put the bag of peas on my ankle, and then completely passed out.

When I woke up the next day, I felt a bit disoriented. I didn't normally wake up to find myself on the coach in my living room. Wiping the sleep from my eyes, I realized that my head and my back and my ankle really hurt. I looked down and saw that not only my left ankle was black and blue, it was also twice it's normal size. *Oh my God. This can't be happening. I thought I dreamt all this!* I thought to myself.

About that moment, my executive assistant Dave arrived at the door for work. I tried, but my entire body, especially my head, hurt so much I found that I couldn't even get up off the couch to open the door. So I just yelled, "Come in!" from my prone position.

When Dave saw me laid out on the couch, he said, "What the heck happened to you?"

"Actually, I slipped and fell down the stairs last night."

"Oh my God." he said. "So, that probably explains why you have a sack of peas on your leg?"

It was slowly dawning on me how late in the morning it must be. I had an extremely important and lucrative interview for the position of personal coach of the most prominent woman philanthropist in India that afternoon. Dave and I also had an important grant proposal for another client due the next day. I had to get up off that couch and get dressed. We had to get to work.

"You stay right there." Dave said. "I'm getting you some coffee, and then we will figure our next move." Dave was an ex Marine so he always had his priorities in order. Coffee *first* and *work second.*

I made myself go to that very important interview that afternoon. I completely underestimated the severity of the concussion I had received from the stair fall. Hard as I tried to cover up my discomfort and disorientation, my inability to focus in the interview was obvious. Even though the choice was between me and another person they were considering, the interviewer told me later that I had not interviewed well, that I didn't "seem myself," and he didn't know why.

When I explained the circumstances, he was extremely upset, "Why in the world didn't you tell me? We could have postponed the interview until you felt better! You were my first choice for the job!"

Ah the beauty of hindsight. That concussion, and my insistence on pushing myself beyond what any normal person would do under similar circumstances, cost me that very important job, including relocating to India.

The political surprise

A few weeks later, I learned that the man I had been working for as communications director in international politics had been skimming money from every single political race I had run, and won, over the past ten years in the form of back end bonus agreements with our clients.

One of our female candidates for U.S. Congress mentioned to me one day, "Hey Mary Anne, did you know your boss is taking a half a million dollar back end winners bonus if we win? I sure hope you are getting at least some of that bonus because it's clear to me that you are certainly doing all of the work!"

In politics, a "back end bonus" is where the client is given a low price up front to run a campaign. If you, as the political consultant, have done your pre meeting polling, you already know from your polling whether your candidate is a "sure win," or not. If your client is a likely winner, political consultants often tack on a huge back end bonus to increase their fees, which the client will pay happily when they win their race.

Until our female candidate for Congress spoke up, I had not known my boss was doing this. Rightfully, I was owed a portion of this money for all my work with our clients. I had to assume he had been doing this all along for the past ten years and had collected quite a bit of money on the races I had worked on.

That afternoon, I marched in to my employer's office and asked, "Why didn't you tell me you were skimming back end bonus money off of my work?"

My employer smiled smugly, "Why didn't I tell you? Well, there's a simple answer to that. You never asked."

I was completely stunned. We were not only colleagues. I thought we were friends. But what he said next was even more shocking. "You know Mary Anne, I have the greatest job in the entire world. I'm like an orchestra leader. I haven't got one creative bone in my body, but I get people like you to do all the work, and I take all the money and the credit too! It's great!"

My response to that was, "Well, you can get someone else to do all your work for you. I quit."

The political consultant already had the perfect comeback, "Well it will take probably six people to replace all the jobs you have been doing for me – and for a shitload less money I might add - but that's cool. Go ahead and quit. I can always find someone to replace you, or anyone else for that matter. No one in this world is irreplaceable."

He was right of course; no one is irreplaceable in politics. Even though I was now out of my only paying job at that time, my concussion had clearly knocked some sense into me. As it turned out, quitting politics and getting away from this man were two of the very best things I ever did in my life; I was making a solid investment in my self-respect, and my health.

Calling God On The Line

After that meeting with the political consultant, I called my dear friend Rina on the phone. Rina was an extraordinarily gifted psychic person, and had been sought after all over the world for her psychic ability. Rina eventually was recruited to work for the U.S. government and Interpol where for years she used her psychic ability to locate missing children who had been kidnapped in the white slave trade. I figured if she could rescue missing children, perhaps she could help me rescue myself.

When Rina picked up the phone I said, "Rina, I need to ask you a very important question. When I first became a soul, can you tell me if God give me a name?"

Rina laughed. "Of course God gave you a name. Every soul has a name given by Source." Rina replied cheerfully.

After everything that had happened to me over the past decade or so, I was quite frankly wondering if my soul name was something like "Loser" or "Idiot" or even, "Masochist."

"Would you please tell me what my soul name is?" I asked tentatively, a little afraid to hear the answer.

"Certainly. Well it's a little hard to pronounce in the English language, but in Sanskrit your name means *peace* and *tranquility*."

I burst out laughing; Rina had to be kidding. "Oh my God, Rina. You have to be kidding me! *I am the least peaceful and tranquil person the world has ever known*!" I said, still laughing.

"Well yes, that's true at this point, perhaps." Rina said, beginning to laugh with me. "But I can tell you for absolute certain that peace and tranquility are where you're headed. You will get there, eventually. I'm sure of it."

Shaking my head back and forth, I said sarcastically, "Yeah right. Sure I will."

"You will!" Rina assured me. "I can see it as sure as I can see the back of my hand right now. Trust me on this one. You will get there!"

The shift in my health began

That stair fall began a two-year battle with my landlords about their negligence over the unsafe stairway, a case which I ultimately won in court. The concussion eventually resolved itself after a few months, but I spent the next two years in excruciating pain and physical disorientation from the fall. I was unable to work. As a result of lack of income, I had to fire my beloved assistant Dave to save money. Due to all the medical bills from cancer and everything else, I was forced eventually to file for bankruptcy anyway.

However, I persevered, one step at a time, even despite the physical and mental pain, and all that incredible amount of stress. After all those various trips around and around on The Roundabout of both my health and work, my life began to shift.

From Me To You

"We can let the circumstances of our lives harden us so that we become increasingly resentful and afraid, or we can let them soften us, and make us kinder. You always have the choice."

~ The Dalai Lama

THRIVE

How do you define a thriving healthy life for yourself? Is it simply the "absence of illness" or is there something more to it?

In 2015, I participated in the Prime Transformation Challenge given by Dr. Jade Teta. After all the health challenges I had already been through, this program was praised by many as just the right thing to reboot my metabolism. I got so much more from this training and Dr. Jade Teta than I ever expected.

The health & fitness industry wants us to believe in a one-size-fits-all approach. However, I learned from Dr. Jade Teta and his programs at Metabolic Effect that actually this is not true. There is no magical diet out there. Did you know that 95% of people who go on diets gain all the weight back? Even worse, 66% actually end up fatter? That's because the approaches they follow never address each person's unique metabolism, psychology and preferences. In fact, that is why most diet and workout programs fail. The real health and wellness search is not about finding a diet, it is about creating the right diet for each of us individually. It's also not about blindly following a protocol, it's about building a lifestyle. Each of us is an individual, as different on the inside as we are on the outside. Our metabolism, psychology and personal preferences are also unique. Any program we follow should work with our differences, not force us to fit their approach. Dr. Jade Teta's programs helped me discover, practice and master the perfect lifestyle that was best for me.

At first, this process of finding the right lifestyle for me was challenging. In fact, one of the things I found most surprising is that the baseline for this program, in addition to the 15 minute exercise routine three days a week, was the practice of mindfulness and a daily sixty minute slow leisurely walk. Being a mostly "power walker" for most of my life, this idea of slow walking was a bit foreign to me. But as Dr. Jade Teta explained, "Slow walking not only is fun and restful, it also brings cortisol, our stress hormone, way down."

Honestly, I must admit I was wondering if a 15-minute workout and a slow walk was enough exercise. But Teta's philosophy is to "work smarter, not harder." Much to my surprise, I discovered this approach was quite efficient and also delivered the results I was trying to achieve. I began to notice things I didn't normally notice while out doing my forceful and determined "power walking." Rather than just push through my walk to get it over with, I began to hear the different birds singing, take in the color of the sky, all the different flowers, trees, and the view. More and more I began to look forward to my daily slow peaceful walks. I could let my mind wander and more fully take in my surroundings. As my stress hormone cortisol came down, I also began to feel much more calm, more aware and mindful.

Becoming a metabolic detective

I also learned to become what Dr. Jade Teta calls, "a metabolic detective." I began to notice and track how different foods affected my hunger, energy and mood. As I noticed what made me feel good, I chose to eat more of those foods. As I noticed which foods made me feel irritated, bloated or uncomfortable, I ate less of those.

The 3 times per week 15 minute sessions of exercises of the Metabolic Prime, Metabolic Aftershock and Metabolic Effect programs did indeed reboot my metabolism. In fact, after nine months on the first program, I lost 33 inches of fat. I went from being a sugar addict, with what Teta calls, "a sugar burner metabolism" to a "fat burning and muscle-building metabolism." But more than anything, as a result of these different programs, I noticed my attitudes about my life and health changing. In addition, the information and training finally helped me create a lifestyle I loved.

One of the principles of the programs from Metabolic Effect is to help us get in touch with our HEC- Hunger Energy and Cravings and also monitoring our SHMEC- Sleep, Hunger, Mood, Energy and Cravings. I began to rely on my SHMEC tracking as a barometer of my overall health and well-being: I watched my Sleep, Hunger, Mood, Emotions and Cravings gradually come into balance. If my SHMEC now goes out of balance for any reason, I can spot that very quickly. Thanks to the program training, I also know how to make any necessary adjustments I need in order to bring myself back into balance.

After a trial and error learning period, I discovered what Teta calls my buffer and trigger foods. These are both foods you love, but one makes your healthy lifestyle easier to manage (buffer foods) and one makes you not be able to find balance (trigger foods). I did my best to keep as many buffer foods in my program as possible while eliminating the trigger foods.

Here is a quick example of buffer and trigger foods: Wine is a buffer food for some people. For these people, having a glass of wine for dinner means they are more likely to eat healthily, less likely to eat dessert and more likely to go to bed satisfied. For others, wine is a trigger food. When they drink wine it makes them drink more wine, eat more food, order dessert and eat worse the next day too. I discovered that red wine was a buffer food for me and so I kept it in my daily diet. If I had discovered through my SHMEC tracking results that red wine was a trigger food for me, I would have eliminated it.

Everyone's trigger foods are different. Teta explained that when we eat these foods, it drains what he calls, "the mental battery." This makes it really hard for our minds to then resist other, even less healthy, foods. I discovered that dark chocolate digestive biscuits are my arch food nemesis. Whenever I ate them, it triggered a binge of, "Oh what the hell, I'll just eat the entire package of biscuits." Next I observed that this triggered a strong desire for salty things like potato chips and other sweet things like candy. Now that I know what happens to me and how I get totally triggered, when I see dark chocolate biscuits on the shelf in the grocery store, I bless them, and keep on walking.

For me now, a healthy life is one where I feel good and in balance, not where I beat myself up all the time for the "bad" things I did. Thanks to Dr. Jade Teta, rather than having a "dieters mentality," watching a scale for my validation, I switched to a healthy lifestyle that I could actually sustain. I now know what to do if my HEC or SHMEC gets off balance for some reason. This has given me a sense of confidence that I know not only what works for me, but also what I need to do to help myself stay in balance.

As a consequence, I feel more peaceful and more at ease overall in my life. As a result of feeling more in balance on all levels of my body, mind and spirit, it was easier to put my entire life into perspective. I began to listen to my heart's desire about the future I wanted to create and what a Thriving life could look like.

The power of deep listening

I once read in a J.D. Salinger novel, "My father turned to me as if he had been waiting all his life to hear my question." Have you ever listened *to yourself* with that kind of focus and respect? Funny how we live our entire lives in this body and we forget to listen to it. Have you ever been listened to by another person like Salinger describes? When you come across a person who listens with true presence, it feels like they are *listening with their entire being*. My husband Rupe listens to me that way now. At first, being listened to and so fully emotionally supported like that felt a little unnerving. I just was not used to that kind of true presence from anyone.

As Abraham Lincoln said, "There are those who listen, and those who wait to talk." For most of my life, that had been my only experience of listening, that people were just waiting to talk and not really listening to me. I only experienced deep listening from people like a minister or therapist. Being listened to deeply from another person, like Salinger describes, creates tremendous trust and allows us to take leaps of faith with them that we wouldn't ordinarily do with other people.

Meet Rupe

In late 2012, I felt so utterly safe with Rupe after I met him it *just felt right*. In fact, when I heard Rupe's voice on the telephone for the very first time, I just had this overwhelming sense of wanting to crawl into his lap, put my head on his shoulder and heave a huge sigh of relief. Hard to believe, but I moved in with Rupe at his home in Port Townsend after I had known him only one month. Every single one of my friends and family thought I had gone completely off the rails. But somewhere deep inside me, I was now listening to a new, budding voice that came with a gut feeling. I began to know it my own real voice.

I was no longer asking everyone else for advice, as Dan the Shaman had suggested back at Miraval Spa in Arizona. I finally trusted my own gut about what was right for me. That strong, calm, clear inner voice said, "This is a good, loyal and trustworthy man. Trust your instincts about him. Trust yourself, Mary Anne."

In September of the following year, I married Rupe. In October 2013, we left the United States and moved to Ecuador. In December of that same year, I started writing my *Footprints in Ecuador Blog* which grew into an audience of 175 countries, and eventually those blogs inspired me to write a full length book in 2015 called, "Words To Thrive By for World Travellers: Footprints In Ecuador." Two years later we left Ecuador and moved to Chile. Six months later we moved to New Zealand, and then to Australia, where we live now.

I have noticed that more and more, just being more authentic, congruent, peaceful and joyful are the real goals in my life. Suffice it to say that after 15 years of being divorced, I gave myself permission to focus all my energy into me, getting totally clear on who I was, and who I wanted to become. Ultimately, I became the person I truly wanted to be. I made good choices along the way and that led me to the conclusion that I was totally happy being alone and that unless someone came along who added really serious value to my life, I was happier being alone. Well that, of course, was the exact moment that Rupe showed up in my life. Go figure.

Each of us have the power to change everything we ever believed about what is possible in our lives. I have now realized that I was never as stuck, lost or hopeless as I had believed. We are all free at any time to expand

and grow beyond any limitations we think are "true." The important question for us to consider is, "What do I actually choose to believe is possible *for me?*"

Most importantly, we need to examine our deepest unconscious thoughts and beliefs in our thinking that are reflected in what manifests in our life. We create our own reality, for better or for worse. If we are not totally happy with what we have created in our current reality, or the choices we are making are not serving us, we can change them. *We are only subject to that which we hold in our mind as true.*

For me, I became aware that it wasn't just about surviving another crisis or heaving a huge sigh of relief that I had dodged another bullet; I needed to learn how to truly feel the joy of life. I needed to learn how to rest peacefully in the flow of The Universe, trusting that the same flow that creates worlds was living and breathing through me also.

I began to trust and surrender to the fact that how things will unfold is always a mystery. I didn't need to know everything or have everything figured out ahead of time. I found myself saying, "I am in the flow and I don't need to know." I began, little by little, to trust the process and believe that the details would become obvious to me, at the right time and the right place, when I needed them. I continue to say this prayer all the time, "God help me. Show me The Way. Show me The Truth. Set me Free."

Author, Pam Grout, uses the term, "Field of Infinite Potentiality," or "FP" for short, to describe how the Universe has the potential to open us all up to some pretty amazing, magical, and miraculous experiences. My faith in God and my spiritual practice has definitely evolved over the years, into the complete trust, faith and surrender I have now. As a result, the people or the things I need most, including abundant health and well being, manifest in my life with ease and grace.

From Me To You

There are two simple steps that can keep you living longer and healthier:

Caloric restriction leads to a longer life. Intermittent fasting does the same thing . . . easier.

Exercising 100 minutes a week adds 7 years to your life.

Start fasting.

Start walking.

CONCLUSION

Clearly, I took exit after exit after exit, both on and off The Roundabout of Health over the years. Now that I have healthier beliefs, much of the previous negative chatter inside my head is no longer rattling about in my brain. After a lot of focus, dedication and hard work, I am thankful to say that I am in the best physical and mental condition of my life.

After appearing like I was headed for a total and complete train wreck in the health department, a few of the major contributors to my great health now have been a daily practice of exercise such as walking, biking, wind surfing, kiteboarding, weight lifting and stand up paddle boarding. I've also reduced my exposure to toxic food and people. In addition, I've cut back completely on reading toxic news media online, and minimalized my exposure as much as I can to other social media. As a result of these simple changes, I feel more calm and peaceful, and I'm also sleeping better than I have ever slept before.

From Me To You

No matter what happens in our lives, we each must find our own way through it as best we can. As the writer Jack Gilbert says, "We must risk delight. We must have the stubbornness to accept our gladness in the ruthless furnace of this world."

BOOK 4

THE KEY OF LOVE

"All shall be well
and all shall be well
and all manner of thing shall be well."
~Saint Julian of Norwich, 1342-1416

INTRODUCTION

Confucius once said, "Wherever you go, go with all your heart." I have to admit that learning how to love myself is something that I'm still working on. I still struggle with both judgment and criticism, of both others and myself. I've read studies which suggest that people don't respond to what we are saying, or how we appear on the outside. They actually respond to who we *are* and *what we are not saying*. This would suggest that what we are actually feeling inside is broadcasting in an outward way far more than our words are.

With time and better perspective, I can see that for much of my life I believed that everyone else was more important than I was. I assumed that this meant I was supposed to take care of them first, even at the expense of myself. I made choices consistent with that belief to the extent of giving up my own dreams and future in order to serve other people's aspirations and lives, such as those of my husband and children. I can now see clearly that my internal resentment over my choices cost me dearly in a physical way in terms of my own health and well-being.

However, even despite my errors in my beliefs and the choices I made as a result of them, I gathered self-confidence, self worth and strength along the way. Eventually, I moved on to taking responsibility for my life. I realized that each of us is on a solo journey through the human existence. I absolutely had to take full and complete responsibility for myself and also for my choices if I was ever going to move forward. When I started my business, My Real Voice, back in 2001, this was the point where I began trusting that I could actually create the things that I imagined and desired.

Since I had joint custody with my former husband of our two kids, we created a week on week off parenting schedule. After being the parent who took care of our kids full time, and then as a result of divorce shifting to becoming a half time parent, this meant I had a ton of time on my hands all of a sudden. In fact, I had a lack of interference from others for a full six months out of every year to do exactly what I wanted to do. I hit certain physical roadblocks during that time as well, such as five cancers, two near fatal accidents along with the experience of a rape. One year alone, I had to manage the death of my cherished dog Biscuit, my bird Birdie, and also all my remaining older female relatives.

However, who is to say that *all* of these experiences were not ultimately in the interest of my highest and greatest Good? All my life, I had always prided myself on being *so tough*. I thought that *force of heart* was the way to get things done, done, done. What I didn't realize then, and that I do understand now, was that my constant use of force was keeping both people, and my greater Good, *away* from me, not drawing them closer.

To Brazil and back

When I was turning fifty years old in 2008, I flew all the way to Brazil to meet the world-renowned healer, John Of God. I wanted to meet a truly enlightened person on this planet and then, I wanted to ask for his help. At that time, my heart felt like a geode, and I didn't know what to do about it. I wrote all about that trip in my first book, *Words To Thrive By: Powerful Stories Of Courage and Hope*, in the chapter entitled, *Transformation: Help Isn't A Four Letter Word*. Here's an update on that Brazil trip now nearly ten years later.

At the time I met with John Of God, I wanted to figure out why I felt so incredibly stuck. I wanted to draw a new partner and a new more abundant life into my experience, but I had been thoroughly unsuccessful. I had tried to outrun my grief, rage and frustration all my life, and now it all had caught up with me, whether I liked it or not. I had tried to manage and control this oncoming train wreck of overwhelm, but ultimately, I could not outrun it.

When I met with John Of God, he insisted I sit near to him in his high-energy field and meditate. After four hours of that the first day, I actually felt a bit more peaceful. John Of God then said he wanted to do what was at that time called "a psychic surgery" on me. I agreed to this procedure, as that was an optional part of the "healing protocol" with John Of God for some people who really needed it.

After the procedure, I spent the next two weeks in my room going out of my mind. Post surgery, I could not read as my eyes hurt so much and I could not go outside because the outside light felt way too bright. I was in pain all over my body where the "psychic surgery" had been done. I had no idea what to do with myself with zero distractions. I began to *cry*. And *pound my pillow*. I just felt completely *lost*. I slipped a note under the door of Heather, our tour guide, who was also the person looking after me at the guest house where I was staying. The note said, "I'm going out of my mind and I don't know what to do. Please help!"

Eventually, Heather came in and talked me down off the ceiling. She was the very first person to teach me how to ask for help. Asking for help in any way from anyone up to that time, had been a really negative "four letter word" for me. I didn't know how to ask for help as I had no idea who to ask for help from. I had always felt profoundly alone in my life and didn't much believe in God or getting any help from there either. I really had no idea how to deal with all of my repressed stuff when it started to come out. Heather explained about The Entities, the various Guides who did the profound healing work through John Of God. She also explained the spiritual rule that no one, not even The Entities, could intervene in my life in any way until I actually asked specifically for help.

My heart burst wide open after that, and for reasons I still cannot explain to this day, I began spontaneously mentally forgiving people I didn't even know I was mad at. Continually, for days on end, I kept asking each of them internally for forgiveness for what I had done to them, and I forgave them for what I perceived that they had done to me. I even asked for forgiveness and release for anything I had done to hurt myself in the past, known or unknown. It was profoundly healing both to my heart and to my head, not to mention to my body.

I can see now that all of these difficult physical and emotional challenges gave me time to analyze how much I truly wanted to be in charge of how I lived my life in a more conscious way. These physical challenges also gave me time to redesign the direction of the future I really wanted to create, with the time I had left. More than anything else, it became exceedingly clear to me that *the only thing that was truly important was the moment and what I chose to do with it.* All along the way, I had known that I had a strong intuition, but I didn't always listen to it. In fact, most of the time, I had ignored it, much to my own peril. I can look back now, of course, and see where different choices would have led to very different results. But all in all, through all of my life's challenges, I can see now that I always did my very best, and made choices that were consistent with my level of understanding and consciousness which I had at that time. This means that if I could have done better, I would have done better and that everything I chose seemed like a good idea at the time. Now, looking back with 20/20 hindsight, I can be more forgiving toward myself, knowing that I always did the best I was capable of and that I always tried to live my life with dignity, integrity and a sharing heart, even when it felt at some moments like there was nothing worth going on for.

I believe that the human spirit is the eighth Great Wonder Of The World. Human beings can carry on through the most difficult of circumstances, the most devastating grief and the most profound of challenges. Even those difficult curve balls life seems to throw us every now and then can be viewed as "sideways blessings." These "sideways blessings" often lead us, much to our surprise, to places we never would have dreamed possible.

From Me To You

"Nobody is superior,

Nobody is inferior,

Nobody is equal either.

People are simply unique, incomparable.

You are you, I am I."

~Osho

SURVIVE

Love can show up in our lives in some very unexpected ways. Periodically throughout our lives, we may receive "gifts in disguise." Sometimes these gifts include very hard choices we all have to make in order to discover who we really are and what being authentic means. At times we may have to make some tough decisions in order to stay true to ourselves in a loving and nurturing way. Sometimes we can only learn this by putting ourselves first.

Hit with a sledge hammer

When I was diagnosed with the first of five cancers in 2009, my children, Sarah and Joshua came to my home. Sarah announced, quite matter-of-factly, "Dad told us we didn't have to take care of a parent."

I said, "OK. I hear what your Dad said, and I understand this is what your Dad believes. What do you both believe?"

Sarah replied, "We agree with Dad."

This was quite a shock and I really didn't know how to respond. "Let me get this straight. You agree with your father that when a person in your family is sick, you bear zero responsibility for taking care of them in any way?"

Sarah looked me straight in the eye, and said, "Yes."

At that moment, I could not believe what I was hearing from my own children. I honestly did not know what to say. I took a deep breath and then tried to clarify once more. "So you both believe that when a member of your own family, someone whom you love, falls on hard times or gets seriously ill, such as being diagnosed with cancer, that is the moment you abandon them?"

Sarah nodded and repeated, "Dad said that we don't have to take care of a parent."

Next I did something I did not previously think I was capable of. I asked them both to leave. I said, "Well if that is true, and that is what you both really believe, then you need to leave my house. I need positive energy around me right now so that I can fight this cancer. I want to be with people who will support me in healing myself. You are telling me that you have chosen not to do that. So, you both need to leave. Right now." And they did.

As I sat at my kitchen table with my head in my hands, tears streaming down my face, I felt more hurt than I had ever experienced in my life. I felt utterly abandoned by the very people I thought would be there for me - my children. I remembered the time I nearly died in a bike accident a few years before. I had said to my Mother, "I'm not leaving my children!" I survived for them and now they were turning their backs on me. I thought, *Well that was a dumb idea, sticking around for them. They couldn't care less about me!* At the time, their words and actions felt unkind, cruel and utterly lacking in compassion.

But that was not the end of the story. As it turns out, my children leaving me was a huge gift in disguise – although I'll admit it did not feel that way at the time, and also it took me a long while to realize it. By leaving that day, my children handed me the keys to my own freedom. By leaving, they set me free to find the life of my dreams. That is the life I am currently living now. Their actions – choosing not to take care of or help me - forced me to confront some difficult but very important questions about myself, and my life:

Who am I living for?

What am I living for?

What am I doing with my life?

How do I see my future?

How do I want to live the rest of my life?

Most of my life I had taken care of other people, virtually to the exclusion of my own dreams, desires and needs. I didn't know that there was any alternative. I lived to serve others. I gave as much as I had, and others took as much as they wanted from me. That day, everything - my personal growth, my spiritual evolution and especially my future - all hung in the balance. Was I going to succumb to the pain, suffering, deep hurt and betrayal I felt? Or was I going to search within myself to find what and whom I wanted to live for and then fight with all my being for that life? I chose the latter. The biggest question facing me was this one: *Who was I going to live for now?* The obvious answer to that question was *myself.*

Putting myself first

The only person you can fully take responsibility for in life is yourself. Learning to love yourself is the most important decision you make in your lifetime. When we decide to take care of ourselves first, we chose the more difficult path of self-discovery. This is our chance to find out what we are really made of, our true opportunity to learn how to get through tough situations on our own. The moment I made that decision to put myself first, I noticed that my entire life began to change for the better.

What I have shared with you above is obviously not your "Hollywood Happy Ending." Real life gives us tough problems to solve in order to make us stronger, both inside and out. As hard as it was for me at the time, my children - by not supporting me - actually gave me an opportunity to develop the strength I needed to push myself forward in my quest to Thrive instead of just Survive.

I feel genuinely grateful now for what I learned as a result of that challenging experience with my kids. I realized that I could still love my kids and choose not to be with them at that time in our lives. I could choose at that moment to give all three of us a chance - and some much needed space - to heal.

Other people stepped forward to help me get through the cancer treatments and therapy. Friends brought cooked food. My agent sent me a teddy bear. Some of my professional colleagues brought groceries to my door since I could not drive. I survived the worst part of the cancer ordeal without my kids, or my family.

I used the time, such as when I lay on the radiation table five days a week for the 33 radiation treatments, to visualize a goal I had set for myself: eating a chocolate croissant at the top of the Eiffel Tower in Paris. After I got through everything, I made that visualization a reality: a good friend and I flew First-Class to Paris. I climbed the Eiffel Tower and counted 690 steps (as high as anyone could climb in 2009). I took the elevator the rest of the way to the top, and then enjoyed a delicious chocolate croissant, just as I had pictured it when I was going through the treatments.

Everything changes

People evolve and grow- if and when they choose to. You can't push another person to develop at a faster pace than they want to. You also cannot force them to change if they choose not to. Likewise, don't expect yourself to grow at a faster pace than you are capable of right now. As a result of my breast and cervical cancer experience, I learned one of life's most important lessons: how to honor and love myself first. Out of that more genuine love, I developed the capacity to show more respect not only to myself, but also to my children and others in my future. For all of this, I am deeply grateful.

From Me To You

Perhaps you cannot imagine how you would react if your children, family or spouse left you at a time of great need. If not, it is time to get some compassion for both yourself and them.

Compassion is a far greater and nobler thing than pity. Pity has its roots in fear and carries a sense of arrogance and condescension, sometimes even a smug feeling of "I'm glad it's not me."

As Stephen Levine says: "When your fear touches someone's pain it becomes pity; when your love touches someone's pain, it becomes compassion."

To train in compassion is to know that all beings are the same and suffer in similar ways, to honor all those who suffer, and to know that you are neither separate from nor superior to anyone.

THE ROUNDABOUT

In my personal Roundabout in the Key Of Love, I had a lot of work to do. At the time when I hit rock bottom in my life, sitting at my kitchen table, I truly believed that that I was not lovable. A thought like that, which I thought over and over again enough times became my strong belief. This belief about myself became reflected in all of my personal and professional relationships, and also my life at that time.

The trip to Mexico

Through God's Grace, I was invited by my dear friends Billie and Tim to visit at their beautiful home in Sayulita, Mexico. Billie and Tim built this amazing healing and yoga retreat center (www.Corazon-Sayulita.com) for people to go to who all have one thing in common: to change the world. I definitely needed my world changed at that very low point in my life.

Not long after I arrived there, I slipped and fell on some gravel in a driveway on the way to the beach. This fall threw my back out again into a very painful paralyzing spasm. The pain was so bad, that I couldn't walk. After that fall, it felt to me that I was doomed to relive and continue the physical pain and suffering I had been going through for the last five years. I felt truly and completely hopeless. The spasm didn't go away for several days and the pain was getting worse. It finally got so bad that Billie called her masseuse friend Lisa for help. Lisa is a very gifted masseuse who travels with the holy man Rinpoche. When Billie called to get me an appointment, she found out that Lisa had just come back into town the day before from a long trip travelling with Rinpoche. Lisa came right over. This coincidence was only the first sign that God's Grace was working in my life, even if I could not see it at the time.

As Lisa was working on my lower back, trying to get my back to move out of the terrible spasm, much to my shock, I found myself suddenly screaming at the top of my lungs: *"I'm everybody's whore!"* I had absolutely no idea where that statement, "I'm everybody's whore" had come from; it had just flown out of my mouth from some deep place, unchecked, and completely uncensored.

"What did you just say?" Lisa asked calmly as she continued to massage my lower back.

I quickly replied, "Oh my God Lisa I am so sorry! I have no idea where that came from. I'm so sorry!"

"Don't be sorry. Just tell me again. What did you just say? I want to be sure I heard you correctly."

I was a little embarrassed but I said again, "I said, 'I'm everybody's whore.'" My eyes were wide and I was at that moment truly puzzled.

"Do you believe that statement, "I'm everybody's whore?" Lisa asked quietly.

"Well," I said hesitantly, "I guess I do. It feels like I've been everybody's whore, helping them get what they wanted, helping them make more money and gain more power and prestige for many years now."

"Hmm. That's a pretty shitty mantra: 'I'm everybody's whore.'" Lisa said. Then she went on, "It seems like that feeling was lodged in your lower back where I was just working. I don't know if you know this but the lower back is where we usually stuff our ideas about support, or in your case it sounds like lack of support. Interesting." Lisa continued to gently massage the area as she spoke.

"Hmmm. That is interesting." I said, still puzzled at my outburst. Nothing like that sudden outburst had ever happened to me before on a massage table.

"But, Mary Anne, is it true?" Lisa asked calmly. "Are you, in fact, everybody's whore?"

I thought for a moment. "It sure feels that way."

"When do you think that feeling started?" Lisa asked, continuing to massage my back a little higher up.

I thought for a long moment and then said, "Well, I think it started with leaving my career as an actress and agreeing to marry my first husband back in 1982. Jeez. That's 30 years ago now. Wow. That's a really long time."

"But is it true now? Now. In this present moment now I mean?" Lisa asked.

"Is what true?" I said, confused.

"That you are everybody's whore?" Lisa repeated.

"I don't know. All I can say for sure right now is that my life looks really bleak. I'm now completely broke, heading to bankruptcy from all my cancer bills. I lost my home due to those medical bills and I don't have a clue where I am going to live now.

"I have no job in sight. I just quit my previous job, where they guy walked away with at least half a million dollars of my money. I have no husband or partner, and I pretty much hate every person in a male body right now. I have no idea right now what I'm going to do or how I am going to manage from here. Honestly, Lisa, I've never felt so lost, alone or terrified in my entire life as I do now." I sighed.

Lisa smiled. Then she said, "I have just the person for you to talk to after this massage. I will see if she has any time available." Claire just happened to have one appointment open before I was scheduled to leave Mexico. This appointment I am sure was what I call, "A Divine Appointment," because it truly changed my life in a very profound way. When we met, Claire's first words to me were, "I hear from Lisa that you have some seriously shitty mantras you need to get rid of." Then she flashed me a huge grin.

All I could do was laugh and say, "Well I suppose I do. My life certainly couldn't get any worse than it is right now."

She interrupted me right there. "Wait a moment. Is that true?"

"Is what true?" I replied.

"That your life as you just said, and I quote, "couldn't get any worse than it is right now.' Is that true?" Claire repeated.

"Well, it certainly seems that way," I said as I began to list off all of my most recent catastrophes: pain and suffering, no money, no job, no house, no man, bankruptcy.

But Claire persisted. "Is it true, your life couldn't get any worse than it is right now? How do you know that is, in fact, 100% true?"

I frowned, "I suppose I don't. In fact, I probably shouldn't even be saying that. It probably could get worse." I was obviously at a pretty low point, without much hope.

Claire went on," You see, when you make blanket statements like that, you are in fact creating your future reality. Are you aware of that?"

I had to admit that thought had never really occurred to me. "I've never really understood that old spiritual saying, 'You create your own reality.' I've always just thought I was really terrible at manifesting anything positive in my life. But hey, my current life is obvious evidence that I'm an absolute master at manifesting lots of shit to deal with!"

Claire ignored my attempt at humor and continued, "I am going to question you on what you just said a moment ago. Is it true, your life 'has been total and complete shit?'"

"Well, up to now, yes." I pouted.

Claire would not let me wallow one bit. "I am going to ask you that question again, and I want you to really think about it. Is it true, that your life has been 'total and complete shit?'"

I had to admit, "Well no…" I said. "But mostly." I whined again.

"Are you 100% completely convinced of that? Can you absolutely know that it's true?"

"Well no." I said, not sure where she was going with this line of questioning.

"How do you react, what happens, when you believe that thought?" she persisted.

"Well, basically, I feel like crap." I admitted. "I feel hopeless. I feel lost. I feel alone. I feel worthless. The world looks like crap and my whole life looks and feels hopeless. Shall I go on?" I said as tears began to roll down my cheeks, and into my lap. I felt totally and completely lost. I had hit rock bottom.

Then Claire dropped another bombshell, "Who would you be without that thought?"

"What do you mean by that Claire?" I cried. "I really have zero idea what you are talking about!"

"I mean, who would you be without the thought of 'My life is and has been total and complete shit.'" she asked again. I really had to stop and think about that one.

Claire then suggested gently, "OK. Close your eyes Mary Anne. Ask yourself that question and just see what shows up. What do you see? What would your life look like without that thought?"

After a moment I admitted, "Well, if my life wasn't and didn't feel like total and complete shit right now, I guess I would be a lot less angry. I would be a lot less stressed and frustrated. I imagine I might be a lot happier. I would sleep better. Basically I would feel a lot better without that thought."

"Let's turn it around." Claire suggested next. "Instead of saying, 'My life has been total and complete shit,' let's turn that statement around."

"What do you mean? How can I say my life isn't total and complete shit when it obviously is at this moment?" I was confused.

"Go with me for a moment on this one Mary Anne. Turn it around. This is not about blaming yourself, or feeling guilty. It's about discovering alternatives that can bring you peace. So let's work on this for a moment and see if we can find at least three specific, genuine examples where the turnaround is true for you in this situation."

I still did not understand what Claire wanted. "I'm sorry. I still don't understand."

"OK go with me here for a moment Mary Anne. This process is the work of Byron Katie. It is about welcoming all your thoughts and experiences with open arms, as it shows you where you are still at war with reality.

"If you feel any resistance to a thought, your Work is not done. When you can honestly look forward to experiences that have been uncomfortable, there is no longer anything to fear in life: you see everything as a gift that can bring you self-realization."

I had to admit it. "Well I have certainly been at war within myself, doing battle with reality for quite some time."

"Exactly." Claire replied. "Wouldn't it be a relief not to be at war with reality any more?"

I sighed. "Yeah. Seeing life as a gift? Nothing to fear? Yeah that would be really nice. But, welcoming all my thoughts and experiences with open arms? I really don't see how that would even be possible."

"Well OK. I get that, loud and clear" Claire laughed. "So let's start small. You are alive right now right? You are breathing? Am I right?" I nodded. "So in fact, if your life was total and complete shit, you would probably be dead right? I mean dead really is total and complete shit as far as life goes right?" Claire smiled mischievously.

I had to laugh at that one "Perhaps."

"So you are breathing. You are alive. It's not total and complete shit, just really rough right now. Let's go with, 'My life is not total and complete shit.' Could you agree with me on that one?"

"I suppose." I said.

"OK good. So let's take another slightly different tack here. How about taking your statement, 'My life is total and complete shit' and turning it around just a little in a different way to something like, 'I'm willing to allow my life to get a little bit better?'" Claire obviously had a quirky sense of humor.

"Look Mary Anne, I am not asking for miracles here, as in your life getting totally and completely better right this second, just a little bit better. Since we both agree now that in fact your life isn't total and complete shit, just really tough, we could take your statement, 'My life is total and complete shit' and turning it around just a little tiny bit. Can you see where I am going here Mary Anne? Could you agree with, 'I'm willing to allow my life to get a little bit better?'" Claire asked hopefully.

I was beginning to see a glimmer of light. I smiled. Claire then asked me to say out loud the following turnaround statements, "My life isn't total and complete shit. I'm willing to allow my life to get a little bit better. I'm looking forward to my life getting better and better."

As Claire was leaving, she said, "I heard from Lisa that another of your shitty mantras is "I'm everybody's whore." I nodded, blushing. "Can you please turn that one around for me?" Claire smiled.

"I'm everybody's Goddess?" I replied, smiling too.

"You got it! Good work! I look forward to talking more with Mary Anne Dorward The Goddess in the future!" Claire said. We both burst out laughing together.

I can see now, over five years later, that this moment talking with Claire was the beginning of my new life of Thriving. My meeting with her changed how I used both my thoughts and my words to create the Thriving life I have today. I've learned that every negative thought I thought, over and over again, created not only my beliefs about myself and the world, but also was creating my future. Thanks to Claire, I was able to understand the life path I had chosen up to that moment, and how I could create a new and improved mindset moving forward. This shift in my mindset began to create a higher vibration around me, which began to attract more and more positive things into my life, including a new partner, who is completely nurturing, loyal and supportive.

From Me To You

If you want to get to the core truth of anything in your life, I invite you to explore the four powerful questions used in The Work of Byron Katie:

The Four Questions

1. Is it true? (Yes or no.)

2. Can you absolutely know that it's true? (Yes or no.)

3. How do you react, what happens, when you believe that thought?

4. Who would you be without that thought?

This process is not about blaming yourself or feeling guilty; it's about showing you where you are still at war with reality and discovering alternatives that can bring you peace.

THRIVE

How I met my husband Rupe, otherwise known as "Mr. Right," is a great example of how when we shift our own vibrations and consciousness first, then we can meet others who are at the same level of consciousness. These are also the people who can support us in our next phase of personal growth and evolution.

How I finally met Mr. Right

Rupe and I both had been married to similar types of people and in subsequent relationships been with similar types of people on and off for the 15 years after each of our divorces. We both had tried the online dating thing with rather disastrous and unsatisfying results. But, we came to the conclusion we would give that online dating process just one more try. Then, if something didn't come of it, we would be content to just quit once and for all. We were both on that last day of the dating service, and planning to quit the following day. At that time, Rupe lived in Port Townsend, which is located about two hours north of Seattle, including a thirty five-minute ferry ride. I was living in Seattle. We were both pretty content with the way our lives were going and had come to the exact same conclusion that unless someone came into our lives who added serious value, we were content to accept that we would happily live alone, and single, for the rest of our lives.

My last date with Mr. Wrong

On this last day of my online dating experience, I accepted a date with a man who seemed fairly interesting on the dating site. He was a drug and rehab counselor. On a Sunday, I agreed to take a walk around Greenlake in Seattle with him. I thought to myself, *What the heck. It's a 45-minute walk. I need the exercise anyway. I'm quitting tomorrow so I guess I'll go.* I arrived and this man was sitting down at the appointed place we had agreed to meet.

The first words out of his mouth were "Well, I guess you can see by now that I lied on my profile. I'm closer to 80 than I am to 60."

That's it. I'm done here! was my first thought. However, instead I politely laughed, and said, "Well can you walk?"

As he got up from the bench, he said "Yes, of course I can walk."

So, off we went on our walk and the conversation around Greenlake was pleasant enough. When we had made a full circle, he said, "Are you hungry? I'm going to get lunch. I'd be happy to treat you to lunch too."

"That would be very nice of you. Yes, thank you." I replied.

We drove our separate cars to the agreed upon restaurant. After we sat down at our table, the first words out of his mouth were, "So you're not going to make me eat anything I don't want to eat are you?" This question caught me by complete surprise.

I barely got the words, "I hadn't planned to…" out of my mouth when this many went on a verbal rant:

"…because my mother used to make me wear everything I didn't eat on my plate. Imagine wearing bananas coming out of your ears"

I was just about to say "Buh bye now!" when our food arrived. I decided that I would be polite and eat my food rather than it going to waste. But I remember feeling that this was truly it for me. I couldn't wait to get away from this strange man. When I arrived home, I was in a sour mood, and went to my computer. There, I pulled up my dating profile and I looked it over very carefully, wondering what in the world I was saying there that was attracting all these creepy, strange and seemingly dysfunctional men. I had a sudden inspiration to erase absolutely everything I had written in my introduction section and leave only one photo. Trusting my intuition, I did.

Next, and to this day, I swear I don't exactly know what came over me, I wrote only two lines on my new profile that would be the first thing any man would read about me,

"If you have truly done your own work on yourself and also gotten over your dysfunctional mothers, your evil ex wives, and your creepy stupid ex girlfriends, please feel free to give me a call. Otherwise, don't bother!!!!!"

For a moment I asked myself, *Too harsh?* And then my immediate internal intuitive answer was a very strong *Nope!* I pushed the button to make this new text on my profile go live online.

Then I thought to myself, *What the heck. I'm taking this all down tomorrow anyway. It won't matter. No man will ever read this and if they do, they will think I have 'anger issues' and won't contact me anyway. I'm so done with this online dating. I will just stay single forever.*

Then, I went on with my afternoon.

Meanwhile back in Port Townsend

Meanwhile, Rupe is sitting at his computer in Port Townsend and was saying to himself, *This whole online dating thing has been a complete and total waste of my time. These women they have set me up with so far are completely needy, lonely, controlling and from not interesting at worst to slightly interesting at best. They all have major issues and problems of ex husbands and ex boyfriends and ex whatever. I'm done with this.*

He was about to delete his profile completely but stopped and intuitively said to himself, *Well the one thing I have never done is do a search in the dating system with my own parameters of distance and qualities I am looking for. So before I go, I will make one last search and one search only and that will be it.*

Rupe plugged in all of his dating parameters - which were just barely far enough out to include Seattle – and pressed send to input it into the dating system. The computer calculated and then the photos of women within his newly written parameters began to come up. The very first photo of all was mine. And of course that photo came with my statement outlined above.

Rupe said his very first thought was *Oh my God, this is a beautiful woman!* Then when he clicked and read what I written, his second thought was *Oh my God! I have to meet this woman! She is totally unapologetic!*

To this day Rupe swears that for him, it was all kind of surreal, like in the movie, *The Matrix*. Rupe said to himself as he looked at my photo, *She. Is. The. One.*

Then, Rupe sat there at his computer for an entire hour trying to talk himself out of his intuition, thinking, *"Oh no this woman won't be remotely interested in me. I'm better off just being on my own.* Eventually, his intuition won out and he sent me a note introducing himself.

I read his note, read his profile and saw all his photos. The first photos of him I saw were of him windsurfing. Turned out that Rupe was one of the early wind surfers in the world, and also was one of the original wind surfing teachers in Hood River, Columbia Gorge area, considered the Mecca for windsurfing in the world. I saw another picture of him on a beautiful white sandy beach and read his words about always finding a way to get out of the dark, dreary, rainy Northwest winters that I equally dreaded.

I remember thinking, *I want to know how in the world he has figured out how to get away for the winter and what job now he could possibly have that would allow him to do that.*

I read his words that were equally unapologetic to mine such as "If you don't like a man who has had many different adventures and jobs in his life and who is not a one note person, then I'm probably not the guy for you."

This man clearly had something that I couldn't put my finger on. Independence? Freedom? Wisdom? Whimsy? Clarity? Whatever it was, I had to know more and we made a plan to talk by phone.

Peace, at last

The first time I heard Rupe's voice, I was overwhelmed with a sense of wanting to rest in his voice, to put my head on his shoulder and sigh a huge peaceful sigh of relief. In fact, we talked for three hours and planned to meet. When we did finally meet each other, I found myself spilling my heart out and telling the real truth of my Journey to this point with no sense of needing to dazzle or impress. It felt like we were old soul friends reunited once again and telling tales of this go round of life. I drove to Port Townsend for a visit, and went back to Seattle four days later. Then asked if I could come back again, which I did the next day. We haven't been parted since.

On the cover of my first book, "Words To Thrive By: Powerful Stories Of Courage and Hope," there is a green crumpled post it note with the word Love on it. I put it there as a kind of private joke. In that book, I wrote that I believed the word Love was the hardest word. Now, seven years later, I am thankful to report that Love is not the hardest word for me anymore. In fact, Love has been my greatest teacher. My guess is whatever word is the hardest one of all for you right now holds an equally beautiful blessing for you, just as the word Love did for me.

From Me To You

Scientists such as the late Dr. Emoto have done amazing research in the field of water research. Here is a healing exercise to charge water with love and gratitude.

The process is simple: Take a glass of filtered water and place it on the table in front of you. Put both your hands around the glass and simply breathe white light through your palms into the glass. Drop into your heart and say, "I love you" and "Thank you" to the water and hold that feeling in your heart. Allow that feeling to pass through your palms into the glass of water. Drink the water yourself, or give it to someone who needs it! Dr. Emoto has proven from his groundbreaking research that water takes on the qualities of the word and intention we send to it into the molecular structure of the water.

CONCLUSION

It is said that there is nothing as powerful in the universe as Love. Have you heard of the Hawaiian doctor who cured an entire ward of criminally insane patients, without ever meeting any of them, or spending a moment in the same room? The therapist was Dr. Ihaleakala Hew Len. He reviewed each of the patients' files, and then he healed them by healing himself. The amazing results may seem like a miracle, but then miracles do happen when you use Ho'oponopono.

You might be a bit skeptical and wonder how this could possibly work. How could you heal yourself and then have that heal others? How could this possibly change anything and why would it affect anything "out there"?

The secret is that in reality, there is no such thing as "out there" – everything happens to us in our mind. Everything we see, hear, every person we meet, we experience in our mind. We only think it's "out there," and therefore, we make the assumption that this "fact" absolves us of any responsibility. However, it's quite the opposite: we are responsible for everything we think, and everything that comes to our attention. This means that we are also able to clear it, clean it, and through forgiveness, actually change it.

There are four simple steps to this method of Ho'oponopono. The order of how you say them is not important. The best part of Ho'oponopono is that we can do it ourselves. We don't need anyone else to be there, and we don't need anyone to hear us. We can just "say" the words in our head, or out loud. The power that is activated by the Ho'oponopono prayer is in the feeling of being willing to both forgive and love. The forces of Repentance, Forgiveness, Gratitude and Love are the only forces at work – but these forces have amazing power.

Ho'oponopono (ho-o-pono-pono) has four steps: "I'm Sorry. Please Forgive Me. Thank You. I Love You."

The Four Steps of Ho'oponopono

Step 1: (Repentance) – I'm Sorry

Whatever needs healing in your life, be it yourself, a person, a family issue you would like to resolve, first we need to acknowledge this by saying the words, "I'm sorry."

Step 2: (Ask For Forgiveness) – Please Forgive Me.

Don't worry about who you're asking. Just ask! Please forgive me. Say it over and over. Mean it. Remember your "I'm sorry" from step 1 as you ask to be forgiven.

Step 3: (Gratitude) – Thank You.

Say the words, "Thank You." It doesn't really matter who or what you're thanking. Thank your body for all it does for you. Thank yourself for being the best you can be. Thank God. Thank The Universe. Just keep saying, "Thank You."

Step 4: (Love) – I Love You.

Say "I Love You." You can direct this "I Love You" to your body, to God, to Mother Earth, to the life giving air you breathe, to the house that shelters you, to your current challenges, to life itself. Say it over and over. Mean it. Feel it. There is nothing as powerful as Love.

That's the whole practice in a nutshell. It is simple and also amazingly effective. I have seen miracles happen as a result of this prayer in both my life and in the lives of others. Again, there is nothing as powerful as Love.

For the love of poetry

I love poetry. I especially love the following poem by Mogh Ruith, titled, *There Is a Pattern*. It speaks well to living a life of deep love from within and how this love is reflected in the world around us if we will but open our hearts to see the pattern there, already laid out before us.

There Is A Pattern

By
Mogh Ruith

The swirling galaxies spreading across the universe

dance the same graceful spiral as does our DNA.

In our every cell, the electrons orbiting each atom's nucleus

reflect the planets, twirling and spinning around the sun.

There is a pattern. There is a pattern,

and it resounds through the world beyond us,

and finds its echo in the world within us.

When we see the moon as dark, hanging in shadow,

it is in truth no less than when it waxed full

and gently illumined our nights with mystery.

The sun continues to radiate its holy fires of life

even after it has dipped below our horizon

and dropped wholly out of simple sight.

There is a pattern.

Day follows night, as surely as night follows day.

The seasons move from growth to harvest and on through decay,

before the exuberance of rebirth in sudden spring.

The pattern repeats inexhaustibly across the millenniums

continually showing us this cycle of life, death and rebirth;

assuring us that dark is always a prelude to light, there is a pattern.

The pattern connects the stars, the trees, and even spiders,

the magnitudes, the moon, and each of our spirits.

And when our spirit rises away from the body,

it does not cease to dance.

The spirit continues to spiral on its way, in its own way,

up and through darkness, moving into light,

and then to more transcendent states beyond

as we waltz through the endless wonders of the universe.

From Me To You

We were born into the exact circumstances that were best suited to bring each of us the spiritual growth and evolution that we planned as a soul. Trust that you knew exactly what you were doing when you chose to come here, no matter what it may look like in your life at this moment.

BOOK 5
THE KEY OF GRATITUDE

"Seven times down, eight times up."
~Taoist saying

INTRODUCTION

You have a right to a Thriving life. It is possible for you to unlock and open all of the other doors to your own Thriving life with the Key Of Gratitude. If you feel that you have made a mess of your relationships, your career, your health or your life up until now, you can change all of them for the better.

At one time of my life, I was deeply struggling in Survival mode, and it was a time when I thought I couldn't stand another minute. Today, I look around and I feel so deeply grateful for my incredibly full and Thriving life. One of the keys to unlocking your Thrive Drive is Gratitude.

Connecting with Native Wisdom

In 1987 I helped develop The Council Program in the Crossroads School in Santa Monica, California. Before I would accept the appointment to become a Council Leader I insisted on being approved and blessed by a Native American Elder. I didn't want to be just another American person who ripped off the sacred ceremonies of the Native American People.

I was blessed through my Aunt JaneAnn to gain an introduction and a conversation with Arvol Looking Horse. At the age of 12, Arvol Looking Horse received the Sacred White Buffalo Calf Pipe Bundle and its teachings. To this day he is the 19th Keeper Of The Lakota Sioux Sacred Pipe descended from Buffalo Woman. Arvol Looking Horse graciously agreed to meet with me to hear my request for a blessing on my work with adolescent kids in conflict resolution in the Council Program. When I spoke with Arvol Looking Horse, it felt like he was looking deep into my soul. He asked me three questions:

1. Tell me about this program of yours?

2. Are you following The Path of The Heart?

3. Are you aware that we approach life from the perspective of not just this generation but for the next seven generations?

I first explained a bit about the Council Program, which had been created at Crossroads School. I explained that I had been invited to develop and to teach in the program for children ranging from 12-18 years of age. I was not aware of the Native American belief of seven generations and so I admitted I did not. I then asked him to explain more about that Native American tradition so that I could incorporate it into my work with the children. As for question number two, all I could answer was, "Sir, in as much as I understand that question at this time, I do believe that following The Path of The Heart is my deepest intention, not only with this Council Program, but also in all that I do."

After an hour of deep reflection, going over his questions and prayer together, Arvol Looking Horse gave me his blessing and encouraged me to go forward with my work, always holding the important vision of protecting the children of seven generations forward, and blessing seven generations back in time. My time with Arvol Looking Horse was one of the most meaningful conversations of my life.

For many years after this conversation, I was involved with this Council program which is now practiced all over the world in schools, corporations, prisons and other places where people gather to work through their differences. One of the core principles that the program of Council is based upon is the statement, Aho Mitakuye Oyasin. Aho Mitakuye Oyasin is a simple yet profound statement. It comes from the Lakota Nation and means All My Relations. It is spoken during prayer and ceremony to invite and acknowledge all relatives to the moment.

The Prayer Of Aho Mitakuye Oyasin

Aho Mitakuye Oyasin. All my relations. I honor you in this circle of life with me today. I am grateful for this opportunity to acknowledge you in this prayer.

To the Creator, for the ultimate gift of life, I thank you.

To the mineral nation that has built and maintained my bones and all foundations of life experience, I thank you.

To the plant nation that sustains my organs and body and gives me healing herbs for sickness, I thank you.

To the animal nation that feeds me from your own flesh and offers your loyal companionship in this walk of life, I thank you.

To the human nation that shares my path as a soul upon the sacred wheel of Earthly life, I thank you.

To the Spirit nation that guides me invisibly through the ups and downs of life, and for carrying the torch of light through the Ages, I thank you.

To the Four Winds of Change and Growth, I thank you.

You are all my relations, my relatives, without whom I would not live. We are in the Circle Of Life together, co-existing, co-dependent, co-creating our destiny. One, not more important than the other. One nation evolving from the other and yet each dependent upon the one above and the one below.

All of us a part of the Great Mystery.

Thank you for this Life.

From Me To You

Peter Kreeft has a nice perspective on gratitude. He said, "I strongly suspect that if we saw all the difference even the tiniest of our prayers to God make, and all the people those little prayers were destined to affect, and all the consequences of those effects down through the centuries, we would be so paralyzed with awe at the power of prayer that we would be unable to get up off our knees for the rest of our lives."

SURVIVE

One year, I had to make a trip to Istanbul, Turkey for work. In between work meetings, my son and I made trips to see all the sights of Istanbul. One day I read in one of the guidebooks that on the Asian side of the Bosporus, there was the best ice cream in all of Turkey. My work associate, my son and I boarded the ferry for the short fifteen-minute ride from the Istanbul side of the Bosporus over to the Asian side.

The Asian side of the Bosporus

Unlike Istanbul, with its ancient mosques colliding with the sights of modern bridges, the Asian side of the Bosporus is filled with modern high end stores and busy streets filled with masses of people. We hopped into a cab and I gave the driver the address of the ice cream store. After driving around in circles for about twenty minutes, it was clear that the driver had no idea where this address was. Since it was lunchtime, we asked him to change course and take us to the nicest restaurant that he knew of. The driver dropped us off at this lovely small restaurant overlooking the Sea of Marmara. There was a platter of fresh fish laid out to the left as we entered and we were taken to a lovely table overlooking the sea, with a linen tablecloth set with silver place settings.

That very morning, while my son was asleep in his bed next to me, I had sat on my bed in the hotel and cried. I felt so depressed. I didn't know what to do. Sitting at the table overlooking the Sea of Marmara, I felt tears welling up again. I was thinking that I didn't want my colleague or my son to see me cry for what appeared to be out of the blue. I was just about to excuse myself to the ladies restroom when I looked up and the waiter caught my eye. He beckoned to me to follow him. I had assumed he saw my discomfort somehow and was taking me to the restroom. But as we went past the front door, past the restroom, into and through the kitchen, out the back door and down some stairs, I knew we were headed somewhere else entirely.

I just "knew" I had to follow this man. For some reason I wasn't at all afraid. When we got to the bottom of the staircase, he stood aside, gestured that I was to go into the room to his left and I did. As I stepped over the threshold, the waiter shut the door behind me. I was dazzled. At first all I could see was light. As my eyes began to adjust, I saw the light was coming from lit candles. Everywhere. As my eyes continued to adjust to the light, I began to see the beautiful colorful mosaics of what looked like holy people, men and women on every wall, floor to ceiling. All around me, there was hammered silver, both in the mosaics on the walls and on the floors. Even the tables were silver. Everything was flickering light. On each of the tables were several rectangular silver boxes, filled with masses of lit tapered candles each one stuck in sand.

My tears began to flow as I stood there in all that dazzling light and color, the light of each of the candles gently bouncing off the mosaics and hammered silver. It was truly breathtaking. *Was all this beautiful light just for me?* I wondered, as I stood there, unable to move. I just stood there and watched the candles burn down to the sand until they each went out. My lunch, my son and my colleague were totally and completely forgotten for a few minutes. All I could think of was, *Thank you. Thank you for this beautiful gift of light and peace and beauty*. When the candles burned out, the light changed in the room and I opened the door and made my way back to the table. By this time, my lunch was cold and my son and colleague had finished their meals entirely.

"Hey what happened to you?" my son asked.

I replied, "I'll show you after lunch."

An Angel in disguise?

When we had paid our bill, I looked for the waiter who had led me to the beautiful experience below filled with so much light. But he was nowhere to be found. *Was he an angel? Did I imagine him?* I wondered. I thought to myself, *Perhaps this was the miracle that I had been praying for.*

When I could not find him, I asked another waiter if I could show my son something just outside the kitchen. He said yes, so I led my son down the back stairs and into the room. Much to my surprise, the tables were now completely empty. All the candles and silver boxes that had held them were completely gone. Without the candlelight flickering off all the silver and the mosaics, the room looked almost normal, like any ordinary room with a few relics on the wall.

My son looked at me and said, "And the big deal here is?"

I laughed and said, "Oh nothing. Just something interesting to see here that's all." I quickly got out my camera and took some pictures, to both cover my confusion and also research this place later. As I was taking photos, I casually remarked to my son, "Let's go find that ice cream now shall we?"

We never did find that ice cream but I did find a connection to a deep part of myself and a profound sense of gratitude that day. I had experienced a true miracle of the heart and I was deeply grateful. I felt healed from my inner darkness by the completely unexpected gift of light given to me from a complete stranger in another land far away from my home.

From Me To You

Hunter Doherty "Patch" Adams was an American physician, comedian, social activist, clown, and author. He founded the Gesundheit! Institute in 1971 and has been active in his work there ever since. Each year Patch Adams organizes a group of volunteers from around the world to travel to various countries where they dress as clowns in an effort to bring humor to orphans, patients, and other people.

Here is what Patch Adams said about gratitude in his own life: "I made the decision to never have another bad day in my life. I dove into an endless sea of gratitude from which I've never emerged."

How can you bring more daily gratitude to your life and to the lives of others?

THE ROUNDABOUT

When you hit rock bottom, what do you do? In The Roundabout of Gratitude, we learn to adopt an attitude of gratitude, no matter what comes our way. In her book, "Fail, Fail Again, Fail Better: Wise Advice for Leaning into the Unknown," Buddhist monk, teacher, author and mother Pema Chödrön tells the story about her very first one-on-one interview with Trungpa Rinpoche, Naropa University's founder. This interview occurred during the time when Chödrön's life was completely falling apart. She went to speak with Trungpa Rinpoche because she wanted to talk about the fact that she was feeling like such a failure, and she didn't know what to do.

However, when Chödrön sat down in front of Rinpoche, and he asked her, "How is your meditation?" Pema Chödrön lied, and said, "Fine."

Next they just started talking, superficial chatter, until he stood up and said, "It was very nice to meet you," and started walking her to the door. In other words, the interview was over.

And so at that point, realizing the interview was over, Pema Chödrön just blurted out her whole story in a nutshell: "My life is over. I have hit the bottom. I don't know what to do. Please help me."

Below is the advice Trungpa Rinpoche gave to Pema Chödrön at that key moment in her life, advice which can also help us when we feel that we have hit whatever we consider to be rock bottom in our own lives.

Trungpa Rinpoche said, "Well, it's a lot like walking into the ocean, and a big wave comes and knocks you over. And you find yourself lying on the bottom with sand in your nose and in your mouth. And you are lying there, and you have a choice. You can either lie there, or you can stand up and start to keep walking out to sea.

"So, basically, you stand up, because the "lying there" choice equals dying. Metaphorically lying there is what a lot of us choose to do at that point. But you can choose to stand up and start walking, and after a while another big wave comes and knocks you down. You find yourself at the bottom of the ocean with sand in your nose and sand in your mouth, and again you have the choice to lie there or to stand up and start walking forward.

"So the waves keep coming, and you keep cultivating your courage and bravery and sense of humor to relate to this situation of the waves, and you keep getting up and going forward. After a while, it will begin to seem to you that the waves are getting smaller and smaller, and they won't knock you over anymore."

That is great life advice. It isn't that the waves of challenge stop coming. Because we train in holding the rawness of vulnerability in our heart, the waves just appear to be getting smaller and smaller, and they don't knock us over anymore. In other words, we are able to work with the feeling of failure instead of shoving it under the rug, blaming it on somebody else, or beating ourselves up. Instead, we begin to have the ability to connect on a more real level with other human beings and accept our vulnerability as a part of our humanness.

When difficult things happen in our life, and we meet them with genuine openness, they become a source of growth, a rich and fertile ground for learning, a source of moving forward with more wisdom and gratitude. That's why, in the Trungpa Rinpoche story, the waves that before were knocking us completely down, begin to appear smaller and have less and less of an ability to knock us over.

As we all go through life, challenging waves are inevitable. Maybe it is the same wave, maybe it's even a bigger wave than the one that hit last year, but it appears to us smaller because of our ability to swim with the wave or ride with it. It isn't that failure or difficult moments don't still hurt. In life things are always happening, like you lose people you love, and all kinds of things break our heart. But we can learn to hold failure and loss as part of our human experience, which connects us at a deeper connection of the heart with other people. For this connection we can always choose to be grateful.

The human soul doesn't want to be saved

Sometimes, however, we're in the presence of suffering so painful we can barely stand to be present to it. Being a witness and standing by a friend or family member in any kind of pain take time and patience, both of which we often lack. However, as Parker Palmer suggests, "The human soul doesn't want to be advised, or fixed, or saved. It simply wants to be witnessed, to be seen, heard and companioned exactly as it is. When we make that kind of deep bow to the soul of a suffering person, our respect reinforces the other person's soul healing resources, the only resources that can help the sufferer make it through."

However many "helper" types are as much or more concerned with being seen as good helpers as they are with truly being present to another person's pain or serving the soul-deep needs of the person who needs help. Others want to apply the "fix," then cut and run, figuring they've done the best they can to "save" the other person."

The flip side is those people who act like your tragedy or dark time is some sort of a contagious disease. I can attest to that latter experience from an example in my own life. When I lost my first child to death at full term birth, many of our "closest" friends, (and especially those who were pregnant and expecting a child at the same time as I was) acted as if they were in danger of catching some sort of a contagious disease from me, "that woman who gave birth to a dead child." These "close friends" gradually kept their distance more and more, and especially as their baby due date approached. After their child was born, I was no longer invited over or allowed to be near their baby. It was very painful for both my husband and I at that time.

A few, however, returned into our lives 10 months later when our daughter Sarah was born. A few more tried to come back into our lives after 3 years when our son Joshua was born, as both children lived and were healthy and thriving. But the hurt from how both my husband and I were treated was very painful, and while eventually forgiven, was never, ever forgotten. Neither of us trusted these people, or called them our friends after that experience.

However, I am grateful for what I learned from the way I was treated during a time of profound loss. I learned that loss is inevitable, and that we will all survive, if we give the pain time and compassion. As a result of this painful experience in my own life, now when I see people who are hurting, I can just sit with them. I know to be a witness to their pain rather than avoiding them, like my friends did when my son died. I just need to say something simple like, "I'm so sorry.' In my experience, you really don't have to say any more than that.

We are all much stronger than we realize. Sometimes it takes a tragedy or horrific loss for us to see just how strong and resilient we actually are. It is at these times we need to remember the immortal words of Winnie The Pooh: "Promise me you'll always remember, you're braver than you believe, stronger than you seem, and smarter than you think."

What we focus on expands

Miles Davis, the musician once said, "My future starts when I wake up every morning." That sounds like a totally obvious statement right? But what is your very first thought when you wake up every morning? Is your first thought when you wake up: "I hate my life." or "This is going to be another incredibly stressful day. I can feel it." What about starting the day in a new and more grateful way? Try exploring creating a new thought as your very first thought when you wake up each morning: "I totally love my life!" or "I am so incredibly grateful for another day of life!" That very first thought you have in the morning when you wake up can set the tone for your entire day. Pam Grout in her book, *E Squared: 9 Do-It-Yourself Energy Experiments That Prove Your Thoughts Create Your Reality* suggests that even before you get out of bed you say out loud and with gusto, "Something incredibly awesome is going to happen to me today!"

She suggests also following that declaration up with dancing around the room and doing fist pumps in the air to a song you love. For me, "Best Day Of My Life" by American Authors always gets me going first thing in the morning with some really great vibes. I even created a "Joy Playlist" on my computer with other uplifting songs which I put on first thing in the morning after my meditation time. (See Appendix for this Joy Playlist.) I can say from personal experience that doing these things first thing in the morning makes for an awesome start to my day! Now, I choose to always start my day follow this truth: "Anything that can go right will go right." As author Pam Grout says, "Once we start noticing all that is going right, that is all we will see."

Remember The Universe is always listening to your mental and emotional broadcasting system: your words and your feelings. If you are sending out SOS energetic calls of distress, The Universe will send you more of that: distress, disappointment and stress. On the other hand, if you send out signals of gratitude, love, and joyful anticipation, The Universe will send you more of that. So choose what you really want the moment you first open your eyes to greet each new day. You will get it.

From Me To You

"Very little is needed to make a happy life; it is all within yourself in your way of thinking." ~Marcus Aurelius

What we focus on from within ourselves expands and then becomes visible in our outer reality. Giving thanks at all times and for all things attracts more wonderful people, ideas, experiences and joy to come into our lives. The more we do a daily gratitude practice the more that appears in our live to be grateful for.

THRIVE

What lives inside each of us no one can ever break. It's never too late to let go gratefully of what no longer serves us and start creating ourselves anew. Elizabeth Gilbert, in her book *Big Magic* says, "This, I believe, is the central question upon which all creative living hinges: *Do you have the courage to bring forth the treasures that are hidden within you?*" What if you just dared to really follow your heart's desire this time? Haven't you waited long enough? It's time, don't you think? Beginning. Right. Now. The past is where we, our former selves, learned our lessons. The future is where we apply the lessons. Let's not give up in the middle. As Ernest Hemingway so wisely stated, "There is nothing noble in being superior to your fellow man; true nobility is being superior to your former self."

From Me To You

The Japanese art of kintsugi (or kintsukuroi) restores a broken cup or bowl by embracing its full history. Rather than disguising the damage, they illuminate the cracks with gold, silver, or platinum. The result is often more beautiful than the unblemished original.

Omid's Safi gives a new perspective on lacquering our own flaws with gold, and not just hiding them:

"We value success, wholeness. Unlike this Japanese art form, we don't yet have a way of looking for what was once broken and has been healed and illuminated. How lovely would it be to find that a cracked and illuminated cup can be even more beautiful than a whole cup. How wise to realize that the broken hearts, illuminated and made whole, can be even lovelier."

CONCLUSION

When I turned 38, I had my first experience of the darkness of depression. During that time, all the powers I depended on -my intellect, emotions, ego, and will -all proved useless. All my feelings went numb, my sense of self was annihilated, my willpower was reduced to nil. Every one of my normal supports collapsed under the weight of my life. It felt like my mind, and I thought at the time my soul too, had betrayed me and become my enemy.

But now and then, even during that dark time, I sensed flickers of the presence of my true Self, the resilient part of me that never left me and had always been within. As my other powers failed me, this core, as savvy and strong as a wild ferocious animal, helped me Survive, and then later to Thrive. My Self, some call it Soul, is the part of me that knows how to persist in the hard times. My Soul Self is like that grounded, gritty life-force that gives "soul music" its name. My Soul Self is strong. It loves life and light. My Soul Self is fierce as it confronts my self with the truth about how and why I got lost in the dark. Together, we find our way somehow, back into the light of knowing again that each of us is all-powerful, magnificent, knowing, and creative.

From Me To You

All souls come to Earth with the purpose of knowing who they really are. We contain the energy of Source within and can use that energy, at will, to help us accomplish anything we desire. As Carlos Castaneda so wisely said, "We can make ourselves miserable or we can make ourselves strong. The amount of work is the same."

BOOK 6

THE KEY OF PEACE

"If I had a prayer it would be this: God please spare me from the need for appreciation, approval and love. Amen."
~Byron Katie

INTRODUCTION

Peace is all about how we look at things. Here's a story that illustrates that point very well:

A very wealthy socialite, we'll call her "Mrs. Smith," lived in the penthouse of a very famous hotel in Manhattan. All the staff of this hotel catered to Mrs. Smith's every need, as she was a very good customer. Late one night, at one in the morning, Mrs. Smith came storming down to the front desk of the hotel in a fit of rage. She screamed, "Someone is playing the piano in the suite next door to me! I can't sleep with all that noise going on!"

The Concierge of the hotel apologized and said, "I am so sorry Mrs. Smith but it is the famous pianist, Arthur Rubinstein who is staying the night in the suite next to you. He must be practicing. I am so sorry. Shall I go upstairs and ask him to stop?"

Well at this news, Mrs. Smith suddenly changed completely. "Thank you. That won't be necessary!" she said as went back upstairs.

The story went on to say that Mr. Rubinstein had made a small mistake that evening in his concert at Carnegie Hall that no one but him would notice. But he felt he needed to come back to his suite play the entire concert again from start to finish, this time perfectly. When Mrs. Smith came back to her apartment, she pulled up a chair next to the wall, sat back and joyfully listened to Arthur Rubinstein play. With her stress level completely down and her heart delighted now that she knew who it was playing next door, Mrs. Smith didn't miss another note of the entire piano concert, and was as happy as she could be for the next three hours!

Think of Mrs. Smith the next time something appears to be a "disaster" in your life. Depending on your perspective, it could become an extraordinary opportunity.

From Me To You

Is there an area of your life that you could embrace in a different way like Mrs. Smith did when she listened to Arthur Rubinstein play the piano? A new approach might bring you peace.

SURVIVE

My life wasn't so peaceful until relatively recently. As a child and young adult, I bottled all my frustration and anger up until it exploded out of proportion to the moment. As I grew older, I nursed a seething sense of moral outrage toward everyone and everything in the world. For many years, I thought anger was my problem. I have come to the conclusion now that really, really angry people are just more energized and mobilized really, really sad people. Now, I understand that my anger was more of an inability to metabolize deep sadness, and a consistent arguing with my reality.

Freak out on a NYC subway

One time, I totally freaked myself out. I was twenty years old, working hard, every single day as a newbie actor in New York City. New York has always been perceived as the land of dreams. You know NYC. As Frank Sinatra sang so well, "If you can make it there, you can make it anywhere."

After a particularly hard week, sending out thirty photos and resumes a day, I just felt like I was getting nowhere. I was done "pounding the pavement," having dropped off my resume to the offices of every agent and casting director I had researched. I was also done dropping my resume off to every place in the city that I could think of where I might get a paying job. I was done doing my various auditions, being number 656, 798 and 932 in line, respectively, for the three open call auditions I had right in a row that particular day, changing my clothes and makeup to fit the three very different characters I was auditioning for in the closest hotel bathroom to the location of the audition. I was exhausted. It was pouring rain. I was soaking wet. I decided to take the subway home.

As I got to the stairs of the 42nd Street subway station, I could hear the squeal of the brakes as the next train northbound pulled into the station. I started running down the hallway, trying to balance my backpack and purse, while I dug into my pocket for a subway token. I saw the train. The doors opened. I slammed in my subway token and blasted through the turnstile. The subway driver saw me running through the turnstile and trying to get to the door fast enough. Right as I got to the subway car door, the subway driver shut it. I could almost hear him smirk.

I don't know what came over me at that moment. Soaking wet on the clammy, damp, urine smelling subway platform with all the people inside the car looking out at me, I started banging on the subway train with my umbrella and screaming. This was a pure moment of blind rage. I didn't care what they all thought. As the train left the station picking up speed, I slammed every window of every car that went by me with my umbrella. People inside the cars actually flinched as I pounded their windows, one after the other until, at last, I was alone standing in the subway station, clawing the air with my umbrella. It may have started with the subway driver, but now, I was pissed off at every single person who had just gotten through their subway doors and was racing down the track to their next stop without me. This beating up a NYC subway car incident happened long before I understood that my anger started within me, and then was projected outward on to everyone and everything in my path.

A few moments after that particular train left the station, I suddenly "saw myself." It was like I "came to" and was suddenly observing some other poor sorry human soul just "losing it." That's when the tears began to flow. I couldn't stop crying. Out came all the tears of frustration of how hard I was working, how nothing seemed to be happening, how I felt I wasn't getting anywhere. More than anything, it felt like I just couldn't seem to move the giant wall in my life that I was sure if I just muscled it hard enough, and long enough, it had to give way. This was a work ethic I had adopted early in life, the "just muscle your way through" approach.

This approach did serve to help me get pumped, motivated and ultimately get a lot of stuff done. But, most of the time it just left me feeling like I wasn't strong enough, clever enough, smart enough, or well, *just not enough*. I certainly wasn't enough to make a NYC subway train stop by beating on it with my little black umbrella.

After I felt my rage and then my sadness, I started actually laughing down there on the urine smelling subway platform. It all seemed suddenly, well, ridiculous all my screaming and my pounding on the side of a subway car. As soon as the tears flowed, I actually felt better. One moment I had been in a fury. The next moment, I was crying. Then, there I was letting the energy of my anger rise into laughter and washing through me. That time my anger energy didn't stay stuck. It moved. And I moved with it.

Three months after I had moved to New York at the age of 20, I had a phone conversation with my younger brother Bob. He had said, "I can't wait to spend time with you when you come home for Christmas!"

I had snapped back at him, "Why the hell would you want to spend time with me? I've been here in New York three whole months and haven't gotten a job. I've barely gone out of my apartment because I'm so scared. I am blowing through all my savings. I am totally lost. I tell you. Lost."

There had been a pause and then Bob said gently, "I don't care about all that stuff. I love you. I just want to be with you. Hang out. Talk. Ride bikes. You know. Like we usually do. Screw that other stuff. It's you I want to see. It's you who I love."

I could not hear what my brother was trying to tell me at that time, all the love he was trying to give. Instead, I was focused on "The Great Story" to tell him when he picked me up at the airport, at the dinner table, our coffee time or, well, wherever. "The Great Story" is filled with accomplishments and glowing reports. That's the story that says, "Hey look at me! I'm so Successful! Talented! Popular! Happy!" I didn't have that story. This was the story I would not be able to tell because at that point, it had not happened yet in my life. I was so confused and depressed, I wasn't sure that it *ever* would. That anger just morphed from hating on myself, to hating on the subway driver, the subway riders and later that night, hating on my entire life.

What was going on

The more I learned to notice and feel my anger rising in the moment, catching myself actually in the middle of the experience and just noticing it, I began to learn more about what was going on inside of me. Catching myself before my rage flipped into a kind of blindness, was very educational. I knew from my own history of experience, that anger was going to happen. But now something significant had changed within me: I could literally feel the anger dragon stir and the energy rise as it began to flick its tail. I began to watch myself get seriously upset, thirty times a day, sometimes even in rapid succession.

But each time I felt the energy of anger or frustration rising, I caught myself and actually began to observe myself right in the middle of the experience of my anger. I just noticed it. I breathed. I felt it in my body. I noticed where my anger energy was located. Chest? Fists? Eyebrows? For example, one day I happened to notice that I feel anger first at the tip of my toes as they start to curl. I started working with the energy of my own anger by simply paying closer attention to *right before* anger got a hold of me and I got completely hijacked.

Depression is anger turned inward

I also didn't realize until a doctor told me so that constant anger was a sign of depression. He told me "depression is anger turned inward." As I look back, that moment of laughing at my anger that day in the NYC subway station was the very first split second in my life where I could see that my anger wasn't actually the truth of who I was. In that moment, my anger was simply a very powerful energy surging through me, based on my internal interpretation of events in my life at that time. I realized that I could make a choice at any time how I was going to interpret it.

Interpreted a different way, hindsight being 20/20 of course, at that time I hadn't failed after three hard months in New York. I wasn't "going nowhere." Far from it. I had just moved 3,000 miles away from home at age 20, into a great big city knowing hardly anyone, learned my way around and how to take care of myself, and figured out more about who I was on top of it all. I also didn't know it at the time that I was beating on the subway train, but I was to act professionally on Broadway only a year later. All that hard work I was doing at that time was actually was leading in the direction of my dream, and eventually, did pay off.

From Me To You

Lao Tzu said, "The best people are like water, which benefits all things and does not compete with them. It stays in lowly places that others reject. This is why it is so similar to The Way."

Nature offers us many examples of peace that we can consider cultivating in ourselves—the strength of the mountains, the resilience of trees, the cheerfulness of flowers. What quality of Peace would you like to cultivate in yourself?

THE ROUNDABOUT

The Roundabout period in the Key Of Peace can be identified most easily by a period in your life that is distinctly lacking in peace. When we lack peace, round and round we go, making decisions or choices, one after the other, and everything turning out worse than the last. It is at times like these that we make decisions too hastily, ones that we discover that we regret later or wonder what we were thinking when we made them. Choosing the wrong person to marry is often one of these kinds of decisions.

I agree to get married and leave my own career when it was just taking off. My brother Bob had died. It was 1982 and I was just turning 24 years old. I was devastated. I was in profound grief. Two years later my teacher and mentor Lee Strasberg died. This double blow of grief was too much at once. I was completely wrecked. Peace for me was nowhere to be found. Next thing I knew I was agreeing to marry someone I didn't know very well because I made a death bed promise to his mother that "I will always take care of him." I don't know why I thought this "taking care of him" promise meant I had to go through with a marriage I wasn't too sure about.

In fact, a month after I had made this deathbed promise and agreed to marry, I woke up one night clawing at my ring finger on my left hand, trying to get the engagement ring off. When I did finally tear it off, still half asleep, I insisted that my now fiancé put it on the other side of the room and get it as far away from me as possible. You would think I would have paid attention to that clue; it was a very clear warning something was wrong.

I went to my therapist at the time and told her, "I really don't want to get married and I don't think I love this man."

She replied, "Well you could do an awful lot worse." I thought by this she meant that I was just being stupid and should go through with the marriage even if it didn't feel right.

At no point in the entire engagement process did I ever consider that all these clues were trying to tell me something. I just believed there was something terribly wrong with me that I couldn't love this man. He was so sure of everything, so clear on his own goals, and so driven to meet them. This man may not have had a lot of things, but the one thing that he did have a lot of was *certainty*. Looking back now, I can see clearly that at that time, with so much grief and uncertainty in my own life, I was looking for anything and anyone who could help me make sense of this terrible dark time, and help me regain control over my life. This man had clarity and self-control in spades. He was charming but also organized, ate and took naps at a regular time each day, was clear, calculating and seemed very powerful. He owned his own apartment in New York, which to me was quite impressive.

I, on the other hand, was a poor struggling actor at that time and thought there was clearly something wrong with me and that I wasn't handling things at all well. At that time I did not know that true peace came from deep within. Instead, I was looking for someone *outside of myself* to give me peace. I can clearly remember saying to myself one day, *This man will save me from myself*. At that time I clearly believed that I was a very bad, weak and lost person. I thought I was heading for sanctuary with this man. What I didn't know at the time was I was ultimately headed for a very different place. Marriage to this man would ultimately cost me everything I held dear.

The audience is listening

When things in my life were at their worst and I had not slept for weeks, in 1997 I met a wonderful therapist named David. Even before he spoke one word, I saw the words, "The Audience Is Listening" appear magically over his head, just like Dolby Stereo used to have in the movie theatre.

David's first question to me was, "Who's keeping you awake?"

I answered, "My husband doesn't snore if that's what you mean." I wasn't sure what he was getting at.

"No let me ask you again." David said. *"Who is keeping you awake?"*

"I have no idea. That's why I'm here." I was getting impatient now.

David sat back in his leather chair and then said, "Let me ask the question a different way. When it was at its worst, the insomnia I mean, *what were you thinking?"*

"Thinking? I was thinking, 'If I don't get my shit together here and quick, my children will starve to death.' That's what I was thinking." I was getting heated now and I could feel my face getting hot.

"And were your children OK at that time?" David asked gently.

"Of course they were OK." I said, confused.

David sat forward in his chair now, and said gently, *"Then who's child is starving?"*

This question felt like an absolute bombshell going off inside me. It totally, and completely caught me up short. Suddenly, me who had not been able to cry in seven months, started bawling like a baby. "It's me. I'm starving to death. It's me. It's me. It's me!" I sobbed as I dropped my head into my hands. *I'm so very, very lost. Where did I go?* I thought, as I bent over, wracked in grief. "Yes it's me. I'm the one who is starving. I haven't done anything, no art, no music, no anything for myself in the last fifteen years since I met my husband. It's me! I'm starving to death!"

Over the next several months we dialogued with the starving child inside of me, the one who was now too afraid to speak up, too afraid to say what she thought, too afraid to have an independent thought of her own, too afraid to express any sense of anger or frustration, too afraid to change.

Dr. Jonathan Wright

The next month I found myself at the office of Dr. Jonathan Wright, a very well respected homeopathic and medical doctor. After putting me through a massive battery of tests he brought me into his office and asked me to sit down. "Well, this probably won't surprise you but you are a wreck, a total and complete wreck. First of all, there are no major minerals left at all in your body. Your body is so run down it is now eating your muscles. That explains why you are so black and blue all over your body. I need at least six months to fix this. Can you give me six months? I promise you will get better if you do exactly what I say."

I had to think about it. At that point, six months sounded like an incredibly long time. "If you can *promise me* that this will get better, then I will hang on for another six months."

Dr. Wright said, "I promise."

Dr. Wright was true to his words. After six months of supplements, colonics, mineral IV's, and specifically following his every medical instruction, I felt increasingly better, both physically and mentally. One by one, the lights within me began to come on again in a house where it had been terrifyingly dark and scary for some time.

The miracle of marriage counseling

When I felt much stronger, I asked my husband to come into marriage counseling with me. His first words to the new therapist when we sat down were, "If you'd just fix her, we'd be fine." This was not exactly a very hopeful beginning to our marriage counseling. Over the months of counseling, my husband just kept repeating at every session, "She's the one with the problem here. An alien has entered my wife's body and I want my old wife back."

After trying every angle I could think of to make things better between us, one day I finally reached a profound level of frustration. "She's not coming back." I said, feeling so tired, and so utterly sad. "I know I agreed to it, and I take full responsibility for my part in all of this, but I feel like I stepped into your script of the perfect wife, mother, friend, hostess, gardener, support person, gourmet cook and collaborator. I just can't play that part of The Stepford Wife anymore."

Tears began rolling down both my cheeks as my words continued to pour out:

"First of all, I want you to know how much I truly appreciate all you have done to support our family. And yes, I can totally understand how you would prefer me playing the role of that "old wife" who serves your every need whenever you ask, takes care of the house and the children, cooks, cleans, does the laundry, so that you can, let's see….what?....have total and complete freedom to go to the gym, work in the morning uninterrupted, have a snack prepared for you at ten, a homemade lunch on the table at noon, a nap at two, work all afternoon completely uninterrupted, a cocktail conversation at five to discuss your work of the day, a gourmet dinner on the table at six, someone to take care of our children so you can leave and go out of town on your fishing trips or off to work, and then call me and tell me you are attracted to some new young girl on the set and I play the part of your totally understanding therapist, and basically do whatever you want whenever you want. So yeah. You wanting to go back to that "old life" makes total and complete sense to me.

I took another deep breath. "However, I am trying so hard to help you understand right now that your old wife is not coming back because she was a total fantasy to begin with. I have tried so long and so hard to be "the perfect wife" of your dreams that I have forgotten who I am, and what it feels like to be a person with their own dreams. I need you to understand that after fifteen years of service, I just can't play that "old wife" part anymore. I don't like the script. I don't like my lines. I don't like my costumes. I just cannot play the part of a fake, perfect Hollywood, Stepford Wife for one more second.

"However, if you would consider creating a new marriage together, one where both of us collaborate so we can both get our needs met, then I am totally all in. Would you be at all open to that?"

My husband sat forward stiffly in his seat, narrowed his eyes, looked straight at me with the coldest expression I had ever seen and then said in a tone snarling with venom, "I haven't the slightest idea what you are talking about. An alien has entered my wife's body. Well I don't like this new wife. I want my old one back."

I exploded. "Since we met, I have tried and tried and tried to give you everything you ever wanted, and do absolutely everything you ever asked of me. I just can't do it anymore. Don't you see? It's killing me!"

My husband repeated tiredly, "I just want my old wife back."

"Even at the cost of my life?" I asked, incredulously.

"Whatever." he replied with a wave of his hand, and then sat back in his chair.

We were obviously at a crossroads.

I wasn't at all sure what would come out of my mouth next. "Well all I know for sure right now is that your "old wife" isn't coming back. While I can appreciate that you preferred the old adoring servant wife to this new one who speaks her mind and who is trying so very hard right now to negotiate a more healthy and balanced relationship with you, I can't play that old wife part anymore at the expense of myself. It seems that you leave me no choice but to respectfully request to be relieved of my marriage vows to you."

"You want a divorce? From me?" He looked at me like I was crazy, and then blinked once as he shook his head. Then he turned away, grabbed his leather briefcase, got up and said flatly, "Well. That's it, then."

I cried out, "Can't you even meet me halfway on this?"

At the door of the office, my husband of fifteen years turned around, and said, "Why should I? I want my old wife back, and that's final." He left the room, slamming the door on his way out.

I turned away from the door and looked at the therapist. He was sitting in his chair, shaking his head back and forth.

"What now?" I cried. "Oh God. What have I done?"

After a few moments, the therapist said "My gut tells me something isn't right here. There is something, and I can't put my finger on quite what it is right now, but *there is something he's not telling us.*" After another few moments of silence, he added, "And furthermore Mary Anne, have you noticed that this whole time we have been working together, your husband never once fought for you, or this marriage?" The therapist shook his head again. Then he leaned forward in his chair and said, "Well, all I can say is that any man who would let you go is an absolute idiot."

Much as I appreciated his kindness at that moment, it was small solace when the world I had worked so hard to build and keep together for so many years, was suddenly burning to the ground in front of my eyes, and I was the one who had just lit the match.

The truth comes out

It turned out that the therapist was right. Many years later, I learned that at the time we had been in marriage counseling, my husband had been involved with another woman. Eventually, this very young woman became my former husband's second wife, and our young children's stepmother. Looking back now, it is clear that during that time of our marriage counseling my husband was just going through the motions so he could say that he had tried. But in reality, he had never really intended to fix anything in our marriage. As painful as that realization was, I am so grateful both for my marriage of fifteen years and that period of counseling as that marriage ended. Both were extremely important in helping me clarify the person who I wanted to become.

The way of the Dark Mother

Vera de Chalambert, MTS, Harvard educated scholar of Comparative Religion suggests that these difficult periods in our lives are when the Dark Mother is "having her way with us." During these dark times of profound discomfort and disorientation, the Dark Mother demands nothing less than total trust as this healing unraveling takes place. Even if this dark path takes us to the point of a full and complete cracking open, all the suffering and pain ultimately help us allow more light of truth in. At this time, Chalambert suggests, "We stop shining of the false light. As our heart breaks, as our veneer cracks, we open to more integrity, more truth, more tenderness. We stop trying to be all things for all people. We become this one small thing, feigning nothing."

At the time of the marriage counseling, I did not agree to change back into the old wife my former husband had insisted was the price to be paid for remaining in our partnership. Instead, after all those years of "shining a false light," I moved on to discover who I truly was and what I really wanted. I began this new journey on a more genuine path to my true self as a "small thing, feigning nothing." At that time, all I knew for sure was that instead of choosing to continue to commit spiritual fascism against myself, I chose to flourish. That choice was the beginning of what later became a healing miracle.

The sleep test

In 1999, I was officially divorced. Eventually, I had recovered enough emotionally to begin thinking about what the next chapter in my life was going to look like. However, I still wasn't sleeping very well during this time. In fact, it felt that for some months I had not slept much at all. My fragile new self, bravely trying to be born out of a long dark sleep of not knowing who she really was, appeared to prefer emotionally thrashing things out during the night.

At my doctor's suggestion, I made my first trip to get a sleep test in a local hospital. When the results came back, Dr. Ralph Pasquale, an esteemed sleep researcher and pioneer in sleep medicine, and the doctor in charge of the entire sleep clinic of Seattle, sat me down. He looked up from the page of results he was holding in his hand, shook his head, then said,

"Well the good news is that you actually slept six of the ten hours you were here at the clinic. However the bad news is that you woke up every other minute. Basically, your sleep study reflects the equivalent of major torture. All of the other doctors here and I have discussed your case at length, and honestly, Mary Anne none of us can understand how you haven't completely snapped by now. Even three days of this breaks most people, and you have been doing this for months now. How in the world are you even still alive?"

This news didn't solve my problem, but it did at least give me some new insights. Dr. Pasquale's medical analysis also confirmed my own subjective experience of how completely debilitating my insomnia actually felt. As bad as the news from the sleep clinic was, finally knowing what was actually going on also felt encouraging in an odd sort of way. From that point on, I began to slowly build myself back up from absolute rock bottom. At the time, I just kept repeating to myself over and over, *Just take your next breath. Just take your next step*. Some days just continuing to breathe was my biggest accomplishment of the day. Eventually, after a lot of hard work and time spent on practicing better sleep hygiene, all areas of my life - sleep, health and well being - came more into balance. During dark and scary times, breathing and walking are sometimes all that any of us can do until we find our way through to the other side of the tough times. Hopefully, we come out on the other end of all these difficult and challenging experiences stronger and wiser than we were before.

A new life

When I began to feel a whole lot better, it was time to start thinking about earning a living. One day as I was thinking over what kind of business I might start, I had an unexpected inspiration. I went to my computer and Googled, "What is people's biggest fear?" The top ten results agreed that pubic speaking was most people's biggest fear, and fear of snakes came in at number two. I thought to myself, *Hmmm. I know a lot more about speaking than I do about snakes, so maybe I can solve that one.* Looking back now, I can see that this was a pretty courageous, some might say ridiculous, or even totally foolish thing to do as I knew absolutely nothing about starting or running a business. However, I can remember saying to myself, *Lots of people start business's all the time. Looks like all it takes is a good idea, passion and lots of hard work. I'm a smart woman. I've got a good idea. I've got lots of passion. I know how to work hard. How hard can this new business thing be?*

One day, I called a very old and trusted friend Richard for advice and said, "I'm thinking of starting a new business about helping people learn to speak better in public. What do you think I should call it?"

Richard didn't miss a beat, "That's a great idea! Perfect for you. You'd be great at that! How about you call it, 'My Real Voice.' I mean that's what people are looking for right? So why not call your business that?"

"What a great idea, Richard!" I said. The next day, I officially registered my new company, "My Real Voice," with the State of Washington.

The first five years of My Real Voice

After my divorce, my kids were living with me every other week. This was a huge adjustment, but soon I discovered that I finally had the time and lack of interference to get something done for myself. I put all my spare energy into building my business. I worked at it seven days a week on the weeks I did not have my kids living with me as working offset the terrible silence in the house. On the weeks I had my kids, I worked every day while they were at school, and then again at night after they went to bed.

One day, my father called. He decided to give me what he felt would be helpful advice about my being a woman in business. "What the hell are you doing? As a woman in business you have four strikes against you: You're female. You're beautiful. You're intelligent. You're white."

I didn't quite know how to respond to that one, so I said, "Uh. Thanks, Dad?"

Despite that withering piece of advice from my father, I carried on and didn't let his words for one single second become either my mantra or my belief system. I will admit, not knowing anything about running a business, I made a few less than stellar decisions. However five years later, by 2007 all on my own, I had single handedly built my business and earned a quarter of a million dollars.

When people ask me now why all the bad things happened to me, one right after the other, and how I could possibly still be alive, I answer, "Well, either God didn't want me, or I was hard to catch!"

From Me To You

No matter what comes your way, remember there are no stressful events, only stressful responses. Everything in life is inherently neutral. During difficult times, we may not feel we can change the cards we've been dealt, but we can choose to change the way we play them.

THRIVE

One of the most important aspects of my Thriving life of today has been learning to say one simple word: "No." Can you say the word "No." as a full and complete sentence, without feeling guilty or having the urge to apologize? Most people I talk to tell me that saying "No." is one of the hardest things to do in their daily lives. Why is it that the tiny word "No." is so hard to say without launching into an explanation? Why can't we just say "No." without worrying what other people are thinking about us? Why do most people find it hard to say "No." in their lives?

We want to be nice

You are probably a really nice and kind person at heart. You want to help wherever possible, even if it means that you give up your own precious time.

As an example of this, one afternoon a young magazine salesman came to our door. I felt compassion for him. I didn't need any more magazines but I didn't want to hurt his feelings as I could see that he was trying really hard to rehabilitate himself. I also knew from personal experience how hard doing door-to-door sales were. But it was also true at that moment that as a family, we really needed to be getting in the car as we were already late to where we had to be.

We're afraid of being rude

Most of us are brought up not to be rude and we're taught that saying "No." is being selfish, unless we have a *really* good reason not to say "Yes." This leaves us scrambling for an explanation and sometimes it's just easier to say "Yes." than come up with something to say that gets us out of the situation or request. Sometimes, we try to be polite and say, "Yes" with a tight smile and then grumble under our breath. Afterwards, we can spend a lot of time kicking ourselves for saying that, "Yes." when we really wanted to say, "No."

Saying "yes" in a crowd

Many of us don't say "No." because we don't want to stick out or be the "odd person out." We all fear being rejected and we don't want to go looking for trouble. But we do need to learn how to stand on our own if we don't agree with the crowd, or it isn't convenient for us to participate.

Fear of conflict

Most people don't want to make other people mad. We all worry if we say "No." to a friend or family member that we might "make waves" or they will get mad at us.

Fear of lost opportunities

No one wants to lose out on possible opportunities for their future. Perhaps you are worried saying "No." means closing doors. It's important at these times that old saying, "When one door closes, another opens." No one wants to burn a bridge and some people take our saying "No." as a sure sign that we are rejecting them. This feeling of rejection could lead to a strained or even severed relationships at worst, or at the very least, a misunderstanding.

Sometimes, it's just easier to say "Yes." than dealing with all of the above. We seem to feel that we have to care for others and their feelings over our own. Enough is enough. Next time you have the urge to say "Yes." when what you really mean and want to say "No." try the following:

5 ways to say no:

Kindly: "No thanks. But thanks for asking."

Directly: "No." (No explanation needed)

Efficiently: "No. That just doesn't work for me right now."

Appreciatively: "Thanks. But, no thanks." (Tone of voice is important)

Considerately: "No. But thanks for thinking of me."

5 benefits of saying no:

You'll get more **time** *for yourself.*

You'll get more **time** for the work *you really want to be doing.*

You'll get more **time** *for your creative ideas and the creation of them.*

You'll get more **time** *for the opportunities you really want to be doing and the time to pursue them.*

You'll get more **time** *to be with the people who are most important to you.*

Do you see a pattern here? **It's time.** By saying "No." you get lots and lots of it. Begin by putting yourself and your needs first, and then take care of others and their needs second. This is like putting the oxygen mask on your face first on an airplane before putting the mask on your child. *You must save yourself first.* You can only truly care for others when you look after yourself first.

Those two letters "No." are very powerful and actually quite life enhancing.

Saying "No." is not a negative. The word "No." is actually a positive affirmation of your needs and desires. Once you start saying a firm "No." instead of the conditioned and automatic response of, "Yeah sure," or the guilt induced, "Uh…..Okaaaay," you might discover yourself saying, "No." actually gets easier the more you practice it. Just possibly, you might also feel a teeny, tiny bit less stressed and resentful. So let's all lose the guilt. Let's all start saying "No." as a full and complete sentence, and without apology. Learning to say "No." as a full and complete sentence is one of the best ways we can start to love ourselves and find our way to peace.

From Me To You

One of the things I discovered along my way to a more peaceful life was the incredibly healing and peaceful music called Wholetones. I often listen to Wholetones during the day while I work or do art. At night I listen to Wholetones Lullabyes and it relaxes me and prepares me for a restful sleep.

Michael S. Tyrrell began developing Wholetones: The Healing Frequency Music Project after he met a piano player who gave him what appeared to be a simple manuscript. Inside that manuscript was the music that would change Michael's life forever. As he began working with it, he discovered 7 hidden musical frequencies that had the power to heal the mind, body, and spirit. This is what makes Wholetones unlike anything else of its kind. Visit www.wholetones.com to learn more.

CONCLUSION

Herman Melville once said, "All profound things and emotions of things are preceded and attended by silence." One way we make peace difficult for ourselves is we keep ourselves busy all the time non-stop, to the point that we don't even leave one moment of silence in our entire day. Just being busy to keep ourselves occupied and not dealing with things leads to a scattered mind. A study published in the journal, *Heart*, discovered that even two minutes of silence can prove to be even more relaxing than listening to "relaxing" music. They based these findings on changes they noticed in blood pressure and blood circulation in the brain.

Recently there was a study done on the benefits of silence on the brain. *Brain, Structure and Function* used differed types of noise and silence and monitored the effect the sound and silence had on the brains of the mice. The silence was intended to be the control in the study but what they found was surprising. The scientists discovered that when the mice were exposed to two hours of silence per day they developed new cells in the hippocampus. The hippocampus is a region of the brain associated with memory, emotion and learning. The growth of new cells in the brain does not necessarily translate to tangible health benefits. However, in this instance, researcher Imke Kirste says that "the cells appeared to become functioning neurons." Silence, and the peace that results, can quite literally grow your brain.

How do we find peace in our daily lives?

Most people in the world today are exhausted, over worked and most days just feel totally overwhelmed. When you ask most people how they are doing, they say, "I just don't know where the time goes! I'm just so busy. I've always got so much to do."

When I was a young mother, I remember being constantly in motion; I never stopped. There was always something important that had to be done: driving my two children around to all their various activities of soccer, gym, tennis, basketball, art classes, drama practice, rushing to pick up something for dinner, making dinner, cleaning the house, putting the kids to bed, never having a moment to myself. For me, it was run, run, run all day long. I woke up and hit the ground running and at the end of every day, I skidded into bed. I was exhausted all the time and emotionally felt stretched to my limit. There wasn't time to think, to read or even take a bath. I was just too busy to make time for anything pleasurable. It was only late at night, after my kids were asleep in bed, their lunches made for the next school day, housework completed at a bare minimum, that I finally felt like I could breathe. It was only then that I went to my "other full time job" and got to my own work at my office desk.

Why do we do this? When did we forget to just sit quietly and be? We are, after all, human beings, not human doings. Are we avoiding something by staying busy all the time in every spare moment? What happened to relaxed, leisurely conversations with friends? There was a period in my own life where even coffee with my girlfriends had to be "fit in" wherever there was space, which wasn't much. For me, the deep conversations, those ones that that spring directly from our heart, so essential and nurturing for our souls, were few and far between except at my weekly appointments with my therapist.

Our habit of being busy

Since I was growing up in the 1960's, we have had so many new technological innovations that we truly believed would make our lives easier, faster, simpler, more efficient. Yet, now, even with all these technological advances in so many different areas, we have no more "free" or leisurely time for peaceful reflection today than we did decades ago. Why is that? Our habit of being busy all the time is also totally destructive to our health and wellbeing. Being busy totally saps our ability to be fully present with those we love the most, and keeps us from forming the kind of community that we all so desperately crave.

For many people, from the poverty line on up, two partners working two jobs is the only way to keep their family afloat. Now, a majority of families are single parent families, or have two parents who are working minimum wage jobs, and can barely afford to put a roof over their head and food on their table. Even people's relaxation these days are full of "extreme sports," a reflection of that same world of overstimulation, masquerading as leisure. Relaxation also often takes the form of action-filled films, or violent video games or high-risk sport.

We used to have one place where we went to work, and one place where we came home after work. Now we have offices, both at work and at home. We have phones, tablets and computers to keep us connected, so we don't miss a call, an announcement, the latest news. Instead of leaving work at the office, or having anything that resembles "down time," we are all on our various devices, all the time. Smart phones, tablets and laptops mean that now there is no division between the office and home. When do we even have time to think through fully what we want to say in how we respond? We don't even shut down the devices until right before we go to bed. And with all that blue light telling our brains that it's the middle of the day, we find that we can't sleep at night either. We are tired, worn out and frazzled. There is no peace in sight anywhere it seems in modern life. How did we lose sight of peace so totally and completely?

How is your heart today?

When did we stop having conversations with those long and deep silences, where we take the time to ponder and discuss the truth of what the person we are talking with has just said? How did we create a world for ourselves in which we have more and more to do and accomplish, with less and less time for fun, rest, and quiet reflection just to be? It would appear that we no longer make time for those rich silences that we are in no rush to fill.

A writer by the name of Omid Safi introduced me to a concept of "haal." In many Muslim cultures, your "haal" is defined as "the transient state of one's heart." For example, when you want to ask a person how they're doing, you ask in Arabic, "Kayf haal-ik?" or, in Persian, "Haal-e shomaa chetoreh?" which means in English, "How is your haal?"

So in reality, when you ask a person, "How is your haal?" you are really asking a much deeper question. You are actually asking them, *"How is your heart doing at this very moment, at this breath?"*

By contrast, in Western society, many people slap each other on the arm and say, "Hey man! How are ya?"

The rote answer of course is, "I'm fine man. I am so busy! It's unreal!"

The inevitable response to that is a smile and a shrug of, "Yeah me too! Geez! Where does the time go right?"

This is the kind of common exchange in modern life these days that passes for a deep conversation. Omid Safi believes that something critical is being lost as a result, and that we need to think about returning to relating more directly from our hearts. Safi suggests, "I am not asking how many items are on your to-do list, nor asking how many items are in your inbox. I want to know how your heart is doing, at this very moment. Tell me. Tell me your heart is joyous, tell me your heart is aching, tell me your heart is sad, tell me your heart craves a human touch. Examine your own heart, explore your soul, and then tell me something about your heart and your soul. Put your hand on my arm, look me in the eye, and connect with me for one second. Tell me something about your heart, and awaken my heart. Help me remember that I too am a full and complete human being, a human being who also craves a human touch."

We need a different relationship to work, to technology, to ourselves. We need to remember we are still human beings, not just human doings. We need to begin to be a healing conversation, one filled with grace and presence, in all of our conversations, no matter how short or long. If we could begin to embrace life where we can pause, where we take the time to reflect and learn how to express the state of our own hearts, we will learn how important and essential that question is for the quality of our lives. Learning how to both ask and answer the question, "How is your heart today?" has the potential to lead us all to a more peaceful life.

From Me To You

There once was a king who offered a prize to the artist who would paint the best picture of peace. Many artists tried. The king looked at all the pictures. There were only two he really liked, and he had to choose between them.

One picture was of a calm lake. The lake was a perfect mirror for peaceful towering mountains all around it. Overhead was a blue sky with fluffy white clouds. All who saw this picture thought that it was a perfect picture of peace.

The other picture had mountains, too. But these were rugged and bare. Above was an angry sky, from which rain fell and in which lightning played. Down the side of the mountain tumbled a foaming waterfall. This did not look peaceful at all.

But when the king looked closely, he saw behind the waterfall a tiny bush growing in a crack in the rock. In the bush, a mother bird had built her nest. There, in the midst of the rush of angry water, sat the mother bird on her nest – in perfect peace.

The king chose the second picture.

BOOK 7
THE KEY OF ABUNDANCE

"Your very body and your very being are perfectly designed to live in collaboration with inspiration, and inspiration is still trying to find you…creative entitlement simply means believing that you are allowed to be here, and that - merely by being here - you are allowed to have a voice and a vision of your own."
~Elizabeth Gilbert, Writer

INTRODUCTION

People in the world today are immersed in a culture of "More. More. More." Thus, many people identify themselves and their feeling of abundance according to their toys, such as their cars and their possessions. Others place supreme value on the balance in their bank accounts. This definition of abundance is based upon a flawed premise that the more I have, the more valuable I am.

The flip side of this premise causes many people to live a life full of anxiety, constantly worrying that other people or the government has the ability to take their possessions, and therefore their identity, away from them. This causes a large portion of humanity in the Western world to constantly focus on not only how to make more of whatever they value, but also a lot of energy and money on how to protect and preserve it. The fundamental problem with this line of thinking about abundance is that it comes with the belief that if you lose what you have, then who you are is lost in the process as well.

Am I what other people think of me?

The second flawed premise of abundance is that I have value contingent upon what other people think of me. But the inherent problem of this flawed thinking is if other people don't like you, then who are you? Women in many cultures are often taught that the only way you can fulfill yourself as a woman is in how you relate to the family, or how you relate to yourself as a mother, daughter, wife. As a result, many women who feel deep within them that they have a calling put it aside because to be away from your children for any length of time according to society makes you a "bad or inattentive mother."

I've learned through losing everything I had, including nearly my life, my sanity and everything I owned, that true health and abundance in life isn't what we achieve or what possessions we have or what other people think of us. We mustn't forget or ignore the part of us that came here to do something powerful. If we ignore it, we abandon ourselves and can become very depressed over time, as I did. Each of us has just as much of a right to have that abundance of personal expression as anyone else. What other people think of us, as we pursue our personal version of abundance that is right for us, is not important. We are a spiritual being having a human experience, not the other way around. We are each on a solo journey, and are only responsible for the lesson plan we chose to explore and master, long before coming here to earth to have our human experience.

Am I someone that is separate from everyone else?

Another flawed way of thinking as far as abundance is concerned is that I am separate and alone. Our ego tries every way it can to Edge God Out. But we all came from a Source, we can call it God or The Tao. This source is everywhere because it created everything. It must be in each of us, because there is no place where It is not. Lao Tzu said, "Let yourself be lived by it." This means that we are already connected to The All in Spirit. All we have to do is figure out a way to align ourselves with a greater *knowing* that we are already connected to it.

Saint Francis of Assisi suggested, "Wear the world as a loosely flowing garment." This way of living suggests that we get to a place where we surrender and have a *knowing* deep inside ourselves that we are not alone, that we are always connected to God, our Infinite Source, and that we're always guided toward that center of our unique version of abundance. We can trust in this deeply connected inner part of ourselves to God and this also means that we don't always have to be struggling and fighting with it. We also don't always have to be in charge. We can allow ourselves to be lived by the Source, whatever our conception of God is, rather than always taking over and trying to muscle things through. Then we can truly move into our own expression of true abundance, fulfilling a calling that is alive inside of us, that we can actually feel if we get quiet enough to let it speak to us.

No one else can ever tell you or decide for you what your purpose or your abundance is. As we truly live our lives according to our own intuitive guidance and what truly feels right for us from deep inside, we will become a life living on purpose and will become more abundant and fulfilled. However, many of us instead of making our choices out of who we really are, our authentic selves, make our choices out of the ego, which edges God, The Source of All Things, out. These kind of choices take us away from finding meaning and abundance in our lives.

My experience is that we can choose to gauge everything based on how we feel. When we need to decide which direction to take, we can ask ourselves better questions such as, "Does this choice stress me out?" "Do I feel anxious when I contemplate this choice?" "Do I feel fearful or angry?" When you are operating out of the part of you that is authentic and connected to the abundant Source of All things, then a calm feeling of peace is always the response you can trust. If I am uncertain, I will say to myself, "I don't need to know. My connection to Source guides me as I go." Then I trust that what I need from the abundant flow of the Universe will show up at just the right moment that I need it.

From Me To You

"I believe in love.

I believe in you.

I believe in me.

I believe in this, the most potent moment in history."

~Jean Houston

How can you make this moment the most potent and abundant moment in your life?

SURVIVE

One of the main blocks to abundance in life is constant stress. In today's busy world, we are all guilty of an addiction to the adrenaline rush of urgency. Things are moving so fast, and so much information is coming toward us every waking moment, most days it's hard to resist the sense that we have to work not only smarter, but also harder. But did you know that if you are in the middle of a task, and you allow yourself to be interrupted for any reason, it takes, on average, at least twenty minutes for your brain to refocus and fully settle back into what it was doing? This means that every time you hear that phone, text or email message "ding!" and you leave what you were doing to check to see who called, texted or emailed you, it will take you about twenty minutes to regain your full concentration again.

Get the most out of your brain

If you want to get the most out of your brain and better store whatever you want to remember in your memory, it's important to consider some alternatives so you can truly get the most out of your work day and your life.

Corinne McLaughlin and Gordon Asher Davidson, authors of *Mastering Time*, suggest the following tips to help you stay focused on your main priorities and drop the urgency to jump from task to task. Stop to consider these tips any time you are feeling scattered to help focus your energy on what's truly important to you:

1. Examine carefully what you have assumed to be urgent. Ask yourself, is this actually urgent? You will find that most things are not as urgent as you may think

2. Consider whether you feel attached to constantly being busy, like many others in our society. Do you feel more important if you are busy? Our attachment to being busy is an energy vampire and sucks us dry energetically.

3. Imagine yourself not being so busy and instead being more relaxed. What comes up for you? What happens for you when you slow down and release some of this busyness?

4. Imagine the "Why" of what you are doing and allow that to drive you instead. Modern life can be a massive barrage of inputs coming into your consciousness every day, every minute.

How to stay focused

In a typical day, do you get up, check your inbox and your Facebook while you are eating breakfast, talking on the phone and paying bills? We all have this crazy idea that becoming a really great "multi-tasker" must be the answer to getting more productivity out of our days. But this belief, and all the actions that come with becoming a more efficient "multi-tasker," may be in fact taking your brain—and a lot of your time—on a detour and with totally unsatisfactory results. As time seems to speed up and more information gets thrown at us every minute of the day and night via the TV, our phones and computers, we tend to think that multi tasking our life is the only answer to getting it all done. I used to be the world's most busy "multi-tasker." But I have learned that multitasking derails me big time.

The average attention span

A survey of Canadian media consumption by Microsoft in 2016 measured the average attention span. Attention span was defined as "the amount of concentrated time on a task without becoming distracted." The survey concluded that the average attention span had fallen from twelve seconds in 2000, to now eight seconds, which means that we now have a shorter attention span than that of a goldfish. For a moment of amusement on this subject, please go here: http://bit.ly/2wUKXx8 Satya Nadella, the CEO of Microsoft said, "The true scarce commodity" of the near future will be "human attention."

Becoming more productive

Multi tasking could even cause you to stall completely, according to Theo Compernolle, M.D., author of *Brain Chains*. Dr Compernolle explains why the human brain is actually not wired to multitask.

Your Brain: Part 1

Your brain is made up of three parts - reflex, reflective, and archiving. Understanding the function of each will help you comprehend why multitasking does not work. The reflex brain is focused on your senses and completely in the now. When you are reading or mindlessly browsing the Internet, for example, your reflex brain is in use. Once a thought has passed, your book is closed or computer is shut down, to your reflex brain, it no longer exists.

Your Brain: Part 2

The reflective brain controls abstract thought. It's what makes the human brain unique among animals, allowing us to remember the past, consider the future, and imagine what doesn't currently exist. The reflective brain creates thoughts. This is what every single person is doing all the time: we imagine, and we make contingency plans based on what we think might happen in the future. The problem with multitasking is that your reflective brain can only handle one thought at a time.

Your Brain: Part 3

This brings us to the third part of your brain: archiving. Your archiving brain is responsible for storing information into your memory. However, it uses the same processor as the reflective brain does during thinking, putting the two parts of our brain in competition. So this means that your archiving brain works best when you take a break from thinking rather than immediately switching gears. When thinking, the reflective brain uses 100 percent of this processor. This means that when you're working (or thinking) hard, there's not too much archiving going on. Most archiving into memory occurs when you're not thinking very hard. Both doctors suggest if you prioritize and complete tasks one at a time, instead of multitasking, you can fulfill the potential of your reflective and archiving brain and essentially become more productive.

But being productive is not the end all and be all of life. In fact, in my personal experience and observation, the stress of modern life expectation of being productive at any cost is actually affecting our overall health, well-being and access to our true abundance in life.

What makes a truly abundant life?

Recently I read an article by Sina Anvari, titled, *Nurse Reveals The Top Five Regrets People Have On Their Deathbed.*

1. I wish I'd had the courage to live a life true to myself, not the life others expected of me.

2. I wish I didn't work so hard.

3. I wish I'd had the courage to express my feelings.

4. I wish I had stayed in touch with my friends.

5. I wish that I had let myself be happier.

It struck me after reading the article that when I look at all the choices I have made over the course of my entire life that I have been working for a very long time to understand my own relationship to these same five regrets. I can see now that I have worked extremely hard to resolve many of these. I lived a life I thought others expected of me, and now I do not. I worked far too hard and it nearly killed me, but now I do not. I did not have the courage to express my true feelings for the most part, and now I do. I did not make time to stay in touch with friends, and now the friends I do have are true ones and I do keep in touch with them. I did not let myself be happier as happiness seemed like a luxury I could not afford. Now, thanks to the choices and changes I have made, I am happier than I have ever been.

Sina Anvari also said in her article, "I learned never to underestimate someone's capacity for growth. Some changes were phenomenal." Over these past five years, phenomenal changes have taken place in my life that, choice by choice, have led me to the abundant life I now live. I also know that I have the capacity, as we all do, to grow into even more abundance from this moment forward.

From Me To You

It's been said, "Wherever you are, there you are." The practice of focusing on abundance can be applied wherever you are at any moment, and to any experience. Remember, what you focus on expands.

If you were focused on lack and one day, you discovered that you had only one dollar left in your bank account, you would probably say, "Oh dear, I'm so broke right now!"

If you were focused on abundance, and viewed that one single dollar as evidence of abundance, then you would say, "Oh wonderful! I have money. I have a dollar!"

The amount of money in your bank account isn't really the point here. The important point to remember is that you have chosen to shift your focus from negative to positive. The Universe will always bring you more of what you are focused upon.

Focusing on abundance instead of lack – in your health, wealth and happiness - requires trust in the process of life. We were born into the optimum circumstances for our growth and well-being. Our lives are unfolding exactly as they should to develop and enhance our growth and well being. The bottom line is that we are only subject to that which we focus on and believe.

So what do you focus on and truly believe about abundance? Where do you see abundance evident in your own life right now? If you feel abundance is somehow lacking in any area, what changes do you feel you could make now in your thinking and belief system to allow more abundance in?

THE ROUNDABOUT

Before we can enter the true flow of abundance in life, I think it is helpful to identify and ask ourselves some new questions around why we get stuck and what we can do about it. What keeps most people stuck? The answer to that question is hidden within our thoughts and beliefs.

A belief is simply a thought that we think over and over again. If we think the same thought often enough, it becomes our belief. Most people share the constantly repeating thought and underlying belief that they don't "have enough" and that therefore, they "are not enough." At the same time, there's also this pervasive belief that somehow, we're all missing something and if we only knew what that something was, and possessed it, we'd all be a lot happier.

We all have this belief that we need more of everything. You name it, we need it: more money, more stuff, more time, more energy, more information, more certainty, more resources, more thinness, more opportunities, more…..everything. We tell ourselves that without having one (or all) of these things first, we can't do what we want – now, soon or in the future. We think there's something missing. This belief that "there is something missing" or we "don't have what we need in order to create what we want," or that we're "just not enough," is the biggest source of unhappiness and dissatisfaction in the world today. It is also the greatest lie that we all tell ourselves.

The big lie

Many people travel their entire lives thinking and believing that one day they will find true happiness when they finally get somewhere. Where they will find happiness they really don't know, but some day, it will be really great. However, this belief in "one day I will find happiness" actually keeps people stuck right where they are, in a perpetual state of longing for more and living in a current state of belief in lack. In other words, a belief in lack keeps people stuck and focused there. It would appear that we're on an endless search for the pot of gold at the end of the rainbow, all the while not realizing that we've been sitting right on top of the pot of gold we've been seeking the whole time. Our answers to everything lie within us.

There's an old spiritual saying, "Like attracts like." Our constant focus on "not enough" is an energy of resistance to the way things are right now. This resistance energy keeps our energy going around and around, perpetually attracting more "not enough" like experiences into our lives.

Our focus on "not enough" ultimately prevents us from ever changing our future, because all our energy is focused on actually creating more "not enough" in our present moment. Before we can create our future abundance, we have to focus on what we want to create instead of focusing on that which we don't. The true reality is that we have everything we need right now to reach abundance in our life. Accepting and loving ourselves, the way we are right now in this moment, is where we must begin.

People always living in scarcity and struggle, with their beliefs that they are "never enough" and "it's always going to be hard," always see the cup as half empty. People who are positive thinkers see the cup as half full. People who understand their true connection to Source Energy see the cup as always overflowing. Each of us are always in the flow, perpetually creating unless we block it. We can come into true alignment in this universe of abundant creative energy and know without a doubt that we are the overflowing cup of abundance at every moment.

How to get into the flow of abundance

Another way we can start the flow of abundance is by ridding ourselves of as much judgment as we possibly can. I know that's easier said than done. It's helpful to try to stop thinking of things as "right" or "wrong." Instead we can simply focus on whether we want them in our lives, or not. We can also try our best to get rid of all expectations of the outcomes of our activities. Instead, when we start an activity, we can choose to do it for the sheer fun or experience of it, in balance with the universe, like a surfboard floating peacefully on the ocean, drifting with the prevailing winds.

We can live fully trusting that The Universe, or God, will direct us to the things we need or want to experience. With help from the Abundantly Creative Universe, our soul, will brings to us all that we desire to understand. The serenity we feel is the energy of the abundance flow.

When we focus on the belief, "I have enough right this moment and I am grateful for this, or something better," we open ourselves fully to our potential for an unlimited abundant life.

From Me To You

In her book, *Big Magic,* Elizabeth Gilbert talks about the creative process. Her words also apply really well to abundance:

"The guardians of high culture will try to convince you that the arts belong to the chosen few, but they are wrong, and they are also annoying. We are *all* the chosen few....Your very body and your very being are perfectly designed to live in collaboration with inspiration, and inspiration is still trying to find you...Creative entitlement simply means believing that *you are allowed to be here,* and that - merely by being here - you are allowed to have a voice and a vision of your own."

THRIVE

Once we begin asking better questions about abundance, and learn to live more moment-to-moment in the abundant flow of the universe, we can begin to Thrive. An abundant life is determined by our belief systems. We need to ask ourselves two important questions: Do we truly believe that an abundant life is possible? Do we believe that we deserve it? Until I figured those two questions out for myself, I knew I would never experience a life of abundance.

For most of us, our beliefs about abundance are determined by the belief systems of others or society around us. Society and our peer group tend to define for us what is "acceptable," and what is "not acceptable." When we make decisions about our abundance based on what society or other people have told us is "correct" or "possible," we let them define what is possible for us too.

Most people live with a deep fear of rejection. Ever since we lived in tribal cultures, to be separated or banished by one's tribe meant death. That's one of the reasons why we tend to choose to stay a part of the tribe at a very deep psychological level, to live according to how society defines right and wrong. It's also why many people live in constant fear and anxiety of the judgment of society.

Many people don't risk daring to be different as they have the impression that they must match with everyone else. These people truly believe that there is one, and only one, way to do things, and that is the way everyone else is doing it. There isn't now, and there never will be, only one way to do anything. Each of us must determine what abundance and what living an abundant life looks like, feels like, and means to us.

What we focus on expands

One thing I have learned is that *what we focus on expands*. My entire focus used to be on all the **difficulties** in my life. At one point I truly believed 'My life is, has been, and always will be total and complete shit." Guess what? The shit in my life expanded.

At that time, I was focused on how **angry** I felt all the time, about everything, and mostly at myself. Guess what? I manifested an abundance of things to be angry about.

At that time, I was focused on how **frustrated** I felt all the time that things weren't going the way I wanted them to go. I believed "How could things get any worse?" Guess what? Everything did get worse.

These days, I focus on my thoughts and beliefs around **abundance** and feeling grateful for this or something better. If we get down to one dollar left before our monthly pensions come in at the bank, we focus on "Yay we have a dollar!" We don't focus on, "Oh my God. How are we going to make it with only one dollar left?" Instead of bracing myself always for the bad thing coming, I look for the good, those "little wins" I can celebrate and feel grateful for.

Guess what? An **abundance** of positive things show up in my life every single day and I find countless opportunities to experience more things to be grateful for. These positive things come to me in the form of **new ideas, new ways of approaching things**, and **new opportunities**.

As a result, I live in an overwhelming vibration of gratitude, from the moment I wake up, until I go to sleep at night. When I focus also on being **thankful** and **accepting** what shows up in my life in the Now, I find I am not constantly at war with reality or focused on the gap between "what I feel should be" and "what is." Instead I accept and am grateful for "what is" and **"I thank God for this or something better."**

How about you? Do you ever pause enough to let in your good? Take a moment right now to focus on what good things you appreciate in your life. What "wins" have you already seen today, however infinitesimally small? Imagine interrupting that negative Nellie inside your head and tell ol' Nellie to just zip her lips for one sec. Hold on to that image of something that went right today, or is going right in your world in general, and say to yourself, "Hey me. Good Job!"

Did you know that twenty seconds is how long it takes to create a new neural pathway in your brain? Yup that's right. In twenty measly seconds we can actually reset the default programming in our brains. How cool is that? So this means that taking just twenty seconds, right now, to say to yourself, "Hey me. Good Job!" is in fact, the beginning of your new abundant life.

From Me To You

All this is full. All that is full.

From fullness, fullness comes.

When fullness is taken from fullness,

Fullness still remains.

Om Shanti, Shanti, Shanti Om

~Isha Upanishad

CONCLUSION

Most older people I know worry about unloading stuff they've collected over the years, stuff that was once useful to them but now prevents them from moving freely about their homes. But the junk I have found that I really need to get rid of now is psychological junk, such as long-time convictions about what gives my life meaning, but in reality no longer serve me. I've found a question that's given me a new sense of meaning. I no longer ask, "What do I want to let go of, and what do I want to hang on to?" Instead I ask, "What do I want to let go of, and *what do I want to give myself to?*" The desire to "hang on" to stuff, or people, or ideas, comes from a belief in scarcity and fear. The desire to "give myself" comes from a sense of abundance and generosity. As Byron Katie says, "Reality is far kinder than all the negative stories we make up about it." With practice, you can manifest positive abundance in your life too.

From Me To You

In her blog, *Five Spiritual Hacks For The Awakening Soul,* Vera de Chalambert, MTS, author and Harvard-educated Scholar of Religion suggests, "Led on by an amusing miscalculation, we fully expect to be saved by awakening, erroneously believing that as we begin living more spiritual lives, we will by-pass the struggles of living a human one.

"Ironically as our spiritual insight increases the opposite happens. As we mature spiritually, the gap between the spiritual and the ordinary begins to disappear - we of course continue to experience challenges, but no longer berate this human limitation.

We stop trying to be special and start showing up as we are; we stop trying to manipulate reality to be as we want, and instead deepen our intimacy with life, as it is. As we surrender our spiritual agenda and embrace our human brokenness, paradoxically self-judgment subsides; self-improvement gives way to acceptance, certainty to mystery."

Every single day, I bow in awe to The Great Mystery which Is eternally abundant

BOOK 8
THE KEY OF JOY

"Ever since happiness heard your name it has been running through the streets trying to find you."
~Hafiz, Sufi Mystic

INTRODUCTION

Joseph Campbell said, "Follow your bliss." This concept of following your bliss suggests that we all have the capacity to choose to do what leads us to a sense of our own personal definition of joy. I can see now that there are certain things that have consistently brought me joy throughout my life such as music, art, writing, travel, great food and beautiful wine. As I have evolved, so has my capacity for joy. Sometimes a moment of joy can even smack you right upside of your head, quite unexpectedly. For me this moment came recently in the form of an Australian nickname.

For those of you who don't know much about Australia or Australians, they are a hearty, lively and loving bunch. They love to party and play and are the most loyal, fun loving group of people you will ever meet in your life. One of the things I find most endearing about Australians is how they give each other nicknames. For example, a guy who has the last name/surname of "Right," gets the nickname of, "Lefty." He is called "Lefty" forever more, until the day he dies. As an "Outsider," meaning you are not Australian by birth, normally you don't get an Australian nickname. It's not mean or anything. It just doesn't happen normally. However, sometimes it does.

I had the distinct honor to receive my own nickname only recently from my native Australian son, Kev. He walked up to me in the kitchen of their home, smiled and said, "I think it's about time Mary Anne that you got your own nickname! How about Mezza?" Then Kev grinned, and announced to the world in a loud, guttural voice, "Mezzaaaaaaaaaaaah" I felt like I was going through some sort of ancient Australian Baptism. I was now "Mezza," and that was that.

A week later, Marnie, my daughter in law, had a set of wine glasses made, with my Australian nickname engraved on them, and she also added a Queen's crown over my new name: Mezza It's official. I am forevermore here in Australia to be known as "Mezza." I have a wine glass to prove it. Not only that, for Mother's Day, Marnie, Kev, and our two grandchildren, Jake and Olivia, sent me a flower arrangement, chocolates and one of my favorite Australian wines, *Pepperjack*. The best part was that the card that had the word, "Mum" written on it. That kind of joy is immeasurable and priceless.

Over the course of our lives, joy comes in all kinds of ways and from all kinds of unexpected places. You never know where or when your joy will come. Sometimes, we find own true and authentic joy after a period of wandering around in the darkness of the desert. But I now know that there is always the promise of a new dawn. A therapist once told me, "When we crack, that's when the light gets in." When joy finally does come to us, we welcome it with open arms, like the prodigal child who has returned after a long absence.

From Me To You

Vera de Chalambert, MTS, and Harvard-educated scholar of religion gives us all a poignant reminder about not trying to run from darkness in her powerful blog, "Kali Takes America." Chalambert suggests, "I think that this moment gives us an opportunity for reckoning only if instead of running for the light, we let ourselves go fully into the dark. If instead of resolving our discomfort too quickly, we consider the possibility of staying in the uncomfortable, in the irreconcilable, in the unsettled. Before we rush in to reanimate the discourse of hope prematurely, we must yield to what is present.

"Receptivity is the great quality of darkness; darkness hosts everything without exception. The Dark Mother has no orphans.

We must not send suffering into exile — the fear, the heartbreak, the anger, the helplessness, all are appropriate, all are welcome. We can't dismember ourselves to feel better. We can't cut off the stream of life and expect to heal. Cutting off the inconvenient is a form of spiritual fascism.

By resolving to stay only in the light in times of immense crisis, we split life; engage in emotional deportation, rather than hosting the vulnerable. Difficult feelings need to be given space so they can come to rest. They need contact. In a culture of isolation, be the invitation to everything…There is a great yearning for change in the order of things, and the Great Mother is leading the revolution."

SURVIVE

Ever since I can remember, I have been fascinated by the image of the Black Madonna. I have travelled to holy wells, shrines and sanctuaries all around the world, which honor her. The Black Madonna is considered by some to be the representative for the Divine Feminine in the world, a principle that was systematically erased from our modern culture, starting about 5,000 years ago. The Black Madonna is found all over Europe—in Sicily, Spain, Switzerland, France, Poland, Czechoslovakia — as well as in Turkey and in Africa and in Asia as Tara in China and as Kali in India. She is also named Our Lady of Guadalupe in Mexico, and sometimes is also called the "Brown Madonna" there.

The Black Madonna calls us to cosmology, a sense of the whole of space and time. Because she is dark and leads us into the dark, the Black Madonna is also cosmic. She is the great cosmic Mother on whose lap all creation exists. Some say that the universe itself is embraced and mothered by her. I was fascinated to learn in my research that the male warriors who were sent in to destroy the early temples dedicated to the Divine Feminine wore literal breastplates on their armor. Did those men really think She could be fooled by that ruse? She knew what was coming, and one might notice that things have been pretty hostile ever since The Boys took over the temples, replacing the chalice with the blade. It was at that time when all of culture on the planet was thrust backwards from Thrive into Survive.

Modern day Christian theologian Mathew Fox speaks extensively about the reemergence of the Dark Feminine archetype into our collective consciousness today. He wrote a blog titled, *The Return of the Black Madonna*, which I really liked. Fox suggests, "The Black Madonna calls us to our depths, to living spiritually and radically on this planet and not superficially and unthinkingly and oblivious to the grace that has begotten us in so many ways. The depths to which we are called include the depths of awe, wonder and delight—joy itself is a depth experience we need to re-entertain in the name of the Black Madonna."

Fox also reminds us that it is really in darkness, "where illusions are broken apart, and the truth lies." I found this to be completely true in my own life. When all my illusions were stripped from me, I had to decide, then and there, what I was going to embrace as *the truth of me*. When we've lost our way in the dark, and the new truths about ourselves that we're searching for are still a bit hazy, metaphors can be useful to help us try to name and describe our subjective experience of both where we are, and where we want to go.

At one point, I can remember sitting in the kitchen, telling my first husband, "I can't keep being the sun that revolves around your planet, keeping you warm. I want my own planet. I want my own gravitational field." My subjective sense at that time of the urgent need I had for my own gravitational field was right on target. However, I was so profoundly tired, and had lost my fundamental orientation to myself to such a profound degree, that I even had my metaphor backwards:

Planets of course revolve around the sun; suns don't revolve around planets.

On one level, I had kept my vow to a dying woman. I believed at that time that this vow I made to her as she was dying meant that I was bound by the words of my promise to "always to take care of" her son, so that she could die in peace. My following through with the marriage a month later could be seen as demonstrating tremendous integrity, no matter how many doubts I might have had about it at that time. My word was indeed my bond, so to speak. Even at the altar, my body knew the cost of what I had just done. After the "you may kiss the bride" moment sealed the deal forever, I burst into tears. The audience thought I was crying tears of joy. In my mind, as tears streamed down my face and then, on to my wedding dress, I was thinking, *Well, at least I kept my word to his mother.*

By the time we arrived at the reception at the Claremont County Club, I had pulled myself together and had resolved to make the best of it. I stuffed my doubts into a box, then placed that box into a dark vault of my psyche, and locked the door. I held my head up, smiled and greeted all two hundred and fifty guests like it was the happiest day of my life. Finally, after doing my dead level best to model myself after the sweet, kind, wise, apron wearing mothers I had watched in My Three Sons and Leave It to Beaver, two very popular American TV shows of the 1960's, I just couldn't keep it up anymore. The beautiful pearls, which every self-respecting woman of that 1950's-1960's era wore around her neck, were covering a scar where a profound spiritual tracheotomy had been performed on me that day at the altar. I had spent years knocking myself out, going against my own planetary nature, and now, fifteen years later, I believed that I didn't even have a gravitational field of my own.

Joy in survival mode

In any Survival period of a person's life, feelings of joy often don't even exist; when you're depressed, the whole world feels flat. I've had three periods of what could be classified as "clinical depression." While I can certainly link these really low periods to actual stressful events that happened, which, quite frankly, would have caused even the strongest person to falter, I can see now that each period of depression that I valiantly fought my way out of, has also blessed me with tremendous gifts of growth.

This new growth, as I was in the process of carving out a *new truth of me*, was like watching the fabled phoenix rising from the ashes. Looking back now, during those dark periods I really don't know where I found the strength. For reasons I cannot explain, I refused to commit what Vera Chalambert calls, "spiritual fascism" against myself; I didn't "send my suffering into exile."

One of my favorite verses in the Bible is "Be still and know that I am God." In that time of profound darkness, I took refuge in the primordial womb of the Dark Mother and stayed still. Waiting. I resolved to stay still and wait, no matter how long it took, until God send me an unmistakably clear sign of my next best step. And as spring invariably follows winter, from the smoldering ashes of all the fear, heartbreak, pain and suffering of my life, the phoenix within me gradually rose. I stumbled at first, unsure, leaden and earthbound, as this truly authentic Mary Anne found a new connection to her Real Voice. (And no, the irony that I had chosen to call my company My Real Voice is not lost on me.)

Gradually, I unfurled my new wings and found that I could now soar on genuine strength, hard earned wisdom, and a deeper understanding of myself. Even though I had "gone off the rails" of my own life for a while, ultimately, it all led to a more genuine self-acceptance, a love and respect of myself that even I didn't know I was capable of. It is said that each of us are born into and live out the perfect circumstance for our ultimate spiritual growth. This was certainly true for me.

Losing the urge to move forward

Human depression is a very interesting state. Since it is one of the things that our current society holds such shame and judgment about, let's take a deeper look at depression for a moment, before we move on.

If you take the word "depression" apart you have the prefix, "de," the word, "press," and the suffix, "ion."

"De" means "the undoing, reversing or ridding of something."

"Press" means "to urge onward."

"Ion" means "the process of."

By the sum of its parts, the word depression means: "The process of losing the urge to move forward." This means that the driving force in your life has been turned off. There's not much joy present. However, viewed from the soul point of view, this state of depression is potentially as *good*, as society judges it as *bad*. The soul views the depressed state as *the ultimate moment of choice*. When depression strikes, all the normal drivers in one's life have been removed. There are no more commands coming from outside anymore, telling us what to do. Instead, there is a vacant space where those orders and automatic societal demands usually reside. Now, it is up to us to *choose what we really want*.

An employment loss can precipitate a period of depression as much as completing a soul lesson can. When a person no longer has their job or spiritual mission urging them onward, they can enter a feeling of disorientation, if not depression. Students may find themselves depressed when they graduate. Depression is also a common occurrence after a divorce. For the primary caretaker, the death of family members, whose care has been labor intensive towards the end, can actually bring on a depression, not the expected or assumed relief the primary caretaker thought would happen. In each case it is time to start over again.

Part of the challenge of getting beyond a time of depression is learning how to make decisions that we have freely chosen for ourselves. We begin to place something new into that "empty space" within us. This is the beginning of reinventing our definition of self. For those who have no concept of their self-worth, a period of depression can cause a feeling of devastation, or even paralysis. For those secure in their own power, this dark time of taking stock and regrouping, can be thought of as a time of freedom.

Depression is an opportunity

The poet, William Butler Yeats said, "It takes more courage to examine the dark corners of your own soul than it does for a soldier to fight on a battlefield." I would certainly agree with him on that. Dealing with depression takes tremendous courage and fortitude, even as it also can be a tremendous opportunity. We have swept the house clean, so to speak, and now we can decorate it as we see fit. But if we've never done that before, how do we do that?

We can begin by creating an inventory of our abilities, our tools, and our desires. We can plan where we want to go, and then begin the trek. It's helpful at these times of transition to try our best to live in the moment. What is done is done. There isn't much value in spending precious time blaming other people or condemning ourselves. We have a new start and it is up to us to decide how to use it. We can choose to seize this new opportunity that has presented itself, whether we feel like we chose it to not, to now explore and showcase our strengths. We have nothing to lose and everything to gain by embracing our newly hatching self.

This new self can make new choices, to follow our instincts into new arenas we have always wanted to explore but may have not had the time or given ourselves permission to do. This approach can help us view depression as an opportunity, an as yet unformed possibility which holds many potential gifts. If we choose to survive it, depression can catapult us into places we had never dreamed possible. Woody Allen said once, "Humor is tragedy, plus time." Eventually after the long Dark Night Of The Soul is over, the Hero's Journey completed, we walk out into the dawn of the new day, with deeper wisdom and hopefully, our sense of humor still intact.

Please Note: If you are feeling really depressed, I suggest you consult with a licensed medical practitioner and/or therapist and get some support and guidance. You will be glad you did.

From Me To You

In his book, *No Mud, No Lotus: The Art of Transforming Suffering,* Thich Nhat Hanh suggests that one way we can begin to create joy and happiness in our lives is to experience the kind of joy that comes from letting go.

"Many of us are bound to so many things. We believe these things are necessary for our survival, our security, and our happiness. But many of these things, or more precisely, our beliefs about their utter necessity, are really obstacles for our joy and happiness.

"Sometimes we think that having a certain something, a career, salary, house, car, designer outfit or partner, is absolutely crucial for our happiness. However, have you ever noticed that even when you have achieved that certain something, it never seems to feel like enough?

"If we look deeply into our fearful attachments, we will realize that they are, in fact, the very obstacle to our joy and happiness. Letting go takes a lot of courage but once you do let go, happiness and joy can come very quickly. Then there will be no need to search for it."

THE ROUNDABOUT

There is always a transition period between any great change in life. Sometimes this moment of change feels like a sudden pivot, for example during a near death or an out of body experience. Periods of profound change can feel much like we have entered a Roundabout, we keep going around until we find the right exit. Sometimes we may miss the "right" exit at first, and then, we keep going around, and around and around in circles for a while longer. One thing is certain, when make the decision to put ourselves *on the path that is right for us*, we will we find the correct exit. At that point, we begin to make the necessary changes we need to, and our life begins to improve.

Hope

I have noticed that in my own life, I've usually taken more than one trip around The Roundabout to find the right answer that helped me to see the right exit. Often my typical pattern has been that I've waited far too long and been too stubborn to ask for help. The consequences have been that I suffered probably much longer than I really needed to. But I firmly believe, even if we have to get ourselves to the point of hanging by the very last shred, of the very last rope, even to the very last shred of hope, there is always another possibility, choice or direction available to us that will solve any difficulty we may face.

So, how do we find our way on to the path of true joy? Sometimes, clues to our joy are in the things that early in our lives held great meaning, lifted our spirits or that we enjoyed. One of the clues to joy for me, and something I have always returned to throughout my life, is music.

When I was ten years old, my family moved from Oakland, California. I remember the day we arrived at our new home in Piedmont, California. I opened the front door and went into the living room. There, in front of the bay window was a beautiful piano. I turned to my Mother and said, "Who is that for?" She smiled and said it was a housewarming gift from my grandparents. I remember staring at this huge baby grand and saying "Wow."

As I stood there staring at the piano, my Mother continued, "Your Grandmother and Grandfather also told me that they would pay for piano lessons for any child in our family who wanted to learn the piano."

I jumped up and down with my hands raised in the air, "Pick me! Pick me! I want to take piano lessons! Pick me!"

My Grandparents had met as music majors at the music department of a nearby University of California, Berkeley. My Grandfather was a violinist and my Grandmother played the piano. For the next two years I had the privilege of taking piano lessons with a local piano teacher and I did regular recitals. My Grandparents didn't miss one performance I ever gave. I loved every single moment of playing piano.

Finding your true path

At age 12, on the first day of seventh grade, I marched into the instrumental music class with teacher Mr. Alan Harvey, even though I didn't play an actual orchestral instrument. On the first day of class, Mr. Harvey came around to each student asking them what instrument they played. Each student, in turn, chirped out what they played: trumpet, oboe, cello, violin. When he got to me, I replied that I had taken piano lessons since fourth grade but other than that, I didn't play anything.

Mr. Harvey, always a very gentle soul, said, "Well Ms. Dorward, I'm sorry to say that we already have a piano player for the orchestra this year."

I immediately got up to leave the class, saying, "Well I love music but if there isn't anything for me to play here, I guess I had better find another class."

Mr. Harvey stopped me, "Wait a minute, Ms. Dorward. Would you consider learning another instrument that you could play with us here in the orchestra?"

I replied with perfect aplomb, "Well, my plan actually was that I would really like to play the piano concerto with the orchestra when I am in in twelfth grade. That is five years from now. So my plan was that I would get an early start by joining the orchestra now. But maybe I could play drums or something else while I wait?"

Mr. Harvey smiled kindly, "Well tell me first, how well do you play the piano right now?"

I answered, "Not very well. In fact that was one of my questions for you Mr. Harvey. Do you know of a teacher who could help me reach my goal? I already know that a concerto is too hard for me right now. But I also know if I practice hard enough, I can learn anything."

Mr. Harvey smiled at that. "How about we make a deal. I really need more string bass players right now in the orchestra. Would you consider learning the string bass if I agree to let you play the piano concerto with the orchestra five years from now?"

I considered his offer. "Well, Mr. Harvey. I hear you have an excellent jazz band too. If you will let me conduct that jazz band now and then, in addition to learning to play the string bass to help you out in the orchestra, you have a deal. I have always wanted to learn to conduct too."

This was clearly a serious negotiation. "As a matter of fact, Ms. Dorward, I need a string bass player in my Jazz Band as well. If you will learn the string bass, and be my bass player in both groups, I will let you conduct the Jazz Band and play the concerto in the Orchestra when you are a senior, five years from now. Deal?"

I smiled. Mr. Harvey smiled. I put out my hand. Mr. Harvey shook it. "It's a deal." we both said simultaneously.

"Now, what's a strong bass?" I asked.

"It's actually called a string bass. And they are over there." Mr. Harvey pointed over to the corner where big wooden instruments were laying down on the floor.

I thought to myself, *Those look like big giant violins. If my Grandfather could play a violin, I could probably play one of those big ones.*

"OK Ms. Dorward now that we have finished our negotiation, please go grab a bow from those hanging on the wall and we will all get started. We've got a lot of work to do!" Mr. Harvey began to move on to the next student in the class when I stopped him.

"Wait Mr. Harvey! If we are going to pull this off, don't forget, I really need a new piano teacher!"

"I haven't forgotten. Please see me after class about that. I have just the right person in mind for you."

That afternoon I called the name on the slip of paper that Mr. Harvey had given me. A woman answered the phone, "This is Leone Evens. Can I help you?"

I did my best to speak in a very grown up voice, like I had heard my Mom and Dad do when they had an important call. "Yes. Mrs. Evens. My name is Mary Anne Dorward and I am a student of Alan Harvey's at Piedmont Jr. High School. Mr. Harvey gave me your phone number."

"Yes, Ms. Dorward. Please go on." Mrs. Evans said.

"Well the thing is this. I am twelve years old and by the time I am seventeen I would like to play the piano concerto with the orchestra in the spring concert at Piedmont High School. This gives us a full five years to prepare. Would you be interested in such a challenge, and do you have space for a new student?"

Mrs. Evens was stunned. She told me later that she had never received a call asking to take piano lessons from anyone other than a parent. "How old did you say you were Ms. Dorward?"

"I'm twelve years old, ma'am." I answered politely.

"How much experience do you have right now playing the piano?" Mrs. Evans asked.

"Well, I have been playing piano since I was ten years old, but I'm not very good at it yet. I didn't have a very good teacher."

Still in shock, Mrs. Evans said, "And your plan is to play the piano concerto with the Piedmont High School orchestra five years from now? Did I hear that correctly?"

"That is correct." I answered, very matter of factly.

"Why don't you come to my home tomorrow afternoon and we will get started. I am also curious, how do you plan to pay for these lessons?" she asked.

"Oh I have discussed the entire matter with my Grandparents. They were both music majors at U.C. Berkeley. They very generously agreed to pay for all my lessons. I am going to reach my goal, no matter what it takes."

"That's wonderful, dear. Here is my address. You can easily walk from school to my home tomorrow. See you tomorrow." And she hung up.

The next afternoon, I went to Mrs. Evans home and she sat me down first on the couch in her living room. Then she said, "I've thought a lot about your request to play a concerto five years from now. I am now going to put on a record of five different concertos for you to listen to. I want you to simply listen, and when your heart feels like it wants to leap out of your chest, we will know that is the right piece of music to pick."

I listened to all five concertos before I gave my answer as to which was my favorite. I wanted to give each of them a fair shot.

"Well?" Mrs. Evans said as she picked up the record player stylus when the last concerto was over.

"It is this one." I said as I picked up the album cover. "The Saint Sean's Concerto in G Minor. That's the piece of music that made my heart leap."

Mrs. Evans smiled a smile that I was to become very familiar with over the next five years. "Wonderful choice. I want you to know this is quite a commitment that you are making here. My plan is to teach you this concerto in smaller sections. You will come for a lesson every week, work very hard and eventually five years from now, we will string all the sections together. How does that sound to you?"

I was ecstatic. "That sounds like a great plan Mrs. Evans! When can we begin?"

"Next lesson." She said. "You've already been here several hours. Great work today."

As I skipped down the front stairs of Mrs. Evans home, I felt on top of the world. I had a plan. I had the music. I had a teacher. I could see the future.

The next five years

For the next five years, I not only learned the string bass to play in the Piedmont High School Orchestra and Jazz Band. I also went every week to Mrs. Evans home to learn each section of the Saint Sean's Piano Concerto #2 in G Minor. Mr. Harvey made good on his promise to also allow me to conduct the Jazz Band. I also practiced my piano concerto every single day for five years.

Soon the concert day was approaching and nightly orchestra rehearsals were added. When the week finally came that I had to play my piano concerto with the high school orchestra, I was so nervous that I couldn't eat or sleep.

All I did was practice piano, before and after school.

The afternoon of the concert

The afternoon before the concert I went to Mrs. Evans home. I burst into tears. I wailed, "Mrs. Evans. We have worked together on this one piece of music for five years. What if I fail? I'm not sure I can do it." As tears dripped on to the ivory colored piano keys, I added, "What if I make a complete idiot of myself tonight? What if I forget every single thing I ever learned here in this room?" Clearly I was losing it.

Wise Mrs. Evans simply said, "Let's both not worry about any of that right now. How about I go into the kitchen and make you a nice hot cup of tea while you dry your tears out here. Then we will simply play through the whole thing and see how we feel then, OK?" After a nice cup of tea and a biscuit, I sat down again at the piano.

Mrs. Evans said, "Close your eyes and imagine you playing the entire piece of music in your mind's eye. When you have done that, open your eyes and begin. Do not stop, no matter what happens. All right?"

I trusted Mrs. Evans, and so I closed my eyes and imagined myself playing the entire concerto, start to finish. When I was done, I opened my eyes and began to play. I did not even notice that Mrs. Evans had left the room. When I was done I looked up. I was the only one in the room. "Mrs. Evans?" I called. Mrs. Evans came into the living room with tears streaming down her cheeks.

"All right. I want to tell you something." She said as she walked over to the piano and took both my shoulders in each of her hands. "I don't care if you play a single note right tonight. Not a single note. You just played the entire concerto flawlessly. You know you can do it. I know you can do it. That is all that matters. What happens tonight doesn't matter. What happened here a moment ago does matter. So tonight, you just go out there and have a good time. Nothing else matters."

I leaned in and put my head on her chest. The only words I could get out of my mouth were, "Thank you."

The night of the concert

The night of the concert was my very first bona fide out of body experience. All I can remember of that night is right before the concert, my hands became extremely cold. Someone handed me a pair of large men's gloves. I remember them being very soft and velvety inside. I remember as Mr. Harvey announced my name, taking the gloves off both my hands, stepping on stage, walking toward the piano and sitting down. I don't remember anything else about playing the concerto except looking down at the keyboard as I lifted my hands off and hearing a roaring in my ears. I remember turning toward the audience and seeing all of them in a blur standing on their feet.

The sounds of "Bravo!" became louder and louder. Eventually, coming out of my daze, I turned toward the audience and took a bow in my homemade dress I had made for the occasion. People told me later that I played "like a woman possessed," and better than they had ever seen me play before. I don't have a single memory of ever touching the keys or playing a single note that night.

My adolescence had been a very full time and with the concert over, it was hard to know where to put all my energy. But soon, it was time to go off to college. I wrote my college application essay on all the things I had learned from setting a specific goal and then meeting that goal of playing a piano concerto with my high school orchestra. The essay was a great success with colleges. In the end I had to make a choice between Stanford University or University of California, Berkeley. I chose to become a music major at U.C. Berkeley, to pursue my current dream of becoming a professional musician, just as my Grandparents had been. There I studied piano performance and played string bass in the University orchestra. During my first two years as a music major at the University of California, Berkeley, when I wasn't in class learning music theory or going to concerts, I spent most of my days in the dungeon of the music building practice rooms, working on mastering the piano and string bass.

The music lesson

My piano teacher and Professor was a Greek man who was both very harsh and fiery in temperament. It's funny to me now that I can't remember the name of this man, but he was a person who had a very strong influence on me for two full years of my college life. He was also one of the people who served to change the trajectory of my life. I remember that moment like it was yesterday. We were sitting in the music room and he was getting frustrated with how I played a particular passage of music written by Claude Debussy.

At one point, he yelled, "Stop! Stop! Stop!" I stopped playing immediately. "Do you know the true meaning of commitment to your instrument?" he barked.

"I guess not." I mumbled to myself.

"What did you just say?" he barked again.

"Nothing." I said, defiantly looking him right in the eye.

"I just asked you a question Ms. Dorward. I expect an answer. Do you know the true meaning of commitment to your instrument?" he barked again.

"No, sir." I replied quite honestly.

This professor had a habit of using the Socratic method in his teaching, using questions to illuminate a point he was trying to make. I had no idea what he was getting at by his question and so I did not have an answer to give him. He went on in a tone of tremendous superiority, "The true measure of your commitment to your instrument is that you practice until your fingers bleed." he said proudly.

"Really?" I replied, incredulously. I thought he was joking. "You're kidding, right?"

His eyes lit up with rage. "I am not kidding. Not in the least, Ms. Dorward." Then he added, showing me his hands, and then turning them over back and forth several times. "You see?" I noticed that his fingernails were ringed with dried blood and he had cuts on his fingers.

"So do you expect me to practice like this?" I said, staring at his hands.

"I do." He replied. "Are you ready to take the next step in your piano practice that will lead you to your true greatness?"

"Yes sir, I am." I replied and I stood up beside the piano. To me, everything was suddenly crystal clear. I looked this Greek Professor right in the eye and said, "I'm quitting the music department as my major." I walked out the door, mid lesson, leaving him speechless.

I started crying the moment I slammed the door to the classroom. *So, what am I going to do now?* I thought to myself as I took a long walk through the U.C. Berkeley campus. Walking has always helped me figure things out, especially at a moment of crisis or indecision. Eventually after a few laps around campus I came up with a new plan. I realized that one of the things I had always liked to do was argue. I thought, *Maybe there's some department here that does that. Or maybe I'll study dinosaurs. I've always liked them.* I mused. Then, with fury and defiance I shouted out loud to no one in particular, "At least I won't be in the practice room dungeons waiting for my fingers to bleed." At that, I smiled and continued the long walk back home.

The experiment

I had always loved dinosaurs so I chose the paleontology department as my as my first non-music elective. Much to my shock and dismay, I failed every single quiz and test. Undaunted, and applying my normal Puritan work ethic, I marched myself into the Teachers Assistant hours every week and discussed the new classwork assignments.

After several weeks of this routine, the Teachers Assistant asked me, "You know you have failed every single test in this class so far right?"

"Yes I am well aware of that fact. That's why I come to see you every week." I smiled, with more confidence than I actually felt.

"Yes. I noticed that." he replied. "And I also know that with me, you can answer every single question accurately. So, I don't understand. Why are you failing all the tests?"

"Well, I'm not quite sure actually. I do know that I am trying really hard but that doesn't seem to be enough to make any real difference."

Next, the T. A. chose a different tack. "So how much science have you taken so far in school?"

"Well, I was only required to pass biology in high school. At my high school, science was considered an elective and it was always offered at the same time block as music. I preferred studying music so I usually chose that."

"Well, that explains a lot." the Teachers Assistant said, thinking out loud.

I tried not to take offense at his comment; even I could see at this point my pursuing any science at a university level, as much as I may love dinosaurs, was rather a waste of time.

I decided to take a different approach. "I think you should know that I have never received even a C in my entire scholastic career, let alone an F like I have here in this class. For me this is quite a shock."

"It must be." he said with a slight grin.

I continued, "But, I think the problem here is that when you explain the question to me, sitting here in your office, I do understand what you are asking. But when I have the test in front of me, the questions are totally worded differently, in all that science language. I don't understand the question so I don't write it like we talk it out here in your office hours."

"Have you considered going back to music?" he asked tentatively.

"Actually, I just quit as a music major last quarter after two years of study in the music department. I just lost my passion for it. It was no longer giving me any joy at all."

"Well what does give you joy, in science I mean?" The T.A. asked.

"Funny you should ask that. I have always loved dinosaurs. So I thought I would come over here to the Paleontology Department to learn more about them. But no one explained to me that in this class, Paleontology 101, that there was only one class the entire quarter about dinosaurs, and I would have to learn everything - from blue green algae up through the ancestry of man!"

The T.A. had to laugh as he said, "I see. Well I can't help you there. It was on the class syllabus. Well anyway, you know the final exam is coming up soon right?"

"Yeah, I do. You have to help me. I can't fail it. My father will absolutely kill me." I said.

"Well OK. Let's get to work then." The T.A. replied, opening up the textbook.

The night of the final exam, I got a call from the T. A. "Well, I've got some *good news* and some *bad news* for you Mary Anne. Which news would you like first?"

I hesitated. "Uhhhh. Let me have the *bad news* first." I said with the phone pressed to my ear, my eyes closed, and my fingers crossed.

"Well, you got a D minus on the final exam." My heart sank. "But the good news is that the Professor and I have talked about you and we have never seen a person try so hard and fail so consistently. So we're giving you C minus for effort. For the entire class grade."

While I appreciated the fact that both the Professor and the Teachers Assistant recognized my tremendous efforts, when I hung up, I realized that there wasn't much of a future for me in science. It was clear that I had to find another direction.

What else do I really enjoy? I asked myself as I was falling asleep that night.

When I woke up the next morning I had an inspiration. I had always loved a great debate and exchange of ideas and so I decided that I would try the Rhetoric Department. I had heard they taught a lot of lawyers how to formulate a solid argument and win their cases. I thought that sounded like fun. I did really well in the Rhetoric Department for a while, until I tried to declare a major in it.

Rhetoric

The Head Professor of the Rhetoric Department at U.C. Berkeley, Mr. Sloan, was the father of a good friend of mine back in high school. One day Mr. Sloan asked me to come to his office for a private meeting. "I've been reviewing your request for a major in our Department. I am sorry to say that we don't have enough classes in our Department to graduate you with the Rhetoric Degree that you have designed." Mr. Sloan said kindly.

"Well I can change my focus within the Department then. I really like it here in the Rhetoric department." I said hopefully.

"I have a better idea." Mr. Sloan said. "Come with me. We're going for a little walk." he said, as he rose from his chair behind his desk. As Mr. Sloan and I walked across campus, I asked what exactly he had in mind for my major. "You'll see." he said with a smile, as we walked.

Eventually we were both standing in front of the U.C. Berkeley Drama Department. "Oh, no you don't, Mr. Sloan!" I cried. "I really, really do not want to be with all those weird drama people!"

"Well I have seen you perform myself while you were in high school with my son David and I think you are quite talented in that department. So I have arranged an audition for you with the heads of the Drama Department this afternoon, in exactly," Mr. Sloan looked at his watch, "Ten minutes."

"What?!" I cried. "What exactly am I going to audition with?" I asked incredulously.

"Well I heard from your Rhetorical argument teacher that last week you performed, and then orally defended the T.S. Eliot poem, *"Four Quartets"* quite admirably. And if I am correct, you also received an A plus grade on your written argument. Isn't that so?"

"Yes." I said begrudgingly.

"Well I thought you could use that poem to audition with. Unless you have something else in mind." Mr. Sloan said with a mischievous smile.

"I cannot believe you are doing this to me Mr. Sloan. You do realize of course that the teachers in Drama teach a sequential series of classes and we are in the spring quarter, which means the students have already been through two full quarters. They will never take me as a student." I said.

"We'll see. Oh here they are now!" Mr. Sloan said.

I looked to his left and three teachers were heading our way. They introduced themselves as Debbie, Dana and Marty. Then Mr. Sloan said, "Well I'm off now! Mary Anne let me know how it all goes!" he said, smiling and winking at me.

While I was furious to be ambushed in this way, I figured, what the heck have I got to lose? I went into the Drama Department and recited my poem.

"We'd like you in class tomorrow at 9:00." Debbie said.

"And I would like to speak to you about taking private lessons with me, on Sundays too." said Dana.

Marty just smiled, and said, "Well done. Quite well done Mary Anne. Mr. Sloan was certainly right about you. Welcome to the U.C. Berkeley Drama Department." And that's how I became a Drama Major at U.C. Berkeley.

One day, Debbie asked me to stay after class. Then she said, "Let's go to my office." When we got there, she sat me down and told me about an audition for "You're A Good Man Charlie Brown" which was being held in San Francisco the following day.

I said, "Well thanks for the idea but I'm going to Tahoe for the weekend."

"Oh. You can't go." she said.

"Oh yes I can." I shot back.

"No really, you can't. You *must* to go to this audition. The part of Sally is so perfect for you. If you won't do it for yourself, will you please do it for me? With any luck, you could get your professional actors Equity card and start your professional career before you graduate from here."

The audition

I begrudgingly agreed to go to the audition the following day. When I got there, I saw several hundred kids of all shapes and sizes. It was my first Equity professional audition and I was completely overwhelmed. I thought to myself, *This sure doesn't look promising.*

I entered the theatre to put my name on the list. I was given "sides," which are the lines you read from the script when you audition. I was given the script for the characters of both Sally and Lucy and I went off into a corner to practice my lines. When it was my turn, and since it was my first ever professional audition, I didn't know exactly how you were supposed to behave. So I just walked out into the Alcatraz theatre where the infamous Gene Persson was sitting, held out my hand, and introduced myself, "Hello Mr. Persson. I'm Mary Anne Dorward. Nice to meet you."

He laughed, shook my hand and replied, "Well, hello there Miss Dorward. You can go up on the stage there, and we'll hear you read."

There were some other people scattered around the theatre but they did not introduce themselves. It was clearly obvious to me now that I was supposed to have just gone directly on the stage. So I turned around, marched up the stairs on the side of the stage, and read the first script out loud for the part of Sally.

When I was done, Mr. Persson said, "Let's try Lucy next."

I said, "Sure. No problem Mr. Persson. But I don't have the script for the part of Lucy."

"Well we will just have to find you the sides for that part then now won't we Miss Dorward?" At that Mr. Person called out to the stage manager, who then went backstage and got the sides for the part of Lucy. She gave them to me.

Then I read the character of Lucy. Everyone in the theatre laughed out loud. I was quite surprised, as I hadn't even practiced the part, and had not expected to get such a strong reaction.

Mr. Persson smiled and said, "You read that very well, especially completely cold and unrehearsed like that. I know your professors sent you in here for the part of Sally. Why not Lucy? You're a natural for her."

I responded honestly, "Well I have no idea about that, Sir. But, between you and me sir, I kinda think Sally is a wimp. Now that I've done Lucy, I personally like her much better. I mean, I guess I understand her better."

"Why is that?" Mr. Persson asked, obviously quite amused.

"Well Sir." I thought for a moment. "Lucy is strong. She's opinionated, and isn't afraid to say what she thinks, even if it doesn't agree with everyone else. She's powerful, and people do what she tells them to. And I guess I have been preparing to play Lucy all my life. I mean, you don't grow up with four brothers for nothing!" I said. At that remark, everyone in the room burst out laughing.

Then Mr. Persson came down to the front of the stage, and said with a big smile, "How do you feel about dying your hair black?"

I smiled back, "Absolutely fine sir. No problem."

After I left the theatre, I thought, *Well that was fun!*

As I was driving over the Bay Bridge to Berkeley, I had a sudden memory flash of when I was twelve years old and our Mother and Father took us all to see "You're A Good Man Charlie Brown" at a theatre in San Francisco. I had loved it. Now, here I was, just 8 years later, meeting the exact same man who had directed that very first premiere of that same play which I had so loved as a child.

When I told my professors on Monday that I had nailed the part of Lucy and been offered the job, they were ecstatic.

Dana said, "Well we all had you pegged for Sally hands down. How did you manage Lucy?"

I laughed and said, "Oh, I just used my memory of beating up on all my brothers, and it all went fine! In fact, it was really fun!"

Disney calls

The next week, Eric a good friend of mine from high school, begged me to come with him and give moral support at a huge audition for Disney. At that time, Disney was on a national hunt for fourteen kids, seven who would go to Disneyland in Southern California, and the other seven would go to Disneyworld in Florida.

In the car on the way, Eric said, "Hey! I have a great idea. Why don't you audition too? It will be great fun!" I hadn't planned on it, but I agreed to audition just for fun, and also for acting practice. Luckily for me, I happened to also have a copy of my acting resume, which I always carried in my purse, just in case.

It turned out to be the hardest audition I could ever imagine. The Disney people wanted to be sure you didn't lie about anything on your resume. So they asked you to recite a single line from every acting part that was listed on your resume. Then everyone auditioning rotated into another room and then were asked to sit down. The people who played instruments were asked to stand up.

"Ms. Dorward, it says here that you play the piano. Please sit down at the piano over there." I walked over to the piano hoping they were not going to ask me to play a part of every piece I knew. But I did have the piano concerto still in my head from the recent concert, so I took comfort in knowing I could at least play a little part of that.

"Play something for us please."

Oh God. It's been awhile, but here goes nothing! I thought to myself. I began playing the opening of the concerto of the Saint Sean Concerto in G Minor.

After a few minutes, the person running the audition then interrupted my playing saying, "That was lovely. Now we would like you to improvise a bit."

Oh noooo! I don't improvise. I have no experience improvising?! I thought as I began to panic.

Then she said, "We'd like you to do an improvisation of *Jack and The Beanstalk*. Now begin!"

Jack and the beanstalk? Is she kidding me? I thought. But I smiled sweetly and said, "I'll give it a try ma'am." I sat there for a moment and tried to remember that story from when I was a little kid. I remembered only that the story had a big giant and a kid who had tried to climb up the beanstalk. I established a large banging low musical sound for the Giant and one lighter one for the character of Jack. Then I imagined him climbing a tall beanstalk, as I moved my fingers up the piano keys.

"That's just great!" The lady with the clipboard laughed, as she stopped me from playing again and looked like she was making a check on the clip board she was holding. "Ms. Dorward you can now move on to the dance part of the audition. Please go through that door over there." she said as she gestured to her right.

Oh God help me. Dance. My least best talent I thought to myself as I headed toward the door to the dance studio. When I got through the door, the dance teacher was obviously annoyed with something or someone; he was yelling at the top of his lungs. I tried to hide from him by quietly and quickly moving to the back of the four lines of dancers up on the stage. I decided since dance was not my strong suit, I would position myself in the middle of any line so that no matter which way we had to turn in the dance combination, I would be able to follow someone else who knew more than I did.

I had not planned on the fact that after each sequence of the dance combination, the lines were rotated forward. After the third combination, I was now dead center in the front of the line on stage. *This is going to be very embarrassing.* I was thinking as the Dance Director counted the starting beats out, "Five! Six! Seven! Eight!" We were about halfway through the dance combination when the Dance Director, after he had looked down, and then back up from his clipboard yelled, "Missssssssss Dorward!" He sounded every bit the authority of a Marine Drill Sergeant.

"Yes Sir!" I said, standing immediately at attention.

"Who taught Youuuuuuuu to dance?" he said with a very obvious sneer.

At that, I heard someone behind me whisper, "Uh Oh...."

To this day, I do not know what came over me at that particular moment. I stayed rigid at attention, smiled my most genuine smile, and yelled back, "NOBODY SIR! But I sure am having a GREAT TIME up here! SIR!"

At this, the Dance Director came absolutely undone. He started laughing so hard that he began to gag. At this, everyone else, including all the other dancers started laughing too. Everyone in the room had seen me flailing, and trying my very best to keep up. Since everyone was laughing, and it was obviously meant to be humiliating to me, I thought the entire audition was all over for me at that point, so I started walking off the stage.

"And where do you think you're going Misssssss. Dorward?" the Dance director said, still laughing. I didn't know what to say or do. "Get back in line Missssss. Dorward! I want to see you do the combination again."

I got back in line and when I heard him call, "Five! Six! Seven! Eight!" for the first time in my life, I completely forgot about everything and everyone else on stage. I just *Danced.*

The offers come in

A few days later, I had an offer to be one of the 14 kids from all over the country to work for Disney. I also had an offer to get my professional acting Equity card as Lucy in "You're A Good Man Charlie Brown." I didn't know what job to choose, as both had their pros and cons. I went to talk with my Professors and we discussed it. They explained to me that a professional Actors Equity card was much harder to get than all the Disney jobs in the world. So I took my first professional job as Lucy in the musical, "You're A Good Man Charlie Brown."

I loved my first experience of life on the professional stage. After two hundred performances, "You're A Good Man Charlie Brown" closed. But very soon, I booked my first National television commercial which secured my Screen Actors Guild professional acting card. I also booked a radio commercial and this allowed me to get my American Federation of Television and Radio Artists professional acting card too. I was totally on a roll. I had every professional certification I needed.

All signs were pointing clearly at a professional acting career. I graduated from the U.C Berkeley Drama Department with the coveted "Mark Goodson Scholarship Award For Outstanding Theatrical Talent." That scholarship money paid for my airplane ticket to New York City. I was going to be a professional actress.

When I was in the fourth grade, I played the character of Mary in "Little Mary's Valentine." Doing that play was my very first experience being on stage and I remember that it was really fun. I remember saying to myself then, *Wow. I want to do more of this!* Until I was writing this chapter,

I had forgotten all about ever saying or feeling that. But, now, nearly fifty years later, looking back in time, it was clear that *The Universe did not forget.* At the time I was ten years old, I didn't know what Broadway even was. Yet, after a few bizarre trips around The Roundabout of Joy in my life, including a brief stop on stage working in San Francisco, there I was *doing more of that.* Just ten years later, as a professional actress living in New York City, I was about to make my Broadway debut.

The lights of Broadway

Just like dancing for Disney, my Broadway debut wasn't a debut I could have ever imagined. Sometimes reality is stranger than fiction. I had been hired to cover for Holly Hunter in Beth Henley's play, *The Wake Of Jamey Foster.* (Holly later starred in the Hollywood blockbuster movies, *The Piano and Broadcast News,* and also starred in the TV shows *Saving Grace.*) I had been on the job for only five days, when Holly's father suddenly died. Since I was the understudy, I had to go on for Holly.

I had watched the play for the previous four nights at the O'Neil Theatre, but had not yet set foot on the stage for a rehearsal. The show was to go on in three hours and I had no idea how loud I would even have to speak in order to be heard. Looking back now, I have no idea how I even performed the entire play without holding a script. On a Saturday matinee day, in the afternoon, I made my Broadway Debut on three hours' notice, and no rehearsal.

Between shows, I went out to dinner with one of the other actors, Tony Heald. (Later in Tony's career, in the movie, *Silence Of The Lambs,* Tony's character was the guy Anthony Hopkins ate at the end of the movie, "with a nice Chanti".) Halfway through our Chinese dinner, Tony asked me, "So, how does it feel to have made your Broadway debut Mary Anne?"

I laughed, "Well between you and me, I'm glad it's over! I'm ready to go home and lie down."

Tony then said, "Well we have another show in about an hour. Aren't you coming?" I had completely forgotten it was a two-show day!

That night, I did it again. *Then* I went home and *collapsed.*

From Me To You

For some people, it is sometimes necessary to do another job for a portion of their time that might not necessarily be their true joy, but a job that allows them to clothe and feed themselves and their family. In this choice, doing a less than joyful endeavor, like doing dishes, cleaning streets, busing or waiting tables or picking up garbage, gives them the thinking time in their heads to plan their next move and joyful passionate endeavor.

THRIVE

Since the period of my life where I worked on Broadway and then moved to Hollywood to work on TV, my life has been full of great adventures in other professions too. First of all I was a parent. After my divorce, I became a very successful International Coach, and worked in both the Corporate world and International Politics as well as in Non Profit. I wrote speeches for Presidents and Prime Ministers and members of Parliament around the world, working in the U.S., the Middle East and Eurasia. It was all very interesting, exciting, and deeply personally and professionally satisfying for me at the time.

It has given me so much joy over the years to help many people all over the world to overcome their fear and loathing of speaking in public, not to mention helping them raise millions of dollars for great causes. I always did my very best to prepare my speakers over the years, no matter what their level or what was at stake for them personally, their company or political race.

However, no matter how much you prepare a client, you never know, or can completely predict what will happen when they get out on stage all on their own. You do your best, as their Speaking Coach, to prepare them for the speech, including their response, pivot or attack they may need to do, but ultimately you can't do the speech for them. The high stakes games of speaking in public can be cutthroat, and there is always a lot at stake. But ultimately, how they handle the tremendous pressure of saying what they say is up to them.

Edgar

One of the people I coached in speaking was the famous Hall of Fame and MVP Designated Hitter, Seattle Mariners player, Edgar Martinez in his first major speech after he retired from baseball.

After his speech was over, he called me on his cell phone and he was in awe: "It was magic Mary Anne! Pure magic! Just like you said, everywhere we wanted them to laugh, they laughed! It was amazing! My whole life, no one really cared what I think. All anyone ever wanted from me, my whole life, was to hit a baseball. That's it. No one ever asked me to speak. Today I spoke, and really hit it out of the park for the first time in my life. Thank you for all your help!"

I was so proud of all the hard work Edgar had put into something that was truly scary for him. I don't know who was more joyful at his success after that speech, him or me!

Patty

Another moment of great joy was a woman politician who had been truly raked over the coals, unfairly in my opinion. Her opponents had even gone so far as to drop horse manure on the courthouse steps where she was a high level judge. I prepped her hard for the political battle ahead and she was not sure that she was going to be able to get through it.

However, she called me afterwards, as I always ask my clients to do after their presentations, and said, "You know, that experience was as bloody as you had predicted. But I walked out of there with my dignity and self esteem intact, and that I owe to you."

This particular politician holding on to her inner strength, despite all odds against her, gave me great joy.

Greg

I was asked to coach a prominent Doctor at Swedish Hospital, Dr. Greg Folkes. He needed to give a speech to raise a million dollars for a new tumor institute. Dr. Greg Folkes was an outstanding and well respected doctor, but he was absolutely terrified of public speaking. However, he was voted by his fellow doctors to give the keynote speech and the main fund raising pitch at the annual Swedish Hospital Gala.

Dr. Greg Folkes and I went over both his speech and the video that was to accompany it. It was clear that the speech and the video were saying the exact same things, and he was in danger of making a common mistake that people in non profit do: overkill, and driving his audience away. I suggested that we cut out everything in his speech that was a duplicate of anything in the video When we did that, there was very little of his speech left.

"What do I do now?" Dr. Folkes said. "I didn't want to give this speech in the first place, and now there isn't any speech left to give!"

I smiled. "Well, I did a little bit of research on you before I came here today. From what I hear, you are an extremely well respected doctor and your staff, patients and colleagues absolutely adore you. You have already built up tremendous trust with them, and now it is time to do the same with your audience in this speech."

"But creating that strong relationship with my staff, colleagues and patients took a lifetime of practice. In this speech I only have less than ten minutes. How can I do that?" Dr. Folkes was nearly in tears.

I replied. "This speech is the place where you get to simply tell the story of why you became a doctor in the first place, and why this new Tumor Institute is so personally important to you. The video will do the rest."

Dr. Folkes was unconvinced. "Are you absolutely sure about that?

I smiled reassuringly. "Trust me on this one. I'm the expert in this field remember? Now, tell me more about why you became a doctor."

Dr. Folkes told me about his history and we wrote that directly into his speech. It was short and sweet. In combination with a professionally produced video, his speech worked like a charm with the audience.

After his speech, Dr. Greg Folkes came off stage, marched right up to me at my table and said, "Well, Mary Anne, I credit you personally with that additional million and a half dollars we just raised. Thank you for your help. Not only did you help us raise an additional million and a half dollars for the Tumor Institute, you also saved my life up there! Thank you!"

Sometimes joy comes from your life, your work, something you create, a mountain you climb either out in the wild, or within yourself. Thriving types of joy can come from an unexpected moment of transcendence such as at the birth of a child or one of profound acceptance as when I received my Australian nickname, Mezza. Whatever it is, enjoy it. It's joy after all. Life is full of it.

From Me To You

The author Richard Bach said, "The bond that links your true family is not one of blood, but of respect and joy in each other's life."

Who are the members of your true family, with whom you share both respect and joy?

CONCLUSION

Sometimes, a feeling of incredible joy can come into your life quite unexpectedly in the form of profound relief from a deep hurt that has been held inside for many years. This kind of joy is another one of those sideways blessings, which only come up in life when it is time for it to be healed.

When my family and I moved to an area of Seattle called Laurelhurst, we had two small children ages 3 and 5. One day not long after we arrived, my daughter Sarah stood out on our balcony with her arms stretched high in the air, and screamed at the top of her lungs, "Is there anybody here who would like to play with me?" I knew how she felt. I wanted to become a part of the new community too, and I wasn't sure where to start.

When Sarah started kindergarten, I joined local non-profit organizations such as the Washington Women's Foundation to meet like-minded women. I started a foundation with my husband to help the local elementary school where our daughter attended. I volunteered to teach music and art classes there. I applied for Washington State Arts grant and raised money to start an art program at the same school. I organized a huge renovation of the school's dreary hallways, and helped create colorful murals in the children's play court. I coached both a boys and a girls basketball team in the evenings at the gym. The teachers at the school joked that they should set up a cot in the teachers' lounge, as I never left.

But no matter how hard I worked at it, the women of that community shut me out of their private parties, their private guilds, their weekend getaways, and their church functions, and I didn't know why. When I divorced at age 40, one of these women named Peggy came to my home one day and announced, "You know Mary Anne, you're making us all feel very nervous."

Quite stunned, I replied, "Nervous? In what way?"

"Well, your divorce for one thing." Peggy said.

"My divorce? How does my divorce make you nervous?"

"Well," Peggy said still standing on the front stoop of my new house where I had recently moved. "There but for the Grace of God go most of us women here in Laurelhurst."

"What do you mean? Just say it plainly so I can understand you." I was truly confused now.

"Well, let me put it to you this way: I am a princess. I have always been a princess, and I intend to remain a princess. You – a beautiful, smart, divorced woman - are a threat to all of us. All of our husbands really like you." She said flatly.

"But I haven't the slightest interest in any of your husbands." I replied.

"Well, we see the way they look at you, and we all have a problem with that." Peggy countered.

"Look, do you think this is easy for me, giving up all of my financial security, living alone, getting a divorce, leaving a home I loved and being separated from my children every week, week on and week off?" I paused, but Peggy didn't say anything, so I continued. "All I have ever tried to do since the moment I came to this town six years ago is help this community, be supportive to all of you and to your children. What exactly do you want me to do Peggy?" I asked, both hurt and bewildered, and trying not to cry.

"I haven't the slightest idea. I just thought I would let you know that you are a threat to all of the women of this town." With that, Peggy turned around, walked back down the stairs of my house and got into her car that still had the engine running. I sat on the stoop of my home for a long time after she left, wondering what I had done to deserve this truly special treatment.

While it was painful to be ostracized in such an obvious way by such a tight knit community, I decided that I would just continue to do my very best to hold my head up, know the truth of myself deep inside, and move on. I focused my energy on my new business, recovering from five cancers, writing a book, and keeping to myself.

Nearly fifteen years later, I was invited to a surprise birthday party of one of the woman of the community named Ginny who had been both my daughter and son's soccer coach. I debated whether to go to the party at all, as I had not seen many of the women from the community in many years. But Ginny had given so generously of her time and energy, not only to my daughter and son, but also to the children of many other families, and that seemed like reason enough to at least stop by her birthday party, wish her well, and drop off a gift.

When I walked through the door, all the heads in the room turned, the laughter stopped, and you could have heard a pin drop. I couldn't help but notice that all the men in the room stood up. My conversation with Peggy fifteen years before popped into my head.

One of the husbands came over to the door where I was standing, gave me a big hug, and said with a big grin, "Wow! Mary Anne. It's so great to see you again! We haven't seen you in so many years! You look great!" As he gave me a hug, I looked over his shoulder, and saw the face of his wife. She was watching this hug and scowling.

I quickly glanced around the room, and saw that all the other women were scowling too. So I quickly disengaged myself from the hug in process, and noticed that several of the other men in the room were now headed my way. I spotted a woman named Lydia on the other side of the room, grabbed a glass of wine off the tray on a nearby table as I passed by, and then sat down next to her. Lydia had been our children's kindergarten teacher many years before.

After exchanging pleasantries of a general nature, I finally decided to ask the question that had been on my mind for so many years: "Lydia, why do all these women here in Laurelhurst hate me so much?"

Lydia had had a few drinks before I arrived, and she laughed as she said, "Well we don't like his second wife any more than we do you, if that's any comfort to you."

This was not exactly the answer I was expecting, but I decided to risk asking the question again as I suddenly had a deep need for closure before I left the U.S. the following week, and moved permanently to Ecuador. "I'm not the least bit interested in what you all think of my former husband's second wife. I'm interested in why you all hate *me* so much."

"Don't you know why?" Lydia laughed again, and then took another large sip of wine. "Really Mary Anne. You *must know* why we all hate you."

"No Lydia, really I don't. I don't recall ever doing anything to any of you that would deserve the treatment I have received for the past fifteen years from every single one of you here in this room tonight. Perhaps you can enlighten me."

As Lydia reached for the bottle of wine on her table and poured herself another glass, she said, "Well for starters look around this room Mary Anne. Take a good long look at all the women in this room, including me. We're all fat, old, over the hill, ugly and we drink too much.

"But now, well, look at you. You are beautiful, smart, funny, thin, wear stylish clothes, have your own business, wrote a book for God's sake, and all our husbands really like you. Are those enough reasons for ya?" Lydia took another long slug of her wine.

At that moment I started laughing, and I just could not stop. Heads turned our way, but I didn't care. I suddenly felt such incredible relief. It was a huge and bizarre explosion of joy. It was like a large, dark cloud suddenly lifted, a cloud that had been following me for a very long time. I felt not only joyful, but also grateful. Lydia had finally spelled out the real truth of why I had been shunned all those years. I hadn't done anything to anyone. The only thing I had done was be myself.

Suddenly, it was also abundantly clear that all of these women in the room were just being themselves too. It was profoundly freeing to realize that no matter how it may have appeared, we were - all of us - just doing the very best we could.

I leaned over and gave Lydia a huge hug and said, "That explains everything! Thank you so much for telling me that. I really appreciate it!"

With that, I stood up and without another word to anyone, I left the party and never spoke to any of the women in Laurelhurst again.

From Me To You

Do you believe that Joy is impossible for you? Well, Theodore Roethke, the Pulitzer Prize winning poet suggests otherwise: "What we need is people who specialize in the impossible."

Did you know that our brains have 130 million photoreceptors, which connect with billions of neurons and synapses, that construct and reconstruct literally anything our consciousness asks for, every single second, of every single day?

So the truth is that each of us is already doing the impossible every second we're awake and breathing. Joy is possible for all of us.

BOOK 9

THE KEY OF IMAGINATION

"I am not what happened to me.

I am what I choose to become."

~Carl Jung, Psychoanalyst and Psychiatrist

INTRODUCTION

I learned how to tap my imagination very early in my life thanks to my Grandmother. From the time I was three, my "Nonny" and I had a private "girl thing" that we did every time we got together. At her home in the hills of Berkeley, California, she kept a large blue plastic water bottle by her front door. This was one of those dispenser bottles you would see on the top of a water cooler. Our blue plastic water bottle was very, very special. We called it, "Our Trip Around The World Jar." Every time we passed the jar, coming in or going out of the house, we would add a coin or two to the jar, even if it was only a penny. The amount of money didn't matter. What mattered was that every time either of us put a coin into the bottle and heard it go "Clink!" we would look at each other with a big smile, nod and then say, "That's for our trip around the world!"

When I was old enough to earn an allowance, I would always reserve a few coins and whenever I went to visit or stay with Nonny, I had these coins in my pocket. Over the years, we watched our pile of coins rise up inside that big blue jar, growing like one of those infamous magic rocks. This is one of my favorite childhood memories.

Tea, cake and details

Whenever I would visit her, Nonny would make tea and serve it in beautiful porcelain cups. She would also serve a piece of cake or a cookie on beautiful china plates. I felt so ladylike and grown up holding my porcelain teacup and plate, talking with Nonny about all the wonderful places we would travel to one day. Our discussions would be filled with exciting details.

One of us might say something like, "Oh how about let's go to see the beautiful Geishas in Japan with their colorful robes!"

The other would respond, "Oh that sounds like fun! Let's add Japan and those pretty Geishas to our list! What colors do you see on their robes? Let's get up and walk like the Geishas do in their high wooden platform shoes."

Then we would put on a record and walk like Geishas, or dance around the room together.

Reality

As I grew older, and I believed wiser, "reality" began to creep into my consciousness. I began to pause by the big blue jar as I came in the door. I would look at the plastic jug, and say things like, "Nonny. Do you know how much a trip around the world would cost? I've researched it. We need a lot more money that what's in that blue jar!"

Nonny would always smile and reply, "Well I'm throwing in a few coins anyway. You never know. They just might be multiplying in there while we're sleeping." I couldn't help but laugh at her fantasy.

Then, as she left the room, Nonny would add over her shoulder, "I really don't think this trip around the world is nearly as complicated as you're making it, Mary Anne. Did you have any more ideas about where you would like to go, and what you'd like to see when we go?"

Eventually, I started to roll my eyes as I passed the jar, saying things like,

"What's the use of imagining something you will never have? It's pointless." Or "You and I both know we'll never take that trip." I began to see the blue jar by the door as "a pipe dream," and this whole idea of taking a trip around the world as a pointless game of "make believe."

No matter what I did or said, Nonny would always smile and throw a few more coins into the big blue jar whenever we came in her front door. She would always say, "For our trip around the world!," even when I pretended that I wasn't listening.

I realize now that my Nonny was the first person to teach me about how to create or manifest what I choose in life. My Grandmother taught me how to be grateful in advance of the things that I wanted to have happen in my life, even if what I manifested showed up in a different way than I expected. Today, one of my nicknames given to me by friends is "The Hilarious Manifester."

Although my Nonny died at age 83, and we never did take that trip around the world together, I have personally travelled extensively for business and pleasure since she died. I have worked in many countries and have learned to speak multiple languages. Wherever I have travelled in the world, I have always thought of Nonny and how much she would enjoy the sights I was seeing, and the different cultures I was experiencing. Many of the things we discussed at our endless tea parties have now become a reality for me, some in very surprising and unexpected ways, just as we had imagined them together so many years ago.

Surprise!

A few years before Nonny died, I complained to her about the men in my life: "It's impossible to find a real man! They're all jerks!" I told her.

She smiled as she always did, and said, "Well, you be careful what you wish for now!"

After many years, many men, and one marriage, I found that they all had fulfilled my very low expectations. Eventually, I had to admit that my "perfect life partner manifestation" needed a bit more refinement. I started to imagine a very different kind of man who would have more of the qualities that I valued, including a love of travel.

After three weeks of following my new partner manifestation plan, and setting aside my many negative "mantras" about men in general, I met my perfect companion. Like Nonny, this man knew from a very young age that nothing was impossible, and that limits were only in your mind. He was kind, funny and fun to be with, just like my Nonny. He also had a passion for world travel as I do. This man became my new husband.

Bringing these things into my life wasn't nearly as difficult or complicated as I had thought it would be all those years ago when "reality" sank the boat of my imagination. Nonny showed me how to visualize things in order to manifest them in reality by trusting that whatever I had conceived (either positive or negative) would eventually come to fruition in my life. She gave me the Key of Imagination.

We don't get what we deserve

What stories do you choose to tell about your life? Most of the time we don't realize it, but each of us are creating our lives in advance when we say things like,

"That will never happen."

"I can't have that."

"Bad things always happen to me."

"I'm totally unlucky in love."

"I'm such an idiot."

In choosing these kinds of negative statements to define who we are, we actually energetically attracting more of the same events, people and experiences to show up and manifest in our lives. The Universe or what

I call Source, doesn't know the difference between real or imagined reality. Each story we tell or imagine in our mind has its own energetic signature, and draws "like energy and experiences" to it.

Someone once told me, *"We don't get what we deserve in life. We get what we think we deserve."* Our individual belief systems are just a collection of the thoughts we think, over and over again. Those thoughts shape everything do, according to our predominant belief systems. What would happen if we put a new frame or a different story together of who we are? By repeating our negative stories, we actually teach ourselves and others who we are and also, how we expect to be treated.

How to change negative belief systems in 3 easy steps

Here's how to identify and change some of the key negative belief systems operating currently in your life:

1. Begin by choosing to pay attention throughout your day to the thoughts that pop up in random moments, or the thoughts that seem to show up repeatedly, in your mind.

Like most people, you will discover that there are lots of negative statements roaming around in your head throughout the day. You can identify a belief system when you hear yourself saying things like,

"I can't get anything right."

"I'm just so stupid!"

"I'm a total failure."

"This will never work out."

2. Next, get a blank journal or piece of paper.

Take your journal or paper with you and each time a negative thought comes up in your mind, write it down. Leave a space below each one. Remember, these are the soul sucking negative things you say to yourself, over and over, every single day.

3. Next, take each negative statement on your list and in the space below each one, choose to turn it around into a more positive, self affirming, non judgmental statement.

For example, "I'm such an idiot" might be rewritten to something like, "Sometimes I make mistakes, but I'm doing the very best I can in this moment."

"Each choice I made in the past was made with the information and experience I had at that time. Today is a new day and I have new information and more experience behind me. Therefore, I have the freedom to make a new and different choice."

"I did the very best I could with what I knew at the time. Every day, in every way, I am getting better and better."

Remember, we don't get what we deserve in life. *We actually get what we think, imagine, and believe that we deserve.* Once we begin paying attention to all those thoughts we think, we will start to notice that they shape the future of our lives. *A Course In Miracles* says that we can choose to change our beliefs at any time and at all times, without exception, *"We are only subject to that which we believe is true."*

From Me To You

In the Harry Potter books and movies written by J.K. Rowling, Sirius Black says the following to the young wizard, Harry Potter:

"You're not a bad person. You are a very good person who bad things have happened to. Besides, the world isn't split into Good People and Death Eaters. We've all got both light and dark inside of us. What matters is the part we choose to act on. That's who we really are."

What part of your own life, light or dark, are you choosing to act on right now?

SURVIVE

How we choose to see the world also influences how we feel about it. A number of years ago, after my divorce, I travelled to the island of Ibiza, which is a very old and mythic place. While Ibiza is famous and best known today as the spot of the rich and famous, jet setters and rock stars who come to vacation there, this island has a long and rich history with many fascinating stories. Some of the stories I found most fascinating were that people there still believe in leprechauns, kids ski the giant salt mountains for fun, and it's where the espadrille shoes were first invented.

Flamingos in the wild

I went to Ibiza specifically to see flamingos "in the wild." I took a tour bus that promised flamingos in the wild, and I could not see one. Not one, single pink flamingo! In my frustration, I finally stood up in the back of the bus, and said quite loudly to the tour guide at the front of the bus, "So where exactly are the flamingos? I thought we were supposed to be seeing flamingos in the wild on this trip? So am I blind? Where are all the pink flamingos you promised?"

As all heads on the very large tour bus turned my way, a lady sitting in front of me turned around and said very calmly and politely, "Dear, the flamingos here on Ibiza are white. Not pink. White. Look again. Out the window."

I did look out of my window again, and suddenly all I saw were white flamingos. Everywhere. Apparently when flamingos are young, they are actually white until they begin to feed on shrimp. Eating shrimp turns flamingos pink, the color we all know so well. I had seen these beautiful graceful white birds standing in the salt flats, their image reflected in the pools, but I did not know that they were, in fact flamingos.

Isn't it amazing that you can live your whole life thinking something is one way, such as "Flamingos are *always* pink." It makes it impossible to even conceive that a flamingo could ever be any other color. I had been conditioned to believe that flamingos are only pink, because I had always seen them at the zoo, or as plastic pink lawn ornaments.

So there I was on a bus in Ibiza, so conditioned to believe that flamingos are pink, that I couldn't even conceive of such a thing even existing such as a white flamingo. As a consequence I literally *could not see them*. My world spun on a dime when the lady on the bus asked me to *"look again."* My whole world was turned upside down at the sight of one white flamingo. Suddenly, all I could see were white flamingos. Everywhere. Our lives are very much like this. We are so conditioned to believe that *things are a certain way*. We may believe that a certain thing is true because that is how it has always been for us, it is what we have always seen, or is something that we have always been told. **We only see what we believe is true for us.**

If you believe, as I did, that flamingos are always pink, a thousand white ones will flutter by your face and you literally will not even see them. When a new experience enters our lives in the form of a person, place or thing, suddenly a new reality is possible. Change is actually inevitable if we are open to it. A new belief, idea or concept is possible because we have seen and experienced it with our own eyes or hearts. Change is slow in coming to full consciousness always. But it will come if we are open and willing to let it in.

From Me To You

Esther Hicks calls the process of using our imagination to create new possibilities, "sending a rocket of desire directly to Source." If we also add, "I am thankful for this, or something better," to whatever we are visualizing in our mind, this lets The Universe know we are open for It to be infinitely more creative on our behalf than even we could possibly imagine as to how our "rocket of desire" request is actually accomplished. Whenever I send one of my own rockets of desire out to Source, I also hold firmly in my mind and heart that "everything is being accomplished with ease and grace."

THE ROUNDABOUT

Creativity and imagination isn't something that only artists have. Creativity and imagination are part of our human nature, and we use them every single day of our lives. Without creativity, we couldn't cook a meal, express an opinion, resolve a conflict, or for that matter sculpt, paint, doodle or draw.

Coloring books for adults have become popular in recent years. Adult coloring books are said to promote mindfulness and reduce stress. Researchers at Drexel University did a study on Art Therapy where they had participants do art for 45-minute periods. They discovered that "art therapy can significantly reduce stress related hormones in your body." This means that you can learn to unlock your own unique and powerful creative energy. Once you do, you can use it anywhere - from the office, to the kitchen to your art studio. Here are some simple steps to help you bring new artistry and imagination into your daily life.

We are creative every day

Almost everything we do in our lives requires at least some measure of creativity. Once you learn how to tap fully into your own unique creative flow, you can use it in any area of your life. The first step toward unleashing the open flow of creativity is to attain a state of openness. This requires clearing away your negative self-image around art. If you feel that you always fall short of being perfect, or doing the right thing (past and present), this will impede your flow of creative energy in the here and now.

In your childhood, or even later in your life, you may have received the message that you were not creative. One of your teachers or a parent may have criticized your creative efforts on a particular project. This doesn't have to mean that you are doomed to failure when it comes to being creative. Sometimes you just need a specific technique in order to eliminate a negative self-perception about your ability to be creative. There are steps you can take to leave these thoughts behind so you can once again express yourself creatively.

People who have a creative blockage always seem to have excuses for not moving forward. Some common things I hear from clients are that they don't have enough time to be creative, or enough money, or that they lack the support from family, friends, or colleagues that they feel they need. Some common obstacles I hear people say are,

"I'm not good enough."

"No one else has tried to do this before."

"I'll embarrass myself."

"I can't."

But none of these things are the real barrier to your success. The real obstacle is within you. If someone held a gun to your head and said, "Do this," of course you would do it. Whenever we say the words, "I can't," what we are really saying is, "I won't," or "I am choosing not to."

At this moment, no one else is stopping you from being creative, or is literally standing in your way. You are blocking yourself. Perhaps you are afraid you will look stupid, or someone will judge you in a negative way. The real truth is that you have chosen to remain in "victim mode," or what I call, "the pity pit," which will endlessly generate excuses to enable you to avoid expressing yourself creatively.

Clearing your creative awareness

Have you noticed your internal dialogue around the subject of creative expression or within your own imagination recently? Are you frequently telling yourself things such as,

"This will never work."

"This won't be good enough."

"No one will like it."

"I feel like I'm wasting my time."

Try to identify the excuses you use most in order to avoid being or doing something creative. Essentially you are using these excuses as a type of negative creativity, using them to help you find a way not to use your imagination to be creative. Simply becoming aware of the excuses you choose is the very first step to overcoming them, to unblocking yourself and your creative energy.

Here is one simple meditation practice you can try right now to begin the process of unleashing more of your creative energy:

Sit comfortably, close your eyes, and pay attention to your breath as it enters and leaves your body. Be aware of your body, and allow yourself to settle into the stillness of the chair or cushion you are sitting on. Listen to the sounds around you. Slowly allow the sounds to fade as you settle down into your own inner world. Rest in this place of openness and peace for a few minutes, or longer.

Now, from that place of stillness, silence, and spaciousness, bring the main obstacle to your expression of creativity into your awareness. Simply observe it, without judgment. Just let the obstacle be there, and as you breathe in and out, simply observe it.

Next, you might imagine holding a balloon or blowing a bubble. You can then place your obstacle in your bubble or balloon, and then blow on the bubble or let go of the string tied to the balloon and simply watch it float away. Gradually, as you inhale and exhale, you will observe the obstacle to your creativity gently dissolving into space. As your obstacle continues to dissolve in your mind's eye, just be aware of the empty space that is left behind, and rest there for a few minutes.

Repeat this breathing exercise until you begin to feel a sense of more openness and spaciousness inside of yourself. The more you become aware of what is blocking your creative flow, and practice clearing it, the more you will discover a more self-affirming and open-minded sense of yourself as a creative person.

This new sense of yourself as a creative person flows from your internal openness and peace which is unchanging, indestructible, and confident. It really doesn't matter whether you are an artist immersed in the act of creating a painting, a cook creating a beautiful meal in your kitchen, or at work in the creative act of resolving a conflict. This full immersion in the creative flow of life brings with it a sense of freedom, playfulness, and joy.

Once you can identify and eliminate your negative self-image around creative and imaginative expression, you will experience a feeling of well-being that will allow your creativity to flow again. You will perceive new openings and opportunities to express yourself creatively that had previously been invisible to you, just like the white flamingos were for me. Your experience of joy in life will naturally increase as you once again begin to imagine and cultivate your unlimited creative potential.

Creativity flows from feelings of joy. You will be able to harness this creativity to manifest what you desire. Love, kindness, compassion, and the ability to include others in your life all come from your experience of joy and imagination. For those people who are not professional artists, there is more good news. It turns out that almost everyone, (75% in one study I read), gets the same stress relieving effects of lowering their cortisol through doing something creative. So this means that whether you draw stick figures or paint an elaborate landscape, everyone benefits equally.

From Me To You

Get some art materials such as colored pencils, markers, paper, modeling clay or collage materials. Take just 45 minutes once a week and immerse yourself in a creative project, any art project, that interests you. People who do this practice report that they feel more relaxed, less anxious, and also less obsessed with what they had to get done. Just a little time doing art also allowed them to put things into perspective. So, do some art and give yourself the gift of lower stress hormones in the process!

THRIVE

As we move into the Thrive section of the Key Of Imagination, I would like to discuss the two schools of learning here on earth: the sledgehammer vs the gentle tap on the shoulder. For most of my life, I've never been a "gentle tap on the shoulder" kind of gal. For much of my life, I've been more the "sledge hammer school of learning" type. In fact, I have tended to receive the sledgehammer more than once, and for the exact same lesson, until I really learn it. I have a feeling that my Guardian Angel must get very frustrated with me. If I were her, I'd want to bang my head on the concrete sometimes.

It been said that we are spiritual beings having a human experience. It might appear that my life has been an example of how the human experience can feel like an absolute battering ram straight to the heart. From another person's interpretation, my life story might be living proof of that great Tibetan saying, "Seven times down. Eight times up." What do I think? From my subjective experience, I would say it's a little bit of both.

Whenever I really want to figure something out, I asked for guidance. Sometimes, I specifically asked to be given a dream to help me understand where I was at that point in my journey, and also where I was heading. One night not too long ago I had this dream:

The Bridge

I saw a rope bridge strung across a huge chasm below. The bridge had rope railing and wooden planks to cross it, but the bridge appeared to end about one third of the way across the chasm. The bridge beyond that point, if there even was one, was enveloped in mist.

I didn't step on to the bridge. I asked in my mind, *How far can I go across this chasm? I only see enough steps for about one third of the way.*

Then, I heard a Voice in my mind reply to my question *Please turn around and look back into the past from where you have just come.*

I turned around and saw absolute devastation behind me; everything was burned to the ground. There was no one, and nothing alive there. Everything was completely charred black.

As I stood there looking at my past, I heard the same Voice ask, *Do you want to go back to that world? That is your Past.*

For a second, this reminded me of the play, *A Christmas Carol*, where the character of Scrooge was forced to look at the Ghosts of Christmas Past. That moment in the play had always scared me, just like this vision of everything burnt to the ground was now scaring me in this dream.

No. I replied firmly in my mind. *I want to see what is on the other side of this bridge in front of me. But I can still only see a little way across to the other side, to the mountains in the far distance above the mist.*

Don't worry. the Voice said. *Just take the handrails and walk out on to the bridge. Oh and one more thing. You must leave your children, your ex husband, ex homes, all of your past life must be left behind on this side of the bridge.*

But...I said.

The Voice interrupted me: *These are the terms to cross the bridge to your future. In order to move forward, you must leave behind every aspect of your old life. You must let even your children go now. They have their own life to live and lessons to learn, and these lessons do not involve you. One day, perhaps, they will attempt to cross over to you, but that time is not now.*

"But...." I said.

Again, the Voice interrupted me, more gently this time: *Crossing this bridge is entirely your choice of course. It is best as if you think of your past as dead to you now, for in truth, you cannot change it. You must move forward, and cross the bridge* to your future if you are to fully live your own life. There is only The Now and The Now is your only point of power. The only person you need to serve in The Now is you.

I turned around, and looked again at the bridge expanse. I felt a little apprehensive and said in my mind, *But looking at the bridge to my future right now, the steps don't reach all the way across. How can I trust that?*

The Voice answered, *Do not worry. Every next step will appear right in front of you, just at the time you need it. You must keep moving forward in your life, not backward.*

I repeated what the Voice had just said, *I must keep moving forward in my life, not backward.*

And by the way, the Voice in my mind added, *your beloved Rupe will be right behind you. He will not let you fall.* In my dream, I turned around and that's when I noticed my beloved Rupe standing right behind me, just as the Voice had promised.

Taking a big breath, I stepped out on to the bridge, grabbed the rails and began to cross the chasm, not looking back.

That was the end of the dream. I woke up with an enormous sense of relief from this message of direction.

From Me To You

I have heard it said we cannot move forward while looking in our rear view mirror at the same time. What part of your past is holding you back from fully moving into your future? What specifically do you need to let go of in order to move forward in your own life?

CONCLUSION

When I began the journey to my own Thriving life, I read a lot of books, explored many programs, talked with therapists and others. All of these things were quite useful. We need to trust our own feelings and intuitive guidance about what we read, and what programs we choose to explore. If a book or program or person resonates with you and feels right, then you should feel free to connect with it and try it out. If it doesn't feel like something you need, forget it. One of the most important lessons I have learned from everything I have studied is this: we don't get the life we deserve, we get the life *we believe we deserve*. Each of us *are only subject to that which we hold in our mind as a belief.*

Health

I believed that growth didn't come without pain and without pain there was no gain. So guess what? I manifested a lot of pain in my life. My over achiever personality even manifested several different forms of cancer, just to demonstrate how creative I could be in the world of illness.

Abundance

I truly believed deep down that I couldn't make it on my own. I believed after my divorce that I would never be able to make enough money to survive, and that I would die penniless like my mother and grandmother did. So guess what? I manifested multiple ways for all my hard earned money to disappear.

Love

As you well know if you read my first book, I believed then that Love was "the hardest word" So guess what? I manifested men who were alcoholics, sociopaths, narcissists and sex addicts as friends, bosses and partners. When I changed my shitty mantras, I made different choices and met my kind, gentle, supportive and loving husband Rupe.

Guidance

As you know now, I come from the self-guided sledgehammer school. So guess what? I didn't listen to my own instinct or inner guidance and so, it's no surprise then that I manifested so many major challenges in my life. I don't recommend this as a life strategy, especially if you want to live to tell the tale.

Peace

Peace? How can a person concentrate on peace when they are so busy surviving? My moment-to-moment life was an absolute nightmare of stress and exhaustion that eventually lead to a complete physical and emotional collapse.

Strength

My strength - physical, emotional and mental - were all severely tested along the way. There were times when there felt like nothing to go on for, and I seriously considered giving up. All I can tell you now about those dark times was that by the Grace Of God, it was not time for me to "cash in my chips" and leave the planet. When people now ask me why I am still alive, I jokingly reply, "Well, either God doesn't want me, or I'm hard to catch!"

Joy

During the period of Survive in my overall life journey, where it seemed that my life consisted solely of just one catastrophe after another, I didn't have much of a belief that joy even existed in the world, let alone that I deserved even one smidgeon of it. Obviously, it took a while to change that belief. Now, thank God, I feel joy every single day.

Imagination

When everything in my life was just so hard, I honestly couldn't imagine anything beyond just doing my best to take my next breath, and then my next step. Sometimes in the period of Survive that is the best we can do until we can imagine new possibilities, enter The Roundabout and then meet our new Thriving life. When my life was at its darkest, I could not imagine that the future Thriving life I have now would even be possible. However, each positive choice I made toward a healthier life improved my outlook and eventually brought me to where I am now. Sometimes, we need to begin with very small steps. First we begin to imagine that our life could become even a little bit better, before our life actually does become a lot better. There is a lot of truth to that wise old saying, "Fake it until you make it!"

Gratitude

During Survive mode, I honestly didn't feel grateful for the quality of my life. But I could be grateful that I was still breathing, I had a roof over my head, that I had just enough money for food. I took comfort in the spiritual truth that "what we focus on expands." The more I felt and expressed gratitude for everything in my life right where I was at that moment, I noticed that I began to have more things to be grateful for.

Freedom

I did not feel free living in America, struggling from one crisis to the next, with debt piling up faster than I could work to pay it off. Eventually, it became clear that both my husband and I could live quite well outside of America on half the cost of my former house mortgage.

This has been true whether we lived in Ecuador, Chile, New Zealand or Australia.

Before we left the U.S. I hadn't realized how much I had accepted subconsciously the subliminal programming from the TV culture of the 1950's that I grew up in. I learned that I had simply created my own version of what I had seen as "The Perfect Mother" in those TV shows, complete with the pearls around my neck, apron over my dress, home made meals from scratch, and fresh baked cookies for my children when they came home from school.

First I questioned the propaganda that I had completely swallowed from my culture of what "A Good Mother" and "A Good Person" were *supposed to be*. Once I understood that all my choices and decisions had been made quite naturally from all that subconscious programming which I had assumed was the only truth, only then did I feel I had the freedom to create a more authentic and honest version of what a more realistic mother and person actually was on my own terms.

Choices

During my own journey of Survive to Thrive, everything in my life was just so hard that at times death seemed to be a completely preferable choice. Even so, I just kept doing my very best to choose the next best step as each new obstacle arrived. I just kept following the clues to the best of my ability, and each tiny positive step moved me forward into a more Thriving life. With the support from therapists, teachers, meditation, reading books and attending programs about new consciousness research, choice-by-choice I began to imagine and create the Thriving life that I really wanted.

From Me To You

Mata Amritanandamayi is known throughout the world as Amma, or Mother, for her selfless love and compassion toward all beings. Her entire life has been dedicated to alleviating the pain of the poor, and those suffering physically and emotionally. The following is how Amma suggests to making peace with ourselves and others:

"Spirituality is loving yourself and accepting what comes. Detachment is the attitude of acceptance, knowing the nature of the world and people. Accept the sugar as sugar and the salt as salt, the cow as cow and the elephant as elephant. Don't try to see the cow as elephant and the elephant as cow. Though sugar and salt look the same, you put salt instead of sugar in the chai and then complain about the taste. The mistake is our own, we mistook salt for sugar.

See each at their own level, and accept them as they are. You may think very highly of someone, but after some period of interaction your opinion might wane. Also, you may think someone is useless at first, but, after spending some time with them, realize how great they are. In both these cases you made someone great and you made someone good for nothing. Both are your creation. That is why you need to see everything for what it really is. Understand the true nature of objects and people, and then live accordingly."

BOOK 10

THE KEY OF FREEDOM

"It ain't what they call you; it's what you answer to."
~W.C. Fields, Comedian

INTRODUCTION

I can remember speaking with a therapist about the subject of personal freedom a number of years ago. He asked me to close my eyes and take a moment to imagine what personal freedom could look like for me. I closed my eyes and suddenly I saw myself inside a dank, cold, dark prison cell with very thick black iron bars, and no windows.

Was this my idea of freedom? A cold prison cell? I thought to myself. If so, it was not a very liberating or free one. I mentioned to the therapist how confused I was at what I was seeing in my imagination. He asked me to keep my eyes closed and take a look around my "prison cell" that had presented itself to me. It was then that I noticed something very interesting and strange. The door to the prison cell was closed, but there was a huge ring of various sizes of black iron and other antique looking keys hanging in the lock on the inside of the cage.

Keys on the inside of a prison cell? That doesn't make any sense at all. Aren't prison keys usually on the outside of the cage to keep the door locked and the prisoner locked in? I thought to myself.

When I mentioned this image and my thoughts about it to the therapist, he suggested keeping my eyes closed, and that I walk over to the door, try to turn the key in the lock on the inside of the cell and see what happened. I went over to the door and turned the key. The key turned easily and effortlessly in the lock and then I heard the classic sound of the door unlocking with a click!

"Wow! It just clicked like it unlocked the door!" I exclaimed in utter disbelief.

He suggested that I push on the door to see if it would budge at all. I did so and the prison door swung wide open, again easily and effortlessly. I was completely stunned. It seemed, at least in this vision of things, that I not only had access to the keys to get me out of my prison cell, I also could walk out of that prison cell to complete freedom any time I chose. I just had to decide to turn the key in the lock and walk out the door. When I explained what I had just witnessed in my mind's eye, the therapist asked me a key question: "So what are you going to do? Are you going to walk out the door to your freedom, or are you going to stay inside the cell like you were before?"

At that, in my mind's eye, I turned and looked back at the black iron bars, feeling again what it felt like at first to believe that I was totally trapped inside the jail cell. Then I turned to my left and saw the wide open door, with the ring of various size keys still hanging on their ring from the keyhole. Our time was up so the therapist told me it was time to open my eyes again.

As I stood up, gathering my purse and coat, I said, "Wow. In this vision, with those keys in the lock inside of that cell, I could totally get out of that prison cell any time I wanted. What do you make of that?"

The therapist smiled and said, "I am more interested in whether you will walk through that door, or stay in that cell of your own making. Give it some thought. See you next time!"

A leap of faith

I have thought of this "prison cell with the keys in the lock on the inside" vision off and on over the years, and especially when I made my choice to finally leave America, leaving all my friends, family and work behind. The single most important thing I had to overcome in my personal pursuit of freedom was overcoming my internal resistance to, and anxiety about, choosing to do something different with my daily life and personal choices than what I had done before. This daring choice meant that I would have to make some big changes. I would have to be prepared to leave old familiar routines, daily habits, my car, favorite foods prepared in favorite restaurants, my favorite coffee and chocolate croissants in my favorite coffee shop, not to mention friends, clients, family, my doctors, my work and my home behind. I wondered to myself, *Wasn't the devil you knew better than the one you didn't know?*

However, by 2013, if I was really honest with myself, even I could see that my life in America had become a kind of prison cell of stress, anxiety and total exhaustion. I felt trapped by the medical and financial system. But was I really ready, even after all that, to open the door and leave it all behind? After all, it had been all I had known for the majority of my life, other than when I went on a vacation out of the country. Was I ready to change all that?

Leaving everything familiar was indeed a tough choice. At the same time, I had always secretly wondered what it would be like to live in a different country. As I look back now, leaving America seemed like a huge leap of faith and at the time I did it, I really wasn't sure if I was ready. But I turned the lock on the prison door of my own making, opened the door, and walked out. While I chose to liquidate whatever I had left, consolidate my assets and take a giant leap of faith to leave everything familiar to me behind, that choice is not for everyone. What I do know for sure is that for me, I have never been happier or healthier in this new life of freedom.

Five years later, I feel like my whole definition of Home has shifted. Instead of living in one home in one place until I died, I'm now like a potted plant who takes her roots with her whoever she goes. Now, my days are defined by three simple choices:

1. What I choose to do that makes me happy.

2. Where I choose to do it.

3. Who I choose to do it with.

From Me To You

The following is a blessing written by the late Louise Hay:

"Today is a time of wonderful new beginnings. I live from the belief that we are here to bless and prosper each other. The safety I seek in the outer world begins with the safety I create within myself. I am always safe and divinely protected. I feel confident about my future.

As I release the past and my fears, I embrace myself, and life, in a whole new light of freedom, compassion, joy, and love. I release any need for struggle or suffering. We deserve all that is good. And so it is!"

SURVIVE

The Key Of Freedom brought me many lessons, trials and tribulations. In the survival period of my life, I stopped asking myself, *Could this get any worse?* because any time I asked that question, it usually did. One of the most important things I needed to learn was mastering the freedom of my mind.

I was raped after a business meeting just before I turned 50 years old. I do remember distinctly while the rape was going on that I said in my mind to the rapist, *You think you are taking my soul. But my soul is mine to give and I don't choose to give it to you.* During the rape, I was amazed at the freedom of where my mind had the capacity to go.

The most surprising thought I remember was one of deep compassion for the rapist: *Who was it who hurt you so badly where you would think this violence was OK to do to any woman, let alone me.* At the time, I was in the middle of reading the incredible book, *Power vs Force*, by David R. Hawkins, M.D. Ph.D. As a matter of fact, I had it in my purse the night that I was raped. I remember glancing over at my purse and seeing the book sticking out of the top of my bag and thinking, *You may think you have all the force here. But I am the one with the Power.*

The Dalai Lama perspective

The day after I was raped, I woke up and remembered that the Dalai Lama had come to Seattle for a series of talks, hosted by The Seeds Of Compassion organization. After the previous night where I had experienced unspeakable violence, I knew I had to get to the University of Washington by the start of his first lecture. All I kept thinking as I walked from my home to the hall was, *I must get to the Dalai Lama's lecture. He will have some wisdom for me. If I listen to him, I know I can shift.*

When I sat down in the lecture hall, I felt rattled, overwhelmed and could not stop my tears from flowing. The more I listened to the Dalai Lama speak, and especially when I heard his laugh for the first time in person, I found that my mind, heart and spirit began to calm. I wasn't exactly sure why this was, but I knew I had to hear him speak more. And I proceeded to attend four more lectures over the course of the next four days.

How to handle violence

I will never forget the Dali Lama's commentary on violence in our world. When someone asked His Holiness about his monks who had been murdered in the monasteries in Tibet, a very somber expression crossed his face. The person asking the question wanted to know how The Dalai Lama managed to tolerate such violence, especially toward people he loved and cared about.

His Holiness The Dalai Lama spoke calmly and with tears in his eyes:

"Well, such violence is hard, very hard. Such violence is not to be tolerated. There is no question about that. But you asked me how I managed to tolerate it. I didn't. What I did instead was to imagine each of the people who murdered my monks as little tiny babies.

"I imagined each one of them as little tiny babies that I was actually holding in my arms. As I imagined myself gazing into their eyes, I tried to imagine each of them as whole and perfect beings, before the difficulty of their family situation or the world got to them, after which there came to be such violence in their minds and hearts.

"I imagined that their experience must have been a violence that would eventually become so great as to allow them to commit murder and other atrocities such as the murders of my monks. In imagining how hard it must have been for these beings, I felt suddenly an overwhelming sense of compassion for them.

"These were now tortured beings, who at one time very early in their lives, were born whole and complete, full of innocence, without a trace of violence within them.

"And I found in doing this, that I could not hate them. I could only feel compassion and love for them and the pain in their hearts that would allow them to commit such crimes against a fellow human being, such as my beloved monks."

I sat in my chair feeling as if the Dalai Lama was speaking directly into my own heart. It felt like he was showing me with his own example how I could turn my attention away from the person and the disturbance of violence that I had unexpectedly experienced the night before.

He was suggesting that I could instead focus my mind and heart with deep compassion toward this man who had at one time been an innocent baby too, full of hope and love and promise. I challenged myself to reflect back on the actual moments of horror and violence during the rape itself.

I found myself remembering and reflecting again what I was actually thinking at the time of the rape:

Who taught you this? Who taught you that it was OK to harm a woman like this? What a small, scared, angry man you must be to act in this way. I know you think that you are taking my soul as you hurt me here and now. But my soul and my spirit are mine to give and I do not give either or them to you here in this moment, no matter what you do to my body.

I realized that even in the midst of the violence itself there was a seed of compassion within me. I discovered that it is also true that despite the violence, we can see ourselves as having an opportunity to grow and evolve, no matter what the other person does or says.

My friends, of course, wanted vengeance, and sought all different kinds of ways to express their own outrage at what had happened to me. I could see that their powerlessness to protect me, and their fierce love for me was so overwhelming that it provoked violence within them that was so profound, they wanted to kill this, "Very Bad Man."

But I begged them all not to meet violence with more violence. I told them what I had learned from the Dalai Lama and they still found it difficult to take in, let alone do. And while I appreciated my friends rising to my defense, I had to focus all my energy on how I was going to forgive. Instead of vengeance, I felt I had to find a way to send love and compassion toward this rapist instead.

Practice makes perfect

I have tried very hard to practice what the Dalai Lama was suggesting to me that day, what he is asking of all of us, as we face violence in our world. Both the rape experience, and the words of His Holiness The

Dalai Lama, became great catalysts for both my growth and personal evolution. I learned that I had the capacity to turn this violence into a moment-to-moment spiritual practice of my own freedom of mind, body and spirit. In learning to focus my mind and heart towards true compassion at all times, I found I could reduce the natural tendency within myself to get caught up in feelings of rage, violation and helplessness that, for most people, are an inevitable result of experiencing a violent assault.

Even a year later, when I learned that this man had given me one of the deadly strains of the HPV virus, which later mutated into cervical cancer at the same time I was diagnosed with breast cancer, still I practiced compassion toward this man. I will admit that to hold true to this practice of compassion as a result of violent acts committed toward me, such as this rape, wasn't easy. But I continue to practice my internal freedom, using this practice of compassion not only toward the rapist, but also toward anyone I feel has taken advantage of my goodwill, been unkind, or stolen money from me, all acts of violence in different ways.

As I look back now on the rape, it was a gift of both great violence and humbling grace. In the end it was up to me to decide how that teaching of compassion and my freedom would be put into action in my own life. Despite periodic flashbacks of the event of PTSD, (Post Traumatic Stress Syndrome,) I refuse to allow that experience of the past to cripple my mind or my body now in the present. Every time this man comes to my mind now, I speak a silent prayer, *May he find peace. May I find peace. May All Beings find peace.*

There is no more violence, pain or suffering being sent out into the world from my mind or thoughts or heart. I am free, and I hope he is too wherever he is. Thanks to the wise words of His Holiness The Dalai Lama, and my willingness to truly try to hear what he was saying about how to embrace violence with compassion, my violent experience became transformed into a prayer of my freedom on the wind.

From Me To You

"Around us, life bursts forth with miracles – a glass of water, a ray of sunshine, a leaf, a caterpillar, a flower, raindrops. If you live in awareness, it is easy to see miracles everywhere. Each human being is a multiplicity of miracles. Eyes that see thousands of colors, shapes and forms; ears that hear a bee flying or a thunderclap; a brain that ponders a speck of dust as easy as the entire cosmos; a heart that beats in rhythm with the heartbeat of all beings. When we are tired and discouraged by life's daily struggles, we may not notice these miracles, but they are always there."

~Thich Nhat Hanh, Buddhist teacher

THE ROUNDABOUT

If I asked you what was the most powerful emotion of all, what would you guess? Anger? Sadness? Grief? Lust? Joy? Well, it turns out that the most powerful emotion of all is *humiliation*.

The Journal of Neuroscience published the results of a unique study that probed deep into human emotions back in 2014. Two Dutch scientists had conducted an experiment in which they exposed test subjects to a wide range of scenarios to evoke some of the most primal human emotions - joy, anger, etc. Subjects were hooked up to an electro-encephalogram (EEG) in order to quantitatively measure their brains' cognitive response to powerful emotions. Turns out that the most powerful emotional experience, as measured by the sheer volume of human brain activity and neurological reaction, was humiliation.

Would you have guessed that? I sure didn't. But I have to admit it makes a lot of sense when I thought more about it. I've certainly felt humiliated a lot of times in my life, and that feeling really stayed with me, long after the humiliating moment had passed. I guess it makes sense though. Deep down we human beings are social creatures. We all, to varying degrees, seek acceptance from the group.

I do understand why conformity is so much easier than standing apart from the crowd, even when the crowd makes absolutely no sense. People who don't conform are often labeled "trouble makers," "instigators," "pushy" and "a pain in the ass." At other times, independent thinkers are also labeled "thought leaders," "cultural creatives," "crazy" and even, "wise." However, what other people think of me is none of my business. My business is the only thing I need to be focused on: being kind, compassionate, caring and considerate at all times, in all places and under all conditions, with everyone as well as myself, without exception. It is my belief that this is the greatest gift any of us can give to the world.

From Me To You

Nelson Mandela is one of the great moral and political leaders of our time. He is an international hero whose lifelong dedication to the fight against racial oppression in South Africa won him the Nobel Peace Prize and the presidency of his country. Mandela spent thirty years in prison. In his book, "Long Walk To Freedom," Mandela reflected on the day he was set free:

"As I walked out the door toward the gate that would lead to my freedom, I knew if I didn't leave my bitterness and hatred behind, I'd still be in prison."

What is holding you back from your own true freedom?

THRIVE

Ultimately, freedom is not found in places, people, or things. Yet we travel to the far corners of this earth in search of "The Answer." We travel by car, bus, bike or plane to a distant land hoping to meet someone - a master, a guru, a priest or average person - who has found "The Answer" and can teach it to us. We watch movie after movie, read book after book in hope of finding this "Answer" without leaving our couch or armchair. We drink alcohol, smoke everything from cigarettes to crack cocaine, try other various mind altering drugs, have amazing sex or pursue an extreme sports thrill or other adrenaline high to hopefully fill our void of excitement on our way to soothing or avoiding our inner angst.

Many of us hope that somehow other people will change according to our ideas of what would make things better; we think that when they do change, we will feel better or at least different than we do now. Those of us who pursue this route are attached to the vain idea that people can or should be able to be different than they actually are.

We try all kinds of both spiritual and other alternatives in an effort to soothe the savage beast inside of us. When nothing seems to work, we get very angry and frustrated with ourselves, the world, and God. In some more extreme cases, when some have come to the end of their rope, they kill themselves in a desperate way out of their constant, unrelenting inner mental, emotional or physical pain.

All of these pursuits are connected to that most vain of human hopes that something *outside* of us is going to finally give us relief, or make us feel happy, content or fulfilled on the *inside*. No matter how hard we work or how much we believe to the contrary, people places or things do not free us from endless desires or ultimately satisfy us. So we keep searching, hoping and buying experiences and stuff, and talking to other people because we are absolutely convinced that one day we will find the

"Perfect Answer" which will finally lay to rest all that has relentlessly drives us for more, more, more, all the time.

However, I discovered that I had things a bit backwards in my thinking and beliefs about this. All of those things outside of me that I was convinced were, are, or one day would be, "The Answer," only served to keep me stuck in Survival mode, and also going around and around in endless circles on The Roundabout of my life. One of the biggest lessons of my life has been that *true Freedom is found within me*. I searched everywhere in the entire world for "The Answer," and there it was inside of me all along, just patiently waiting for me to discover it! What an irony, right? And people say that God doesn't have a sense of humor!

My connection to the Love of God within was where I discovered my Ultimate Freedom lies, and this Love is complete, nothing needs to be added to or subtracted from It. Now, this Love travels with me wherever I go, and lights up the world for me so I can truly See. This Love is expressed through me to whomever I meet along the way in my travels, whether it is only to the corner grocery store or the far reaches of Africa. This discovery for me was "a real mindblower" as they say. Thomas Kuhn calls moments like this a "paradigm shift," which he defines as a "willingness to see things differently from an expanded perspective."

It would appear that my personal "paradigm shift," required a combination of severe suffering: physical and emotional pain, profound grief and loss, terrifying fear and debilitating shame. My journey to Freedom also included searching the world over until I was willing to acknowledge and accept that my cherished beliefs of what I was absolutely convinced must be "The Answer," were actually not correct or even true. When I discovered that I was *only subject to that which I believed as true*, I was able to finally surrender myself to another reality entirely. Before I believed and fully participated in all the content of the world's glamour, and then I finally let utterly and completely go of it all.

In an All-Inclusive Moment, I surrendered my entire being into a completely different context of God The Universe: Love.

Letting go

I can see now that my thoughts are actual things with energy and form, and each of us does indeed "create our own reality." Every thought we have is attached to a feeling, which is attached to a story, which perpetuates other thoughts and feelings ad infinitum in our minds. I now finally understand that our thoughts are caused in part by repressed and suppressed feelings. When we make the choice to let those feelings go, without condemning, judging or resisting them, and without trying to modify or change each feeling in any way, the millions of other thoughts attached to them also disappear over time.

My brother Bob had told me many years ago to accept "the power of my mind to move all obstacles out of my way." The Shaman Dan told me I "could change my life in an instant." Dr. Sun, the Quigong Master proved to me that any erroneous belief I accepted as true, whether created by me or given to me by someone else, had the potential to manifest as an illness. He also taught me, "understanding and letting go of mistaken beliefs could heal me." Now, I can finally understand what they were all trying to communicate: the power is within us to conquer any and all pain, suffering, and even that which we call "terminal" illness. It is up to each of us to bring any and all remaining mistaken beliefs up to a conscious level, and then correct them, so that we can create our own version of a truly healthy and Thriving life.

Ego juice

In order to be able to let go of some of our more negative and difficult feelings and beliefs, sometimes it is necessary to go a few steps deeper under them to discover the payoff or "ego juice" that we receive and actually crave from both ourselves and the outside world. These payoffs often showed up in the form of the "ego juice" of emotions of pity and sympathy. When we tell our terrible stories over and over again, we fuel and reinforce our own perception of ourselves as a helpless victim. When we secretly hope for, or even actively solicit, comments from other people such as, "Oh you poor thing," what we are really craving is that they acknowledge and validate our suffering. This craving for acknowledgement of suffering is a really clever form that the "ego juice" payoffs take, as they serve to prevent us from ever getting out of our own self pity.

At the same time, when we tell these negative stories about ourselves over and over again, this keeps us stuck, always focusing our mind and also our beliefs on our "negative past." The unfortunate consequence of this choice then energetically draws in and manifests more of the same type of negative experience in our present moment, and serves to confirm a basic and profound spiritual principle, "Like attracts like."

As I started really paying attention, I noticed that there were a few places in my life where my own craving for "ego juice" surprised me. I noticed that within my own overblown sense of "moral outrage," I was fueling a relentless desire to help or to change others, solve all the problems of the world, and save all those whom I considered to be the downtrodden or needy. I also noticed other forms of this "ego juice" within myself as the adrenaline boost of anger over both all the suffering I saw in the world, and all the suffering I had been through in my own life. It was so easy for me to say things like, "That just isn't fair." and "Why me?"

As I began to pay even closer attention, I noticed that the more "moral outrage" I focused upon, the more my own mind quite effortlessly created more things for me to notice and be upset about, both around the world and in my own life. In another mind blowing instant I saw that I was actually creating a world of rage and attack thoughts within my own mind; I was creating a literal hell on earth for myself everywhere I looked. As I began to pay attention and examine each thought I had, both about the world and what I had been through in my life, I finally came to a rather startling conclusion that everything happening in each person's life was unfolding according to the level of expectation and consciousness that I - and everyone else - held within their own minds.

If each and every person created their own subjective reality at every moment according to their specific level of consciousness, then *there is no one single truth that applies to everyone*. Rather all "truth" is a subjective conclusion that each of us make which makes sense only to us. This suggests that everyone and everything are perfect just they are, and so nothing actually needs to be changed or fixed. It was actually a huge relief to discover that everything in this visible world was unfolding just as it needed to, and that I was not actually responsible for fixing anyone or anything.

I also learned that not only were every single one of my choices in perfect alignment with what became my reality, I was also the only person responsible for the further evolution of my own consciousness. It became increasingly clear that everything I had experienced and endured in my life had been perfectly designed for making my deepest and most profound growth possible. This meant that at every single moment, I was having exactly the experience I needed, in the perfect form, amount, and degree to facilitate exactly the lessons I had chosen to learn in my life.

The Pathway Of Surrender

One of the most important actions I took was to release my "victim story" so that I could embrace a new interpretation of my life story. While I had the creative power of the Source from which I came to create a living hell for myself, full of pain and suffering, I also had complete free will to design heaven on earth, full of joy and peace. Which reality I chose to create was totally up to me.

One day, I hurt myself badly practicing kite boarding in too heavy winds for my skill level. Soon after that, while sitting at the beach drinking coffee with my husband, I was swarmed with biting ants, mosquitos and flies. In a matter of a few minutes, I was covered with bites, and I counted at least twenty-five bites on my stomach alone. Between the pain and itching I was absolutely miserable. I decided to practice a new "Letting Go" technique I had recently read about in *Letting Go: The Pathway of Surrender*, the final book written by David R. Hawkins, M.D., Ph.D.

As I began to put the concepts of this book into practice, I realized that the words, "pain" and "itching" in relationship to biting insects were just programs I had accepted. I noticed that in reality, if I was "in pain" or "itching" from a bug, mosquito or ant bite, I was actually only feeling a specific body sensation. If I added all the victim stories I had about "Mosquitos always bite me and never seemed to torture anyone else," or "These things 'always' happen to me," the bites got more painful and the itching also became worse. When I attempted to let go of or surrender the labels of "pain," "itching" and "suffering," I noticed that I also had many additional feelings of anger and frustration.

I began to notice other angry attack thoughts and negative feelings that were attached specifically to mosquitos and biting flies. I observed that whenever I turned my attention specifically to the discomfort of my many bites, I felt the strong emotion of hatred for every part of nature too: the sand that bred the ants, the wind that had caused my pain and suffering during my "kitemare" accident, the water that bred every mosquito, and every tree that let the biting flies and mosquitos stop and rest upon them. I noticed that was even angry at my own body for being born with "sweet blood" that any biting insect within a hundred miles seemed to sense and come looking for.

Following the instructions in *Letting Go: The Pathway of Surrender*, I did my best to release each thought as it came up – no matter what it was - with the words, "I surrender this to you Oh Lord." As each thought and feeling came up, I just kept on releasing all the energy behind each of them, over and over. Eventually, underneath all that anger, and feelings of victimhood, I began to notice a different emotion that was beginning to make itself known; this emotion was moving me toward tears. As I allowed my tears to begin to flow, I identified many feelings of helplessness which were attached to the words, "Why me?" I did my best to simply release that feeling of helplessness too.

Eventually underneath it all was a terrible agonizing feeling of primal terror of being doomed to spend my entire life in agonizing suffering and pain. I did my best to surrender all the energy behind that primal terror, and all those victim stories I had been telling myself. After I fully released and surrendered my terror, suddenly there was a stunning silence. There were no thoughts. No feelings. No suffering. Nothing. I couldn't even feel any pain or itching. I actually felt truly and completely peaceful for the first time in my life. This complete and utter peace was so unexpected and delightful I began to laugh. Over the next few days, I observed that I healed much faster from all the bites. The best part was the inner peace and total freedom from any and all suffering continued long past the time that all the bites had healed.

Over time, as I experimented moving both in and out of this truly peaceful state, I learned that in order for me to remain longer in a totally peaceful state, all I had to do, was to completely surrender to God any and all negative or difficult feelings as they came up, layer upon layer. Now, any time I notice that my mind and ego are suddenly becoming busy, busy, busy, kicking into high gear with my opinions or judgments about everything and everyone, I surrender all of those opinions and judgments' to God too. Invariably, my peace returns.

Mind chatter

Have you ever noticed that our minds do a kind of endless, and rather meaningless color commentary non-stop while we are awake? Our minds appear to be constantly rating, judging and grading everything and everyone.

"Wow! You are amazing!"

"Oh that was certainly a really stupid thing to do. What was that person thinking?"

"That person certainly does think they know everything now don't they? People like that are so incredibly annoying."

"I really hate that….fill in the blank."

Have you noticed that this voice in your head never shuts up? One time I asked my mind, very politely, to "Please stop thinking." It could not do it. On it went with it's endless "blah… blah… blah…" thoughts. That's when I began to get even more curious.

The Kitchen Sink

As a kid living in the Bay Area, we had this amazing ice cream shop called Fentons Creamery. It was everybody's favorite place to go to either celebrate or commiserate. While there was delicious food like their legendary crab sandwiches, most people went to Fentons for the ice cream. My favorite ice cream was Swiss Milk Chocolate, a yummy, creamy, malty, heavenly rich chocolate chip. That ice cream was my version of heaven on earth.

At Fentons, you could also order things like a "Black and Tan," layers of chocolate and coffee or toasted almond ice cream, alternating with caramel and chocolate sauce, all topped with a massive dollop of whipped cream and a cherry. Another choice was a "Black and White," vanilla ice cream alternating with chocolate and marshmallow sauce. I swear either one of these were massive, with the ice cream piled high over the fountain glass at least 18 inches tall (a little under a half a meter.) These confections kept any kid busy for at least half an hour. Sometimes it took two of us to finish one.

However, there was another "piece de resistance" on the menu at Fentons: The Kitchen Sink. This bad boy came delivered to your table in a large metal sink. Whoever came up with this idea probably thought it would appeal to buff football players trying to outdo each other in terms of their machismo. The Kitchen Sink had every single flavor of ice cream (35 of them at last count), every single sauce - chocolate, caramel, marshmallow - nuts, cherries and whipped cream, all sitting on top of an entire bunch of bananas?!

So as I said earlier, my politely asking my mind to stop thinking exercise was kind of like trying to get through eating A Kitchen Sink at Fentons…never gonna happen. The mind *thinks*. That's what it *does*. That is *it's true nature*. So I just decided recently not to fight my mind anymore. Instead, I decided to treat it like a very sick and deluded child who needed my care and compassion.

I also have compassion for myself knowing that that sometimes I am just not able to resist the slings and arrows of my outrageous thinking. My very clever ego mind still gets away from me sometimes, rambling and ranting. At those moments, I feel tempted to respond, "Get back here and sit still you rebellious two year old child!" However, then I stop and remind myself that it is always my choice, and I always have the freedom as to whether I will respond to the thoughts in my mind or not. I try to keep in mind the wisdom of the words of W.C. Fields who said, "It ain't what they call you; it's what you answer to."

Our Monkey Minds

This new approach has changed the game of Mary Anne's Inner Monkey Mind forever. My mind used to be a very scary place to go alone, like walking into a hall of mirrors in a fun house. Thoughts would go through my head like,

Do I really have thunder thighs like my brother once said?

Do my children hate me?

Should I buy that gadget I saw on TV that promises to save me loads of time?

Are my friends just pretending to like me?

Am I completely unlovable?

While even as I could recognize that my thoughts were at times way out of proportion and distorted, my mind was just like when I saw myself reflected in those fun house mirrors; it was perversely compelling, fascinating, and at time quite funny. But now at least, I didn't have to believe everything I thought. When I didn't have any attachments or aversions to anything, I was free.

I know now that I have the capacity to simply feel any feeling that comes up in my mind, without labeling it or putting even a name on it, and then let go of the energy behind that feeling. I know now that I have the capacity to stop identifying with my more distorted thoughts, feelings and beliefs as true, or even real.

At the deepest level of my Being, now I know that I am only subject to what I hold in my mind as true. By the same token, I know now that I am only subject to a negative thought or belief if I say it applies to me. Beyond everything is my true Self, rock solid and infinitely fluid. God is in charge of a beautiful and loving universe the moves from perfection to perfection. At the deepest level of my true Self I now know that I am totally and completely free to choose my reality, and what I believe, at every moment.

Judgment

One day not long ago, I was meditating on the idea of releasing all judgment of myself, and others. All of a sudden, I heard in my mind, *Who made you everyone else's judge, jury and executioner? You judge everyone and every thing, all the time, every single moment of every day. What actually makes you think you can do a better job than God, The Source of All Creation? Do you have more power than That which created and continues to create everything in The Universe, ad infinitum, World Without End?*

I really had to stop and give this idea some thought. If it was true, then I no longer would have to feel a relentless urge to *"fix"* everyone and everything that crossed my path. For a fleeting moment all I felt was what can only be described as Unconditional Love and monumental relief. Everything, including me, was in an endless dance together with God Creating Itself. It was *Perfect*. It was as if God said in a silent transmission to the deepest part of my own Heart:

"I am All knowing and All Creation. It is not your job to fix or change even one iota of anything that exists in my Perfect Creation. Everything that exists in the Universe is perfect just exactly the way It Is, and that includes you Mary Anne.

Your acceptance of, and surrender to, the Perfect Beauty Of All That Is is all you need to do now. All Is Love. Surrender the heart of your being into the Perfect Love that Is, and you will finally know forever in your heart the perfect Peace that passes all understanding.

From Me To You

Dr. Joe Dispenza, one of the pioneers in the science of epigenetics, and author of *Breaking The Habit Of Being Yourself* and *You Are The Placebo* suggests, "Our thoughts, beliefs and emotions have a huge impact on our health and ability to heal. The latest science reveals that we are not victims of unchangeable genes, nor should we buy into a scary prognosis. The fact is we have more control over our health and life than we have been taught to believe. This is very good news indeed."

CONCLUSION

I recently heard an amazing story about a polar bear. This polar bear lived in a zoo and the zoo management where he lived decided to redesign his habitat. To keep the polar bear safe during the process of creating this new and much more beautiful, expansive habitat, the zookeepers created a large cage and put the polar bear inside.

After a very short while, the zookeepers noticed something strange. The polar bear demonstrated a behavior it had never shown before. The polar bear would pace to one end of the cage, rear up on its hind legs, and then turn around, pace to the other end of the large cage, and then rear up and down again. This pacing behavior would go on for hours and hours until the polar bear finally exhausted itself and went to sleep. The next day, the pacing and rearing up and down would resume.

As the zookeepers became increasingly concerned about what appeared to be this polar bear's nervous and obsessive behavior, they did everything in their power to speed up the renovation of the polar bears new habitat. Eventually, after nine months, the zookeepers opened the door to one end of the cage and stepped back. The polar bear came up to the open door, and right where the door had been, the polar bear reared up on its hind legs and down again, turned around and paced back to the other end of the cage and did the same thing.

Next, the zookeepers removed the other door at the other end of the large cage. The polar bear kept going from one end of the cage to the other, with the same rearing up behavior, as if in a trance. Next, the zookeepers took down the sides of the cage and the polar bear continued to pace from one end of the cage to the other, doing the same behavior. *The polar bear believed that it was still in a cage, even though the cage wasn't there.*

Eventually the zookeepers put a leash on the polar bear and dragged it out of the area where the cage was and led it out into it's beautiful new habitat. The polar bear looked back one last time at where the cage had been, turned back around, and then bounded off into its new environment.

I think we humans act very much like that polar bear at times of profound change in our lives. We all tend to pace back and forth in our very narrow cages of belief about who we think we are, what we are capable of, and what we believe is possible for us. All the while there is a huge, grand, amazing and wonderful world out there to explore. We all have the capacity for freedom. If we dare to take a leap of faith, turn the key to our prison door and walk out, we can embrace our freedom once and for all.

From Me To You

I have found the following Forgiveness Prayer to be enormously healing and freeing for my mind, body and spirit. The healing power of this prayer is limitless, and it has truly changed my life at a most profound level.

Forgiveness Prayer

"If there is anyone or anything that has hurt me in the past, knowingly or unknowingly, I forgive and release it.

"If I have hurt anyone or anything in the past, knowingly or unknowingly, I forgive and release it.

"If I hurt myself in the past, knowingly or unknowingly, I forgive and release it."

Note: Our "past" consists of anything prior to "this breath." If this prayer is done at the end of the day, it has the potential to clear any negativity that builds walls of separation both within us, and between us and other people. Working with this prayer for 32 days consecutively has the potential to heal what now may feel like insurmountable chasms of pain and separation in relationships with self, God/Spirit/Source, other people, and any past situation that has happened in our lives. It is not necessary to know the root cause of anything; we just have to be willing to forgive. Forgiveness is the key that opens the floodgates of Love. Working with this prayer was quite transformative for me. Try it and see if it works for you.

BOOK 11
THE KEY OF POWER

"Wisdom tells me I am nothing.

Love tells me I am everything.

Between the two my life flows."

~Nisargadatta Maharaj

INTRODUCTION

In order to accomplish their agendas and goals, people, governments and social structures in the world generally rely on varying levels of force, from cleverly subtle to profoundly cruel. On the other hand, all of the truly positive transformation and evolution over the centuries of human life in the world - spiritual, political and social - have come about through a full understanding and use of power. One of the most pivotal events in global history, and one of the best displays of the concept of true power that I can think of, came about through the mind and actions of one very humble person: Mahatma Gandhi.

Mahatma Gandhi was a small, ninety-pound man who single-handedly overcame the British Empire, which at that time ruled two-thirds of the face of the globe. Gandhi not only brought the British Empire to its knees, he effectively ended a century of colonialism. Gandhi accomplished this by simply standing for a powerful principle: the intrinsic dignity of man and his right to freedom, sovereignty, and self-determination. Fundamental to these principles, in Gandhi's view, was the fact that such rights are a human right, by virtue of the divinity of his creation. Gandhi believed that human rights are not granted by any earthly power. Gandhi considered these human rights, like those of the "unalienable rights" written into the United States Constitution, to be inherent in the nature of man himself and by consequence of his creation.

The violence used by the British Empire, and other Empires over the centuries, have all used force as a means of control and domination. In contrast, Gandhi forbade all use of violence, because both he and his cause were aligned with power. Gandhi was a man who expressed universal principles. As a result, he was able to unite the will of the people around him in India. In the course of world history, when the will of the people is united and aligned with universal principles, it is virtually unconquerable. Gandhi demonstrated to all people around the world the true power of "selflessness" versus the force of "self-interest," which up until that point had been exemplified by the British Empire.

Personally, the concept of true power mystified me until relatively recently. For most of my life I had the concept of power totally confused with the concept of force. It was my belief - and life strategy - that if I applied enough energy or force over time on whatever it was I wanted to accomplish – a door I wanted to open, a job I wanted to have, something I wanted to learn, a person I wanted to change – whatever it was I wanted would give way. I felt that I was guided by the sheer force of my focus, hard work, and intention, and this made me feel strong. In fact, I was completely convinced that this sense of strength was what power was supposed to feel like. Eventually my consistent application of force in all areas of my life led me to two very important conclusions:

1. However strong my force, will or determination was, it never fundamentally changed anything. People always and at all times are who they are by virtue of their level of their consciousness. This means that they only change when they are ready and willing. People are always doing the best they can with what they know and believe at that time. Hawkins reminds us over and over to keep this truth in mind, "If people could do better, they would do better."

2. The force of my own will, tenacity and determination most definitely helped me persevere as I overcame many difficult life challenges, but my application of force never brought me any lasting peace, love or joy.

I now understand that my strong belief that force was far superior to power was mistaken. After many attempts over the years to work, reason and intellectualize myself out of difficulties, I finally learned that no amount of force was ever going to help me learn to love myself, or help me evolve into a truly Thriving human being.

My use of continual force rather than power also contributed greatly to the major suffering of my life. Just like a ship whose bearing is one degree off compass will eventually find itself hundreds of miles off course, my consistent use of force steered and locked my life course on the destination of illness, exhaustion and frustration. In essence, by using force instead of power, I actually created survival mode for myself in every area of my life.

With time and perspective, I can see now that much of my life was the true definition of insanity: trying the same unsuccessful forceful approach, over and over, and expecting a different result. When I realized that I had been banging my head against the same futile wall of force, over and over again for decades, I tried to avoid sinking into despair or harsh judgment of myself over all the time and energy I had already spent in what was clearly misguided effort and energy. Instead, I did my best to have compassion for myself remembering that it truly was the best I could do with what I knew and understood at that time. I reminded myself over and over that if I could have done better in any situation - and with using less force - I would have.

Eventually, as I found better information and teachers of integrity, I learned that all I really needed to do was adjust my technique not my aspiration. One day this particular statement of Hawkins hit me right between the eyes, "We change the world not by what we say or do, but as a consequence of what we have become." At that moment, I chose to set a different course for my life of simply Being, not being busy doing or talking all the time. I began to steer my ship towards the very different destination of power.

Much to my surprise I discovered this destination lead to true and lasting wisdom: less is always more, being is more joyful than doing, surrendering is more peaceful than fighting to be right, and the use of power rather than force would lead me back to my true Home as a soul. After a lifetime of searching the world "out there" for all the answers I was seeking, I was to finally discover that the answers to all of my most important questions would be found "in here," deep within me. As far as the state of enlightenment, and his own subjective experience, David R. Hawkins, M.D., Ph.D., reassured me, "The state doesn't have to be sought; it is always within us."

From Me To You

Whenever we attempt to learn something new, we may fail many times before we are able to acquire the necessary skills and understanding we need to master it. The Tibetans have a wonderful and wise saying, "Seven times down. Eight times up." As long as we keep trying and don't give up, that is all that matters.

Learning in life is a never-ending process. Ultimately, every moment of our lives is always a choice between which aspect – positive or negative – that we're going to allow ourselves to act on and become. Each decision to choose a positive action of integrity over a negative one lacking in integrity has the power to transform both our lives and the world. Remember, as Hawkins said, "We change the world not by what we say or do, but as a consequence of what we have become."

SURVIVE

The all-time bestseller, *Man's Search for Meaning*, was written by a Jewish man who had just lost everyone he loved, and everything he owned, in the Holocaust. When Viktor Frankl, emaciated from the concentration camps, returned to his beloved Vienna, no one was there to meet him. His mother had been gassed at Auschwitz. His brother had been killed in another camp. His wife, Tilly, had starved to death in the women's camp at Bergen-Belsen. Now, he wondered, what was the point of his life?

Frankl later said, "I decided not to commit suicide—at least not before I had reconstructed my first book, *The Doctor and the Soul*. After Frankl finished that book, friends who read it asked him to write another book, this time about his personal experience in the concentration camps. Viktor Frankl poured out *Man's Search for Meaning* in just nine days. Seventy years later, his book remains a classic guide for people of all faiths. In fact, Mother Teresa encouraged all of her novitiates to read *Man's Search for Meaning* as part of their spiritual formation.

The terrible cruelty and inhumanity of The Holocaust was the epitome of the use of force. However, in his book, *Man's Search for Meaning*, Viktor Frankl spoke about where true power lies within every human being: "Everything can be taken from a man but one thing: the last of the human freedoms—to choose one's attitude in any given set of circumstances, to choose one's own way." Frankl also added, "When we are no longer able to change a situation, we are challenged to change ourselves." To me, Frankls's decision to change himself in relation to his devastating circumstances is the essence of the concept of true spiritual power.

Each of us must dig deep within ourselves in order to access sufficient courage to face our suffering. Next, we must find a way to figure out how to survive whatever devastating experience we are faced with. Finally, we need to learn how to create a Thriving life beyond our suffering. Each of us must discover a way to make meaning of our lives, and that meaning must include our suffering as well as our triumphs. As we attempt to do this, another thing to keep in mind is that we cannot expect other people to understand, or even empathize with, our suffering. They are suffering too in their own way, even if that may not always be obvious to us. According to Alexander Vesely, (Vicktor Frankl's Grandson,) his Grandfather always said, "Never compare suffering. Everyone has their own Auschwitz."

Each person's life journey is their own path and composed of millions of choices they make along the way. While it may be tempting for us to judge, the truth is that only God has the full picture of everything that each person has been through. Only God knows the choices they were faced with, the choices they made, and ultimately the choices that they have had to live with.

So how can we make meaning out of our suffering? Viktor Frankl suggests that there are three ways to help us uncover meaning in the truly dark periods of suffering in life:

1. The "Creative" way - write a book, make a movie, create a business.

2. The "Experiential" way - encounter another person, love them in their singularity and uniqueness, or go somewhere that changes your life.

3. The "Attitudinal" way - this is the path for those who face unavoidable suffering such as an incurable illness or the Death Camps. You can't escape the condition, but you can choose your attitude toward it, and fill it with meaning, which becomes an inner triumph.

No matter what challenge I have faced in my life, especially the deepest and most profound dark moments when I felt that I had lost my will to live, Fankl's three ways outlined above helped me to both uncover meaning, and also to survive.

Logotherapy

Another aspect of Viktor Frankl's work I have found really helpful during dark times is his concept of "Logotherapy." The word "Logos" comes from the Greek word, "meaning." The word "therapy" is related to "healing." So "Logotherapy" means "healing through meaning." Frankl struggled to have faith in humankind after the war. Through "Logotherapy," Frankl created a theory of humanity which might at first appear simple, but was actually quite profound in its implication: always look for the best in people. Frankl was not interested in the worst version of anyone or spending any time analyzing that. Frankl focused in on the "best version" of you, and then acted as if you were already there. He would say, "If you take a man as he is, you make him worse. If you take a man as he can be, you help him become who he can be, the best version of who he is."

I discovered that using this approach has an uplifting effect on both me and other people. (Note: Frankl meant "women" too—he used the male pronoun for all people that was in common use at the time.)

Frankl never denied the horrors of humanity. He had come out of the Holocaust, one of the worst possible savagery human's ever inflicted upon one another. What I found most profound of all was *his attitude about this savagery*, how he witnessed and re-contextualized it in his own mind: "After all, man is that being who invented the gas chambers of Auschwitz; however, he is also that being who entered those gas chambers upright, with the Lord's Prayer or the Shema Yisrael on his lips."

I want to be extremely clear here that Viktor Frankl never said that the situation at Auschwitz was "meaningful." Instead, he focused on looking at the idea of what meaning could possibly be derived by understanding what led to the Holocaust in the past, so that human beings of the future would have a chance to prevent it from ever happening again.

We can use this powerful way of looking at suffering and apply it to our own lives as well. We may discover that our suffering does not have any inherent meaning at all. However, we can make the choice to ascribe a meaning of our own to our suffering. This choice can become a powerful catalyst for deep understanding and resolution within our hearts, so that whatever difficult experience we have had does not repeat again in our lifetime, and we gain a powerful internal freedom from it. Sometimes, that is the very best we can do, especially when someone has been inordinately cruel, or a past situation haunts us or feels absolutely unresolvable. We forgive, not because it is necessarily deserved, but because we choose to allow peace within our own hearts. In so doing, we also choose to release ourselves from future suffering in relation to that person or situation which we may feel is absolutely unreconcilable.

Hitler, Mother Teresa and Death Eaters

Throughout my life, I have also taken great comfort, insight and inspiration from Frankls' words, "There's a Hitler and a Mother Teresa in all of us." None of us are perfect. We all make mistakes, which we later regret when we discover that we have chosen the less than positive option in a given circumstance. By the same token, there are times where we even surprise ourselves with our amazing capacity for generosity, compassion, forgiveness and understanding. In the Harry Potter movies, the character of Sirius Black tells the young wizard Harry Potter: "The world isn't split into Good People and Death Eaters. We've all got both light and dark inside of us. What matters is the part we choose to act on. That's who we really are."

To make the positive choice from the place of power is the greatest of all challenges and accomplishment in human life. What part of your own life are you choosing to act on right now? Choosing between the Mother Teresa or Hitler - the Power or Force aspects within us - will always determine both our level of consciousness, and also our destiny. Any choice made from integrity changes both our present and our future. Choosing power over force in any situation impacts our ability to move out of Survival mode into The Roundabout, and ultimately our ability to truly Thrive as well.

I would not presume to tell anyone how to live their life. All I can do is share what I know from my own life experience and hope that sharing both my perspective and the tools that I found useful along the way, will help steer you in a more positive direction. What worked for me might not be the best choice for you. It is up to each person to create meaning out of his or her own life experiences, and to find their own way to their unique version of a Thriving life. In the end, everyone's journey in life is between them and God alone.

From Me To You

In her book, *Big Magic,* Elizabeth Gilbert poses what she considers "the fiercest question of all: "What would you do even if you knew that you very well might fail?' In other words, '"What do you love doing so much that the words *failure* and *success* essentially become *irrelevant?* What do you love even more than you love your own ego? How fierce is your trust in that love?" Your answers to those questions have the power to change your life in a radical way." Gilbert goes on to suggest, 'This, I believe, is the central question upon which all creative living hinges: "Do you have the courage to bring forth the treasures that are hidden within you?"

Why not follow your curiosity and live your life doing all the things you love? There is true power, wisdom and potentially a beautiful future in that choice.

THE ROUNDABOUT

There were many trips around The Roundabout as I learned how to let go of the use of force as a way of life. At first, I couldn't believe how many times a day that I noticed how my ego wanted to take over everything in my never ending fight to be right, how many self righteous opinions and judgments I had of everyone and everything, and also how much anger, frustration and constant adrenaline rush this all created within me. I discovered that learning how to surrender to the power of God was harder than I ever expected, and was to become a moment-to-moment spiritual practice for me.

I just kept at it, surrendering each challenging feeling and experience as they came up, surrendering each time I caught sight of yet another area of force I had been using or relying on. This process went on every waking moment, and quite frankly, at first it was exhausting. During that period, I took great comfort in the words of the 14th-Century Christian Mystic Meister Eckhart who said, "The outer work can never be small if the inner work is great. And the outer work can never be great if the inner work is small."

Mystics and Sages throughout recorded history have all pointed their students toward spending as much time and focus as possible on realizing their "inner greatness." These Mystics and Sages have confirmed from their own subjective experience that everything in the visible world seen with our eyes actually comes from the inner planes. While for me this idea was a bit unsettling at first, it strongly suggested that each of us indeed does create our own version of reality from within us. If that is so, then we must also have the power to change our outer reality from within. There is a traditional Sufi saying which promises: "He who tastes, knows," but I was not fully convinced just yet. While I could intellectually agree that tasting chocolate is more delicious and compelling than studying its chemical components, I didn't honestly know for sure what this saying actually meant in a spiritual context.

Stonehenge and The Sword

About this time, during a meditation I was reminded of a significant experience from years before, and one I had completely forgotten about. This experience had taken place inside Stonehenge, under the direction of Emma Restall Orr, British neo-Druid, Priest and Joint Chief of the British Druid Order (BDO) at that time (with Philip Shallcrass.) Before the ceremony, Emma had instructed me to buy a replica of Excalibur, the fabled Sword of Kind Arthur. I was instructed to look for it in one of the shops in Glastonbury and then bring it with me to the sacred Druid ceremony, which was to begin at dawn the following day.

As the sun came up through the Eastern Gate of Stonehenge, I was instructed to hold my sword up to the light of the sun. Next, Emma poured sacred water from the Chalice Well of Glastonbury from one end of the blade to the other. She then blessed both the sword and me.

Next Emma instructed me to lower my sword and pierce the tip of the earth of Stonehenge about one inch in depth. Intuitively I felt something terrifyingly powerful would happen if I did what she had asked of me.

I vigorously shook my head, "No." I kept my eyes firmly locked with Emma's as I kept shaking my head, back and forth.

Emma shouted in a startlingly powerful and commanding voice, "Do it! Now!"

I took a deep breath, lowered my sword from over my head, and pierced the earth of Stonehenge with the tip of my sword. All of a sudden a jolt of tremendously powerful energy came up from the earth, through the blade, and into my hands. Then this energy spread out from both my hands into and throughout my entire body.

That's the moment when my steel broadsword began to melt. The blade softened of its own accord and began to bend. It kept bending over toward me until it reached a full C shape, with the handle of the sword completely parallel with the ground. As I stared at my own two hands holding the impossible, time seemed to stand still. I felt a Presence that was incredibly soft, gentle, loving, melting, and paradoxically, simultaneously rock like, immutable, and all powerful. My experience of this Presence as I held the sword went on for a time.

Then, for reasons I cannot explain, it was as if I was suddenly "snapped out of it," like going from zero gravity to gravity again. At the same time, the sword blade suddenly snapped back to straight again. If I had not had a really firm grip on the hilt, this powerful, electrical energy would have sent the entire sword flying completely out of my hands. In spite of that incredible brute force, somehow I had managed to keep a firm grip on the sword.

I was of course completely freaked out by what had just occurred. I was holding a sword that was made from such strong inflexible steel that I physically could not bend with my hands even if I had wanted to. Yet when I pierced the tip of the earth, this same sword had turned fluid, effortlessly folding over into a complete C shape with absolutely no force at all on my part. Then, as if it had a mind of its own, the sword had returned, not only back to solid steel, but also back to its original shape. It was like something out of a science fiction movie.

Once again my eyes locked with Emma's. She had a rather enigmatic look on her face. I then heard Emma say quietly, "Very good. That's enough now. Remove your sword."

After we left Stonehenge that day, I asked Emma to explain this powerful experience to me. First we discussed the energy of Stonehenge. She asked me if I knew that the U.S. Air Force and the Royal Air Force would not fly over Stonehenge, because every time that they did, their navigation systems became disabled. I had not known that. Then she asked me where I thought the energy of Stonehenge really was. I just smiled. My own recent subjective experience with the sword had confirmed where it was: under the ground.

Emma further explained, "Most people believe that the energy of Stonehenge is above the ground, radiating from the huge rocks arranged in a circle. In fact, the powerful energy of Stonehenge runs in a circle just one inch below the ground." So that's what I had tapped with the tip of my sword. When I asked Emma why she had not explained to me in advance what was going to happen, she smiled mischievously and said, "It was a surprise." When I asked why she had done this Druidic ceremony with me she said simply, "You needed it." Then she clarified her reasoning further, "I felt you needed to have an experience way beyond your ordinary thinking mind. The energy of Stonehenge jolted you out of the illusion of this world and into The Real Reality."

For a long time, I didn't understand what Emma meant by "The Real Reality." However now that I was getting farther away from my ordinary way of relating to the outside world, and was being guided further to the world within me, I realized that my sword experience at Stonehenge had been an advance preview of things to come in my spiritual journey. It was a brief glimpse of the true power and Ultimate Reality of God, that only now, nearly twenty years later, I was just beginning to understand.

Alchemy

One of my favorite books is Paulo Cohelo's, *The Alchemist*. The concept of the proverbial "search for one's heart's desire," and being willing to search to the ends of the earth to find it, had always really spoken to me. This idea had also piqued both my interest and curiosity. I knew that Cohelo's book was a fairy tale on one level, but at another level I really wanted to believe that he was showing me The Way. Was Cohelo actually saying that we have the capacity to "turn ourselves into the wind?" Did this become literally possible when we finally became one with Ultimate Reality?

I had certainly tried everything I could think of up to that point. I had read book after book about everyone else's spiritual journey, attended what felt like hundreds of seminars and workshops, and experimented with many different types of spiritual modalities. I worked with a guru and did a mantra for a few years. While the experience of doing this mantra daily focused and calmed my mind considerably, it did not provide me with the ultimate answers I was after. I meditated, did yoga, Quigong, trained to level two Reiki healing, studied crystal and sound healing, went to meet with numerous psychics, shamans, psychologists and psychiatrists, snorted cocaine, ate peyote mushrooms and marijuana brownies, and even tried LSD once. Even focusing all my intention and efforts on anything that could be reasonably considered "of a spiritual nature," I was only to discover I wasn't any closer to the Ultimate True Reality than when I started. Instead, I had overwhelmed, exhausted and depressed myself without having any conclusive answer to my two most important questions:

Who am I?

Where is God hiding?

Ultimate Reality and The Burning Bush

In an article titled, *Beyond Reason: The Certitude of the Mystics from Al-Hallaj to David R. Hawkins*, by Fran Grace, Ph.D., I was introduced to *The Book of Certainty*. *The Book of Certainty* was written by Abu Bkar Siraj ad-Din. In his book, he explains the Three Levels of Knowledge in Sufism by analogy to the Burning Bush: the Lore of Certainty, the Eye of Certainty, and the Truth of Certainty. In Sufism, The Burning Bush is the Sufi symbol for The Ultimate Reality.

1. Those who heard about the Burning Bush from Moses possessed the lowest degree of knowledge called the "Lore of Certainty." This is hearsay, third-person knowledge attained via reportage from another person.

2. Those who possessed the next level of knowledge, called the "Eye of Certainty," have actually seen the flames of the Burning Bush, such as Moses did when he was approaching the Burning Bush.

3. Finally, the "Truth of Certainty" is considered the highest level of knowledge. This knowledge belongs only to those who have become one with the Burning Bush, and are consumed by its flames.

In the same article, Grace introduced me to the supremely accomplished scholar, Al-Ghazali, known as "The Proof of Islam." I found Al-Ghazali fascinating. At a crucial point in his academic career, Al-Ghazali came to see himself as a hypocrite because he spoke of sublime truths that were merely the truths of others, not his own. Fully realizing that, he left his academic post to become a wandering Whirling Dervish. He did continuous Sufi practice for many years; his intention was that the stories about spiritual realms might be verified, both in his own heart and subjective experience. "Only then," Al-Ghazali declared, "could I teach anyone anything with any real authority."

Al-Ghazali identified three levels of research and experience he considered to be his own personal spiritual map.

Knowledge of God gained through his own study.

Faith gained through his hearing about the spiritual experiences of others.

Experience gained by fruition of his first-hand experience with Divinity/Reality.

After reading about Al-Ghazali's spiritual journey, I realized I might have had plenty of knowledge and faith, but I didn't have anything even close to the "Truth of Certainty" that Al-Ghazali was talking about. Like Al-Ghazali, I'd also reached a dead end with all my knowledge gained through study and reading about the spiritual experiences of others. I had read and tried everything I could think of, and at this point in my spiritual search, I felt that I had run out of options. Now I was determined, whatever it took, to finally have my own subjective and irrefutable experience of God, to see the Face Of God for myself.

The only place that I really had not looked was deep within myself, and so I resolved to travel into that unknown. When at first I truly tried to silence my mind it felt like I was spinning in circles just like a Whirling Dervish. Previously, I had prided myself at my ability to analyze and store massive numbers of facts and data to be brought out at just the right moment to impress my listener whoever they happened to be. But, I discovered that just because I might know a lot *about* China, that did not make me *Chinese*. I then realized that in truth, I had no idea where my thoughts even came from. The thoughts in my mind were clearly an endless and incessant stream of "blah-blah-blah." What was all that noise of constant thinking streaming inside my head all the time? After a period of time I came to a rather amusing and startling conclusion: I did not actually "know" anything. Not only did I not know what any of the stuff in my mind really meant, I could now see that all my thoughts were pure conjecture, opinions and judgments. Round and round and round I went inside my mind; it often felt like I was splitting endless spiritual hairs. During this period, some of the questions I often asked myself were, *What was the Real Truth of anything? How far down this Spiritual Rabbit Hole am I willing to go? Where does this Spiritual Journey end?*

It was about that time I noticed another very interesting and curious thing start showing up in my life. In the Epistle to the Galatians of the Bible, I had read about the fruit of the Spirit: "But the fruit of the Spirit is love, joy, peace, patience, kindness, goodness, faithfulness, gentleness and self-control." I thought those qualities sounded really good, and they were certainly spiritual, so I challenged myself with the task of mastering each fruit of the Spirit. Yet, each time I firmly resolved within myself to be more loving, it would appear that I was given endless opportunities to observe all my thoughts and feelings that were *not loving*.

As I tried to move closer to peace, I was confronted with everything, both within myself and in the world, which were *not peaceful*. As I tried to focus on joy, I was confronted with everything about myself that was *not joyful*. As I tried to become more patient, I noticed all the different areas of my life that I was *not patient*. Every single fruit of the Spirit appeared to bring up everything in my life that was its opposite. Was this progress? I had imagined that mastering the fruits of the Spirit would ultimately make me feel better, not worse. It became abundantly clear that I obviously had a lot more to clean up within myself than I had ever expected. I was confused and frustrated indeed.

Prior to this point, my Zen Teachers had suggested that I place all my focus on "the space between the thoughts." My thoughts always came at a relentless pace, with what appeared to be zero space between them, so focusing on what appeared to be a non-existent space never worked for me. Another Teacher just kept recommending, "Keep silent. Pay Attention." When I tried to do that, I always wondered what exactly was I supposed to be Paying Attention to? When I had tried really hard to Pay Attention to my mind it just seemed full of noise. When I had tried to Pay Attention to the things of this world, everything just appeared to be relentless chaos. Another Teacher suggested, "Meditate on the words, "I Am That I Am." To me, that instruction had sounded a bit like a Dr. Seuss book. David R. Hawkins, M.D., Ph.D. suggested, "Pay close attention to the 1/10,000 of a second *before* the thoughts." When I heard that one I thought, *How is that even possible?* Another teacher admonished me, "Stop talking so much. God is in the silence." Yeah right. Me? Keep my mouth shut? Stop talking? Was he kidding?

After my apparently failed experiment with the fruits of the Spirit, I began to wonder if Enlightenment, what some Mystics call "Unio Mystica," was some sort of a Cosmic Joke. Even with all my time and effort, anything even resembling peace of mind, love, joy and patience felt farther away than ever. I even wondered at one point, *Were the fruits of my Spirit rotten?* It's clearly one thing to read a book about

Enlightenment, or read a travel magazine about the marvels of the Taj Mahal. It's quite another thing to actually travel there, sit in it, walk its grounds, and breathe its air. I tried to take comfort in the fact that every spiritual Teacher recorded throughout time has said that the search for the Ultimate Truth of Enlightenment "is the hardest work you will ever attempt to do."

At this point, you might be asking yourself, "Jeez. Why doesn't this woman just give this all up, go sit on a nice beach somewhere warm, and hook up to an endless IV drip of pina coladas!" I have to admit that I asked myself similar questions too during that time like, *Is all this spiritual work really worth it?*

The un-learning process begins

When hiking an unfamiliar trail, I would much prefer to learn about the various conditions of the trail from the hiker who has just come down from the top of the mountain than from the one who is reading a guidebook at the start of the trailhead. Similarly, I have found the books written, and the maps that have been drawn about the spiritual journey from Mystics and others throughout the centuries extremely helpful in my search for Truth. But ultimately, even Mystics like Sri Nisargadatta Maharaj suggest, "All knowledge is ignorance." Nisargadatta also said, "To know that you do not know is True Knowledge." At a certain point in the spiritual journey, the serious student is counseled to "Throw away all the books and just Be."

I began a process which can best be described as un-learning. I let go of all I thought I knew, and discarded all the conflicting spiritual guidance I had read. I also stopped comparing myself to other people and their spiritual journey. I was determined to have my own verifiable subjective experience of God. At first, not working so hard at everything all the time and just Being felt very strange. But then I began to notice that something rather strange and miraculous was beginning to happen: As I withdrew all of my preconceived ideas and opinions about everything, I noticed that everything and everyone around me began to reveal their own inherent beautiful truth. Suddenly I saw God everywhere, in everything and everyone, including myself. It would appear that Love had been in and all around me the entire time!

From Me To You

If you have reached what feels like a dead end in your own spiritual search, please don't give up. All the answers you are seeking truly do lie within you.

THRIVE

When asked to give an answer as to how the universe works, Sir Arthur Eddington, the British physicist, said, "Something unknown is doing we don't know what." Today, when my friends and family ask me to explain, "What exactly is your plan?" and "What exactly are you up to right now" the most honest and true thing I can say is, "Well, the best answer I can give you is that The Universe is up to something with me, I just don't know exactly what that something is."

Flow

Many people actually already have personal knowledge and experience of a temporary timeless Flow. A common description of these states is that "the ordinary orientation in time and space is lost." This is similar to what happens to me during a deep meditation, creating art or while kiteboarding. During these activities there are the moments in which the constant chattering of my ego mind is muted, if only temporarily. Flow, or what some people call, "The Zone," often occurs when people are engaged in some sort of activity that they truly love, such as creative work, love-making, athletic or stage performance, the birth of a child, religious and patriotic ritual, meditation, dying, or other similar kind of experience that goes beyond the normal everyday one.

While many of us have transient moments of Flow, as in intense joy, or self-transcendence, it is quite rare for such a state to be permanent. Historically, after reaching Enlightenment, most such beings remain in what is termed, "God-Shock," and are completely unable to speak about it. As William James tells us in his classic *Varieties of Religious Experience*, the Mystic experience is "ineffable." Very few people ever speak of such a state of transcendence or make reaching the ineffable an actual goal for their lives.

Can you even imagine a conversation about two people aspiring to achieve Enlightenment on a typical street corner of today?

Two men meet on the street. One man says to the other, "So what are you up to these days, Joe?"

"Ah, not too much, Ron. Just trying to reach the ineffable."

"You are completely out of your mind, Joe!"

"Yup. I'm working on it."

People who have a Near Death Experience, or another major life event, sometimes choose to leave what is considered "the real world" in search of some Higher Truth. As a result of this choice to follow their hearts, and their version of a higher calling, the current consumer driven culture often considers these people "crazy." The rare individuals who do successfully make this spiritual attainment their life work we refer to as Mystics, Sages, and Saints. In our modern day we have the example of Mother Teresa who worked with the lowest of the low on the streets of Calcutta, and Gandhi who created a movement, which ultimately toppled the British Empire. I humbly aspire to reach the highest level of spiritual attainment that I am capable of, and only God knows what that is.

The inner pathway

I can describe my current life as following an inner directive, which might best be described as an inner pathway. This inner pathway points me toward the ultimate journey toward full realization of Self. I may never get there in this lifetime, but it's nice to know that the inner pathway is open to all who choose it and is free of dogma, dues, or membership. All that is required is a willingness to surrender within to God anything that is not Truth, and to show kindness, compassion, forgiveness, and a reverence to all life on the planet, including oneself, at all times and without exception. This is no small task.

There are certain core principles held to be true across cultures which I am trying to practice on a day to day basis: love is more powerful than hatred; truth sets us free; forgiveness liberates both sides; unconditional love heals; courage empowers; and the essence of Divinity/Reality is peace and love. The research in consciousness done by David R. Hawkins, M.D., Ph.D., and his *Map Of Consciousness*, has also helped me to understand the important principle of "that which weakens our life energy is to be avoided: shame, guilt, confusion, fear, hatred, pride, hopelessness, and falsehood." On the other hand, "That which uplifts life is to be followed: truth, courage, acceptance, reason, love, beauty, joy, and peace." I just try to do my very best each day and also say the following prayer, "God help me. Show me The Way. Show me The Truth. Set me Free."

I am acutely aware that in all humility I do not always succeed at practicing any of these things, even with my best of intentions. But I figure that is why this spiritual journey has always been called "A Practice." There is always plenty for me to practice that's for sure!

Mystics and Maps

Mystics who pursue an understanding of Ultimate Reality may be viewed as intrepid souls who traverse the spiritual realm much like Marco Polo traversed the geographical realm of the world. Whereas many Thirteenth-Century Europeans were content in their belief that there was "no such thing as China," Marco Polo pressed on with single-pointed perseverance to discover unknown lands. Reaching the farthest possible destinations, he returned home to Venice to share his maps of The Silk Road. However, upon hearing Polo's accounts of other lands, skeptics dismissed him as deluded. So it has always been with the Mystics.

Mystics have ventured into the farthest interior realms and reached the ultimate destination, "Unio Mystica." Like Marco Polo, the Mystics remain certain of the realm they have experienced, even if this territory is largely unknown to the majority of people. The Mystic testifies to the existence of a realm beyond ordinary perception. The Mystic has attained, so Hawkins tells us from his own subjective experience, the "highest state of the spiritual life: an unquestioning trust in God's wisdom, where there are no more questions or needs and from which nothing is hidden." That sounds really appealing to me personally.

At this point in my life, I have chosen to live a very different path from when I was younger, and I realize that this choice may not make any sense to anyone else but me. I'm totally OK with that. In the past, I was full of moral outrage and working so very hard to change the world in the name of "being helpful." Now, I no longer focus on changing anything or anyone. When I look on all things and people with love, appreciation, gratitude and open-mindedness the beauty of every living thing reveals itself quite naturally and without effort.

Now all I see is God's power, a shimmering energetic reality everywhere, in everything and everyone. This Loving energy is the true beauty and radiance of God, The Ultimate Reality. Being able to connect with this powerful and Loving energy is a tremendous gift, and beyond anything I could ever have imagined with my human mind. It seems amazing, and somewhat amusing to me now, that I ever thought God was hiding from me. Hiding in plain sight is more like it. Now that I have developed a more expanded vision, I know that the energy of God lights up the world and everything in it.

From Me To You

"To realize the constancy and steadiness in your life is to realize the deep nature of the universe. This realization is not dependent on any transitory internal or external condition, rather it is an expression of one's own immutable spiritual nature. The only way to attain the Universal Way is to maintain the integral virtues of the constancy, steadiness and simplicity in one's daily life."

– Lao Tzu

CONCLUSION

The true spiritual journey Home is between each soul and God alone. I am blessed that through the Grace of God I finally understand that all the answers I searched for my entire life were never to be found in a person, book, the world, or even in my own mind. The ultimate destination of "Always," the ultimate Truth, Love and Peace of the Self is discovered and realized within.

Each one of us, through our own unique contribution, changes the world not by what we say or do, but as a consequence of what we choose to become. Each minute internal progression that any person living on this planet makes towards love and integrity uplifts the whole of existence. Our choices are indeed the Master Key, the key which opens the door to our unique version of a Thriving life. We simply need to truly believe that we have the power to choose to move any obstacle out of our way, and that we can completely change our reality at any moment.

These days, my life is very simple. For me now, Heaven on Earth is sitting in a deck chair overlooking the ocean, feeling the sun and soft breeze on my face, and listening to the birds sing as I drink a beautiful cup of coffee made by my beloved husband exactly the way I like it. When I ride my kiteboard, leaning back in my harness with one hand on the kite bar and my other hand trailing along in the water, I feel a joyful communion with the wind, the water, and the Grace of God. Every moment, my soul continues the eternal dance of the creative unfolding of God through me, and I am at peace with the fact that the concluding chapter of the book of who I am to become is yet to be written. Wherever my path leads from here, I take great comfort and inspiration from the words of Mother Teresa who often said, "The Mystic is simply a pencil in God's hands."

ABOUT THE AUTHOR

Mary Anne Dorward, PCC, is an International Author, Speaker, Coach, Actress, Blogger and World Traveler. From the age of 17, Mary Anne was an actress on Radio, National Television, Broadway and Hollywood. In addition to founding her own company, My Real Voice, Mary Anne has served as Communications Director and Chief Communications Strategist for companies and political campaigns around the world. She has coached World-Class Athletes, CEO's and Humanitarians, as well as Heads of Nonprofit Organizations Internationally. Mary Anne is committed to being a positive force in the lives and companies she touches through her writing, coaching and speaking. Mary Anne now lives with her husband in Oceania where she joyfully and peacefully spends her days creating art, playing music, gardening, doing yoga, stand up paddle boarding and kiteboarding.

Speaking

Considered a Thought Leader around the world, Mary Anne delivers her inspiring, timely, uplifting and spiritual messages with tremendous humor and style through her speaking and teaching Internationally. To book Mary Anne for a speech, please contact her at www.WordsToThriveBy.com.

Also by Mary Anne Dorward

Words To Thrive By: Powerful Stories Of Courage and Hope

Words To Thrive By for World Travellers: Footprints In Ecuador

Survive To Thrive: 11 Keys To Unlock Your Thriving Life

ACKNOWLEDGEMENTS

Thank you to my early readers. Your feedback has been invaluable: Janice Barnard, Richard Bingham, Paula Boucher, Mary Garripoli, Paul Goode, John Kremer, Cici Christiansen Lee, Charles Louvau, Derek Mueller, Amos Lukumba Mutale, Eric O'Del, Ellin Anderson Purdom, Catherine Eaton Skinner, Liz Talley, Billie Taylor, and Urs Winzenried.

Thank you to Julia Whippo for your technical brilliance and support.

Thank you to Dr. Guan Cheng Sun for teaching me Quigong and also for teaching me the wisdom that cancer tumors come to teach.

Thank you to Sonya Cockram and Jason Lewis, Owners of West Oz Kiteboarding. You introduced me to the joy, challenge, and true grace of kiteboarding. Thanks to you, kiteboarding has become both a passion, and an essential part of my Thriving life.

Thank you to Kevin and Marnie Webb for teaching me the depth of the Australian Heart.

Thank you to my children, Sarah and Joshua Schenkkan for teaching me the power of Love and Peace.

Thank you to my husband Rupe for being the best life companion any person could wish for. My Thriving Life truly began when I met you.

Thank you to my Spiritual Teachers, all along the way.

And finally, Gloria in Excelsis Deo!

FOR FURTHER EXPLORATION
aka
MY VIRTUAL BOOKSHELF

There are so many helpful and transformative books and programs to choose from. Each of the references listed below are ones that have contributed in an extremely positive way toward my personal growth and Thriving life. Please note: this list below is in no way intended to dispense medical advice. Please consult your own medical practitioner before beginning any new approach, medical or otherwise.

Body
Supplements for Men and Women

Dr. Al Sears, Anti-Aging Telomere Support

Teloessence

For more information and to Order Teloessence: http://bit.ly/2urhzht

Flexibility and Strength

Thomas Hanna

Somatics: Reawakening The Mind's Control Of Movement, Flexibility, and Health

Callan Pinckney

Callanetics: Ten Years Younger in 10 Hours

Jade Teta

Metabolic Aftershock

Metabolic Effect

Metabolic Prime

For more information: www.MetabolicEffect.com

Pain Relief

Pete Egoscue

Pain Free for Women: The Revolutionary Program for Ending Chronic Pain

Dr. Lou Fehmi, PhD and Jim Robbins

The Open Focus Brain: Harnessing the Power of Attention to Heal Mind and Body

Food

Marco Canora

Bone Broth: Brodo: A Bone Broth Cookbook

Donna Gates

The Body Ecology Diet: Recovering Your Health and Rebuilding Your Immunity

Nancy Harmon Jenkins

The New Mediterranean Diet Cookbook: A Delicious Alternative for Lifelong Health

Kefir and Villi

Kefir Grains and Villi culture

Order here: www.yemoos.com

Olive Oil

Fresh Pressed Olive Oil Club

Order here: www.freshpressedoliveoil.com

Transformational Programs

The Work by Byron Katie

The Work

For more information go to: www.thework.com

The Programs Of Paul Scheeley

The Abundance Course

For more information go to: www.learningstrategies.com

The Programs of Dr. Robert Anthony

The Secret Of Deliberate Creation

The Tao of Thriving

For more information go to: www.robertanthony.com

Books

Alice Bailey

Glamour: A World Problem

Brene Brown

Rising Strong: The Reckoning. The Rumble. The Revolution.

The Gifts of Imperfection: Let Go Of Who You Think You're Supposed To Be and Embrace Who You Are

Pema Chödron

When Things Fall Apart: Heart Advice For Difficult Times

Fail, Fail Again, Fail Better: Wise Advice For Leaning Into The Unknown

Getting Unstuck: Breaking Your Habitual Patterns and Encountering Naked Reality

Dr. Joe Dispenza

You Are The Placebo: Making Your Mind Matter

Breaking The Habit Of Being Yourself

Wayne Dyer

The Power Of Intention

Clara Pinkola Estes

Women Who Run With The Wolves: Myths and Stories of the Wild Woman Archetype

Untie The Strong Women: Blessed Mothers Immaculate Love for the Wild Soul

Viktor Frankl

Man's Search For Meaning

Elizabeth Gilbert

Big Magic: Creative Living Beyond Fear

The Signature of All Things

Pam Grout

E Squared: 9 Do-It-Yourself Energy Experiments That Prove Your Thoughts Create Your Reality

E to the Tenth Power: Manifesting Magic and Miracles Is My Full Time Gig

Art and Soul Reloaded: A Year-Long Apprenticeship to Summon the Muses and Ignite Your Daring Audacious Creative Side

David R. Hawkins, M.D., Ph.D

Along The Pathway to Enlightenment

Devotional Nonduality: Discovery of the Presence of God

Healing and Recovery

I: Reality and Subjectivity

Letting Go: The Pathway of Surrender

Power vs Force: The Hidden Determinants of Human Behavior

Reality, Spirituality and Modern Man

The Eye Of The I: From Which Nothing Is Hidden

Transcending The Levels Of Consciousness

FOR FURTHER EXPLORATION

William James

The Varieties Of Religious Experience

Byron Katie

Loving What Is

Who Would You Be Without Your Story?

Getting The Love You Want

A Mind At Home With Itself

Anne Lamott

Bird By Bird

Help. Thanks. Wow. The Three Essential Prayers

Bruce Lipton

The Biology Of Belief

Sri Nisargadatta Maharaj

I Am That

Anita Moorjani

Dying To Be Me: My Journey from Cancer, to Near Death, to True Healing

Christiane Northrop

Goddesses Never Age: The Secret Prescription for Radiance, Vitality, and Well Being

Making Life Easy: A Simple Guide To An Inspired Life

The Wisdom Of Menopause

Women's Bodies: Women's Wisdom

John O'Donohue

Anam Cara

Bless The Space Between Us

Helen Schucman

A Course in Miracles

Cheryl Strayed

Tiny Beautiful Things: Advice on Life and Love from Dear Sugar

Jill Bolte Taylor

My Stroke Of Insight: A Brain Scientist's Personal Journey

Alan Watts

Become What You Are

Poetry

T.S. Eliot

Hafiz

Mary Oliver

Pablo Neruda

Rainier Marie Rilke

Robert Frost

Rumi

Music

Michael R. Tyrell

Wholetones

Wholetones Lullabyes

Order here: www.Wholetones.com

My Joy Playlist (See: Key Of Gratitude)

Best Day Of My Life, American Authors

Odds Are, Barenaked Ladies

You Sexy Thing, Hot Chocolate

Overjoyed, Stevie Wonder

I'm a Believer, The Monkees

True Colors, Cyndi Lauper

Celebration, Kool & The Gang

I Got You (I Feel Good), James Brown and His Famous Flames

Happy, Pharrell Williams

SURVIVE TO THRIVE

Life Is Better With You, Michael Franti

Three Little Birds, Bob Marley

What A Wonderful World, Louis Armstrong

Say Hey (I Love You), Michael Franti

Harlem Shuffle, Rolling Stones

Fall, Peter Mayer

You Are So Beautiful, Joe Cocker

End Of The Line, The Traveling Willburys

GLOSSARY OF TERMS

Assumptions
What we believe is true. Marshall McLuhan said, "Most of our assumptions have outlived their uselessness."

Birth
Choosing the human physical domain can only be done by agreement with the individual will. So all humans have, by agreement, chosen this pathway. David R. Hawkins, M.D., Ph.D. said, "All humans have, by agreement, chosen this pathway. Consciousness research confirms that all persons are born under the most optimal conditions for spiritual evolution, no matter what the appearance seems to be. You don't get born without your approval."

Consciousness
It is like infinite space that is capable of awareness, and is a quality of the Divine Essence. "Consciousness is the unlimited, omnipresent, universal energy field, carrier wave, and reservoir of all information available in the universe—and, more important, it is the very essence and substrate of the capacity to know or experience, to perceive or witness. Even more critically, consciousness is the irreducible, primary quality of all existence—the formless, invisible field of energy of infinite dimension and potentiality, independent of time, space, or location, yet all-inclusive and all-present. Consciousness is an impersonal quality of Divinity expressed as awareness, and is non-dualistic and nonlinear." ~ David R. Hawkins, M.D., Ph.D.

Context
The total field of observation predicated by a point of view. Context includes any significant facts that qualify the meaning of a statement or

event. Data is meaningless unless its context is defined. To "take out of context" is to distort the significance of a statement by failing to identify contributory accessory conditions that would qualify the inference of meaning.

Duality

The world of form characterized by seeming separation of objects, reflected in conceptual dichotomies such as "this/that," "here/there," "then/now," or "yours/ mine." This perception of limitation is produced by the senses because of the restriction implicit in a fixed point of view.

Ego (or self, with a small s)

The ego is the imaginary doer behind thought and action. Its presence is firmly believed to be necessary and essential for survival. "The ego could be called the central processing and planning center; the integrative, executive, strategic, and tactical focus that orchestrates, copes, sorts, stores, and retrieves. It can be thought of as a set of entrenched habits of thought that are the result of entrainment by invisible energy fields that dominate human consciousness. These entrenched habits of thought become reinforced by repetition, and by the consensus of society. Further reinforcement comes from language itself, as to think in language is a form of self-programming. The use of the pronoun "I" as the subject, and therefore the implied cause of all actions, is the most serious miscalculation we make, and this error automatically creates a duality of subject and object. Put another way, the ego is a set of programs wherein thought follows certain decision trees that are variously weighted by past experience, indoctrination, and social forces; it is therefore not a self-created condition." ~ David R. Hawkins, M.D., Ph.D.

Enlightenment

A state of unusual awareness that replaces ordinary consciousness. The self is replaced by the Self. The condition is beyond time or space, is silent, and presents itself as a revelation. The condition follows dissolution of the ego. Everything is realized to be autonomous, rather than the result of causality.

Flow

A temporary state of being that is intensely pleasurable and where "the ordinary orientation in time and space is lost." This "peak experience" can happen at any time, but usually occurs when people are engaged in some sort of activity that they truly love, such as creative work, love-making, athletic or stage performance, the birth of a child, religious and patriotic ritual, meditation, dying, or other similar kind of experience that goes beyond the "normal" everyday one. While many of us have transient moments of "Flow," as in intense joy, or self-transcendence, it is quite rare for such a state to be permanent. Historically, after reaching Enlightenment, most such beings remain in what is termed, "God-shock," unable to speak about it. As William James tells us in his classic *Varieties of Religious Experience*, the Mystic's experience is "ineffable."

Focus

The latest research shows that humans currently have less focus and attention than a goldfish. (See: http://bit.ly/2wUKXx8)

Forgiveness

Forgive others, not because they need it, but because you deserve peace. And by the way, while to forgive is commendable, at a later stage of one's spiritual growth and discernment, one sees there is actually nothing to forgive. There is no "other" to be forgiven. Everyone's ego is equally unreal, including one's own.

Forgiveness Prayer

"If there is anyone or anything that has caused me harm in the past, knowingly or unknowingly, I forgive and release it. If I have hurt anyone or anything in the past, knowingly or unknowingly, I forgive and release it. If I have hurt myself in the past, knowingly or unknowingly, I forgive and release it." (See: Prayer)

Freedom

"Be still, and know that I am God." ~The Bible

Gloria in Excelsis Deo

Glory To God In The Highest in Latin.

Gratitude

Do you have "a toe tag" today? If you don't, you're still alive. Be grateful.

Ho'oponopono (ho-o-pono-pono)

Another very effective prayer for forgiveness is Ho'oponopono. Ho'oponopono has four parts: "I'm Sorry. Please Forgive Me. Thank You. I Love You."

Joy

Joy can be complicated, messy, and exquisitely beautiful and transcendent, sometimes all at the same moment. The Sufi mystic, Hafiz of Shiraz said, "Ever since happiness heard your name it has been running through the streets trying to find you."

Karma

In essence, individual karma is an information package (analogous to a computer chip) that exists within the nonphysical domain of consciousness. It contains the code of stored information that is intrinsic to, and a portion of, the spiritual body or soul. The core represents a condensation of all past experiences, together with associated nuances of thought and feeling. The spirit body retains freedom of choice, but the range of choices has already been patterned. Karma really means accountability—every entity is answerable to the universe. Choosing the human physical domain can only be done by agreement with the individual will. This means then that all humans have, by agreement, chosen this pathway.

Knowledge

Will Rogers said, "It ain't what you know that causes trouble. It's what you know for sure that just ain't true that's the problem." Sri Maharaj Nisargadatta suggested, "To know that you do not know is True Knowledge." He also said, "All knowledge is ignorance."

Laughter

Laughter is one of the greatest gifts of human life. If we understood the serious business of laughter, and how much it represents some of the highest spiritual truths, we would do it more often.

Love

Love is one of the most important lessons we came to earth in order to learn. As Martin Luther King, Jr said, "Darkness cannot drive out darkness; only love can do that. Hate cannot drive out hate; only love can do that."

Non-duality

"When the limitation of a fixed locus of perception is transcended, there is no longer an illusion of separation, nor of space and time as we know them. On the level of non-duality there is observing but no observer, as subject and object are one. You-and-I becomes the One Self experiencing all as Divine. In non-duality, consciousness experiences itself as both manifest and un- manifest, yet there is no experiencer. In this reality, the only thing that has a beginning and an ending is the act of perception itself." ~David R. Hawkins, M.D., Ph.D.

Peace

When I am in deep meditation, doing a piece of artwork, playing music, gliding along on my kiteboard with my hand trailing behind in the water and my mind focused only on the current second, or when I am stand up paddleboarding in the morning when the sun is up and the water is so glassy and beautiful, I find that I can expand my sense of Peace. "The Peace that passeth all understanding" is the goal. Taking a few deep breaths is step number one. Doing something that we truly love is step number two.

Prayer

Below are a few prayers that have served me well:

1. God help me. Show me The Way. Show me The Truth. Set me free.

2. Ho'oponopono (ho-o-pono-pono): I love you. I'm sorry. Please forgive me. Thank you.

3. The Forgiveness Prayer: If there is anyone or anything that has caused me harm in the past, knowingly or unknowingly, I forgive and release it. If I have hurt anyone or anything in the past, knowingly or unknowingly, I forgive and release it. If I have hurt myself in the past, knowingly or unknowingly, I forgive and release it.

Positionality

All positionalities, are voluntary; they are programs, not the real Self. The positionalities are structures that set the entire thinking mechanism in motion and activate its content. The world holds an endless array of positionalities that are arbitrary presumptions, and totally erroneous. According to David R. Hawkins, M.D., Ph.D., "Primordial positionalities are: (1) Ideas have significance and importance (2) There is a dividing line between opposites (3) There is a value of authorship— thoughts are valuable because they are "mine" (4) Thinking is necessary for control, and survival depends on control."

Self: (capital S)

"The Self is beyond, yet innate in, all form—timeless, without beginning or end, changeless, permanent, and immortal. Out of it arises awareness, consciousness, and an infinite condition of "at home-ness." It is the ultimate subjectivity from which everyone's sense of "I" arises. The Infinite Reality does not even know itself as "I," but as the very substrate of the capacity for such a statement. It is invisible and All- Present. The Self is the Reality of reality, the Oneness and Allness of Identity. It is the ultimate "I-ness" of consciousness itself as the manifestation of the unmanifest. Thus only can the indescribable be described." ~ David R. Hawkins, M.D., PhD.

Spiritual First Aid

To relieve an emotional upset try the following:

1. Thump "The Thymus" The thymus gland is located behind the upper breastbone. Thump that area with a closed hand and say at the same time, "Ha-Ha-Ha" rhythmically three times, and then, after a pause, do it three more times. Smile while doing that and picture something or someone that you love. That could be a divine figure or even one's favorite pet. (The thymus is the controller of the acupuncture energy system, and is related to one's overall immune health, which is prone to suppression by stress.)

2. Next, breathe spiritual energy from the base of the spine up to the Crown Chakra. On each inhalation, picture it as Light. It flows from the base of the spine to the crown of the head. Even a few breaths done in this way will cause a very noticeable effect.

3. While doing the breathing, think or sound the syllable, "Om," as you proceed with the above. (The "O" is pronounced like the name of the letter "O").

4. Picture someone you love.

5. While involved in this process, find within yourself the willingness in your heart to surrender anything and everything to God, and recommit your devotion above all else.

The above instructions will lift you quickly and easily out of the arena of emotional conflict and distress. It does not take practice and the results are obvious, even on the first try. This can be followed up by prayer and meditation that focus attention on the whole picture of what one is witnessing, rather than getting stuck and involved in any of the specific details. This approach restores equanimity and tends to keep one at the level of witness rather than at the effect of the details with attachment to a specific outcome. Note: This method was originally taught by Dr. John Diamond.

Subjectivity

Life is lived solely on the level of experience, and none other. All experience is subjective and nonlinear; therefore, even the linear, perceptual, sequential delineation of "reality" cannot be experienced except subjectively. All "truth" is a subjective conclusion that we make. All life in its essence is nonlinear, non-measurable, non-definable. It is purely subjective. Each human is creating their own subjective reality at every moment.

Suffering

"The true Mystic's knowingness is that the world is perfect as it is, including its suffering. Mystics often see suffering as the means for spiritual growth." ~David R. Hawkins, M.D. PhD.

The Purpose Of Life

Henry Miller summed up the purpose of life very well: "The aim of life is to live, and to live means to be aware, joyously, drunkenly, serenely, divinely, aware."

The Universe

Hafiz, the Sufi mystic said, "Ever since happiness heard your name it has been running through the streets trying to find you."

Truth

While many people throughout time have argued relentlessly about "who is right," the truth is that Truth is relative, and only "true" in a given context. All truth is only so within a certain level of consciousness. Perception is not reality. "Truth is radical subjectivity. With the collapse of the illusions of duality, including the supposed "reality" of a separate "self," there remains only the state of the Infinite "I," which is the manifestation of the Unmanifest as the Self. Truth has no opposites, such as falsity or "off-ness." Nothing is hidden from the Field Of Consciousness. Any attempt at Self-definition, such as "I Am That I Am" - or even just "I Am" - is redundant. The Ultimate Reality is beyond all names. "I" signifies the radical subjectivity of the state of Realization. "I" is in itself the complete statement of Reality." ~David R. Hawkins, M.D. PhD.

Why We Are Here

Souls come to earth to learn specific lessons that they themselves have chosen. Their spiritual journey is thus between them and God alone. Consciousness research has determined that people, only move up in consciousness an average of five points in a single lifetime. This suggests that it's entirely possible that one soul may have chosen to master only one particular level on the Map Of Consciousness, rather than proceeding in their spiritual journey all the way to Enlightenment. Souls can also drop like a rock from higher levels of consciousness if they become consumed with greed, anger or envy. So again, each individual soul's spiritual journey is between them and God alone.

Consciousness research has also proven that a soul will always choose to be born into the exact circumstances, culture, family and location on the planet that is the most optimal for their own spiritual growth. As David

R. Hawkins, M.D. PhD. said, "All humans have, by agreement, chosen this pathway. Consciousness research confirms that all persons are born under the most optimal conditions for spiritual evolution, no matter what the appearance seems to be. You don't get born without your approval."

Wisdom

The best definition I have ever heard of wisdom is from Sri Nisargadatta Maharaj: "Wisdom tells me I am nothing. Love tells me I am everything. Between the two my life flows."

www.ingramcontent.com/pod-product-compliance
Lightning Source LLC
Chambersburg PA
CBHW030217170426
43201CB00006B/112